Masculine Pregnancies

Masculine Pregnancies

Modernist Conceptions of Creativity and Legitimacy, 1918–1939

AIMEE ARMANDE WILSON

Cover art: "Square from a glitch-quilt in progress" (foraged handmade inks and gold paint on watercolor paper), Amy E. Elkins, 2022.

Published by State University of New York Press, Albany

For information, contact State University of New York Press, Albany, NY
www.sunypress.edu

Library of Congress Cataloging-in-Publication Data

Name: Wilson, Aimee Armande, author.
Title: Masculine pregnancies : modernist conceptions of creativity and
    legitimacy, 1918–1939 / Aimee Armande Wilson.
Description: Albany : State University of New York Press, [2023]. | Includes
    bibliographical references and index.
Identifiers: LCCN 2023009065 | ISBN 9781438495590 (hardcover : alk. paper) |
    ISBN 9781438495613 (ebook) | ISBN 9781438495606 (pbk. : alk. paper)
Subjects: LCSH: Pound, Ezra, 1885–1972—Criticism and interpretation. |
    Faulkner, William, 1897–1962—Criticism and interpretation. | Cather,
    Willa, 1873–1947. My Ántonia. | Barnes, Djuna. Nightwood. | Pregnancy
    in literature. | Masculinity in literature. | Women in literature. | Sex role in
    literature. | Modernism (Literature) | LCGFT: Literary criticism.
Classification: LCC PS3531.O82 Z8946 2023 | DDC
    810.9/354—dc23/eng/20230621
LC record available at https://lccn.loc.gov/2023009065

10 9 8 7 6 5 4 3 2 1

Contents

Acknowledgments   vii

Introduction   1

Chapter 1   A Cultural History of Gender and Reproduction   19

Chapter 2   Literary Obstetrics: Ezra Pound and
the Midwives Act of 1902   43

Chapter 3   Pregnancy in Faulkner's Artist Novels: Masculinity,
Sexology, and Creativity in Interwar America   71

Chapter 4   The Mannish Woman as Fertility Goddess:
How Narrative Makes a Legitimate Mother Out
of Ántonia Shimerda   93

Chapter 5   " 'Conceiving herself pregnant before she was' ":
Parental Impressions and the Limits of Reproductive
Legitimacy in *Nightwood*   127

Coda: Masculine Pregnancies beyond Modernism   161

Notes   167

Bibliography   189

Index   207

Acknowledgments

This book was written over six years, three states, four houses, and three departments. As a result, there are many people who came into contact with the ideas in this book and helped foster the project along; more people, indeed, than I could possibly mention here. So to anyone who lent an ear, suggested a source, nodded encouragement, or corrected an error, thank you.

There are, however, several people who deserve special mention. First, my writing group partners. Their steadfast support as I worked on the book makes them feel like fellow travelers and co-authors. If book writing were a board game, toiling away in complete isolation would be a chute, and a good writing group would be a ladder up to square 100. My writing groups included Marie Brown, Liz Foley O'Connor, Marike Janzen, Ani Kokobobo, Ari Linden, Brad Osborn, Ravenel Richardson, and Nick Syrett. Their wisdom helped me see which ideas had potential, while their graciousness and wit helped me let go of ideas that were lacking. Any lackluster ideas that remain in the book are my fault, of course.

The members of the Space Between Society: Literature and Culture, 1914–1945 have heard excerpts and early versions of every chapter. Their questions and suggestions pushed my research in productive directions. Listening to their ideas never fails to reinvigorate my excitement for the study of the interwar period.

I found the perfect editor in Rebecca Colesworthy. Her editorial acumen is complemented by her expertise in modernism and gender studies; truly a trifecta for this book. She happens to be a delight to work with, too. She saw promise in this unusual project, and for that I am grateful.

Thanks to the anonymous readers of the manuscript for their insight, generosity, and discernment. The book is better for their assistance.

To the scholar and artist Amy E. Elkins: the cover image for *Masculine Pregnancies* is her *Square from a Glitch-Quilt in Progress* (foraged handmade inks and gold paint on watercolor paper), 2022. Her consideration of modernism and craft can be found in the luminous *Crafting Feminism from Literary Modernism to the Multimedia Present* (Oxford UP, 2023). Conversations with the experts at the Spencer Museum of Art at the University of Kansas—including Kris Ercums, Kate Meyer, and Luke Jordan—helped me reconceive my abstract, text-based ideas in visual mediums. These conversations allowed me to articulate my vision for the book's cover and led eventually to the Elkins swatch.

To the Humanities Program at the University of Kansas for the time, space, and camaraderie I needed for thinking inter- and cross-disciplinarily. The Women, Gender, and Sexuality Studies Department at the University of Kansas welcomed me with open arms when the Humanities Program closed. Even though I've been a member of the WGSS department for only a short while, it already feels like an intellectual home.

To Maria Bonn and John Wilkin for use of their Orcas Island house for a writing retreat. Tami Albin and Sherri Brown helped me think through ideas at a pivotal moment.

To the College of Liberal Arts & Sciences at the University of Kansas for a pre-tenure research intensive semester. A Faculty Travel Grant from the Hall Center for the Humanities at the University of Kansas provided funding for a research trip during this semester. I spent several weeks at the Beinecke Rare Book & Manuscript Library at Yale University. The librarians, researchers, and support staff are as kind as they are smart.

To Robin Goodman, for giving me the confidence to think I could write books as well as the practical tools to do so.

Finally to Josh, my cooking partner, adventure buddy, comedian, sounding board, occasional therapist, and companion in cat-wrangling.

The cats were very helpy, too.

Chapter 2 is derived in part from an article published in *Feminist Modernist Studies*, 2019, 212–231, copyright Taylor & Francis, https://doi.org/10.1080/24692921.2019.1622173. Chapter 3 is derived in part from an article published in *The Space Between: Literature and Culture, 1914–1945*, 2018, vol. 14.

Introduction

"New York is not renowned for its gallantry where pregnant women are concerned," writes A. K. Summers in the graphic memoir *Pregnant Butch* (2014), "so imagine how often you're offered a seat when most people take you for just another **fat guy** on the subway. It's strange, but pregnancy increased my ability to pass" (bold original, 2). What would have happened if Teek, the author's alter ego and titular pregnant butch, insisted on taking a seat because of her[1] pregnancy? I suspect at least some of the passengers would have accused Teek of lying, mocked her (the other "fat guys" showing off their stomachs and asking for seats, too), and possibly even demanded that Teek show proof that she is pregnant. Since her large belly would not suffice, I suspect that "proof" would mean biological evidence of female embodiment: show us your tits if you want a seat.[2] When confronted with the presence of a masculine pregnant person, many people resist giving up their more familiar narratives ("just another fat guy" as opposed to a masculine pregnant woman) and instead challenge the person's legitimacy: are you really pregnant? Elsewhere in the memoir, Teek is forced to demonstrate her legitimacy as a pregnant person, as a parent, and as a person deserving common courtesy because her comportment is not feminine.

A character like Teek may seem to emblematize issues that arose in the twenty-first century. For many Americans, queer pregnancy ideologically began in 2008 with the appearance of Thomas Beatie, a man who was assigned female at birth, on the *Oprah Winfrey Show* to discuss his pregnancy.[3] This perception of queer pregnancy as a recent or futuristic phenomenon has at least some grounding in fact since the biotechnology that would allow trans women, cisgender men, and others born without ovaries and uteruses to gestate human offspring is only now on the horizon. Yet these kinds of reproductive embodiment have always been possible in fiction.[4] Indeed, reimagining pregnancy is a hallmark of several genres, most obviously dystopias such as *Brave New World* (1932). Nevertheless, a recent spate of memoirs about nonbinary embodiment and reproduction are often discussed in the popular press as though queer pregnancy is a new literary subject without a history. Among other points, *Masculine Pregnancies: Modernist Conceptions of Creativity and Legitimacy, 1918–1939* demonstrates that the masculine pregnant woman is not a new character type but instead one with a literary history that stretches back more than a century. Queer people have always reproduced and had lives shaped by reproductive decisions; what is uncommon is the recognition of their presence in works of literature before the twenty-first century.

This book explores the relationship between masculinity and pregnancy in Anglophone literature published in the years between the First and Second World Wars. It focuses on depictions of what I call "masculine pregnancy"—mannish pregnant women and metaphorical male pregnancy—in the works of Djuna Barnes, Willa Cather, William Faulkner, and Ezra Pound, with comparative discussions of works by Charlotte Perkins Gilman, Olive Moore, Jean Toomer, and Virginia Woolf. I argue that these modernist writers combined masculinity and pregnancy to give shape to their ideas about reproductive and creative legitimacy. The book considers one of many strands of transatlantic modernism. Barnes, Cather, Faulkner, and Pound were all born in the United States, but Barnes and Pound spent significant portions of their careers abroad, and Faulkner and Cather thought globally even if they wrote locally. These four authors incorporated transatlantic political, social, and scientific debates into their works, and these debates inform my readings of the selected texts. These readings highlight a fact that is still rarely acknowledged in literary criticism or elsewhere: not all pregnant people are feminine people.

The first half of this book considers texts in which most of the depictions of masculine pregnancy attempt to delegitimize the biological children and literary "offspring" of women and queer people; the second half of the book looks at texts that generally treat queer (pro)creation sympathetically. This two-part structure is motivated by principles Heather Love lays out in *Feeling Backward: Loss and the Politics of Queer History* (2007). Love delineates two of the important aspects of literary scholarship: the "critical function," which reveals "the conditions of exclusion and inequality," and the "imaginative function," which illuminates "alternative trajectories for the future" (29). Love is careful to explain why literary scholars must attend to these functions jointly rather than directing attention to one or the other:

> Both aspects are important; however, to the extent that the imaginative function of criticism is severed from its critical function—to the extent that it becomes mere optimist—it loses its purchase on the past. . . . The politics of optimism diminishes the suffering of queer historical subjects; at the same time, it blinds us to the continuities between past and present. As long as homophobia continues to centrally structure queer life, we cannot afford to turn away from the past. (29)

Roughly speaking, my analysis of metaphorical male pregnancy attends to the first function by revealing that certain modernist authors attempted to use these metaphors to position women and queer people as illegitimate creators. My analysis of mannish women attends to the second function by offering alternatives to the usual ways of imagining queer pregnancy.

To be more specific, Pound and Faulkner used childbirth metaphors to position virile men as the only legitimate creators of literary and physical offspring alike, while effeminate men and masculine women appear in their works as unnatural usurpers. In these works, feminine people—be they women or men—produce bad and therefore illegitimate art; masculine women might be able to produce legitimate art, but only so long as they do not reproduce (and they always reproduce eventually, since the female body's drive to reproduce is supposedly unstoppable). The purpose of such depictions is to shore up the idea of the Author as a heterosexual, masculine man. Nevertheless, my analysis of Cather and Barnes demonstrates that these exclusionary efforts were published in the same time period as texts by women writers that radically reimagine reproductive embodiment. Barnes and Cather shift our attention away from the realm of metaphor by depicting the pregnant bodies of mannish women in *Nightwood* (1936) and *My Ántonia* (1918). (Faulkner's *If I Forget Thee, Jerusalem* [1939] is a special case because it includes both exclusionary depictions of masculine pregnancy and imaginative ones.) Toward the imaginative function, my reading of Cather and Barnes helps us see a different literary trajectory for queer pregnancy by showing that it has a trajectory at all. Like the broader public, literary scholarship tends to position queer pregnancy as a recent phenomenon coinciding with the rise of modern reproductive technologies.[5]

These two halves of *Masculine Pregnancies* give space to the critical and imaginative functions, thereby balancing the sobering reality of exclusionary politics with a politics of optimism.

Rethinking Masculinity, Pregnancy, and Modernism

I began writing this book with a working theory: experiences like Teek's—pregnancy increasing her ability to pass as a man—are due in part to the unthinkability of masculine pregnant women. This unthinkability stems from a common worldview that links pregnancy with femininity; because femininity is defined and shaped by race, the version of this worldview that circulates in the United States is implicitly associated with whiteness, "born of the impulses to differentiation and hierarchization" (Schuller ch. 3).[6] Despite the significant inroads made by LGBTQ+ activists, femininity is still often talked about as a by-product of or precursor to pregnancy, as though femininity "goes with" pregnancy. As a result, masculine women are outside the realm of what many people conceptualize when they think about pregnancy. Teek references the association between femininity and pregnancy when she expresses concern that her masculine embodiment will prevent conception: "I worried that **butchness itself** might preclude my chances of getting pregnant. The more **feminine** the woman, the more fertile, right?" (bold original, 11). Teek admits her logic is faulty—"warning! flat-earth-society-style reasoning" (ibid.)—but the historical association between femininity and pregnancy is hard to dislodge, even for a butch woman trying to conceive a child. The conceptual adjustment is harder still for the strangers who encounter Teek. The femininity-pregnancy linkage is so tight that Teek's fellow passengers are *more* likely to perceive her as a man because that fits into their understanding of gender more easily than a pregnant butch. The pregnant man, a cousin to the pregnant mannish woman, is familiar as a comedic trope in the arts and pop culture, but his presence has historically been restricted to the realm of fiction, showing up in novels, stage productions, film, and TV. Most Americans do not expect to see a pregnant man or mannish woman in memoirs or the "real world"; much less are they willing to take masculine pregnant people seriously as legitimate claimants to reproductive rights, privileges, and justice.

The unimaginability of masculine pregnancy, especially pregnant mannish women, extends to academic communities. Indeed, when telling colleagues about my project I was often asked, "Is it about trans men?" The question suggests the limits of imagination in Western scholarly communities surrounding queer pregnancy; within the academic spheres of literary criticism and gender studies, anecdotal evidence suggests that pregnant mannish women are even less imaginable than pregnant trans men.[7] To be clear, trans male pregnancy is far from firmly ensconced within the realm of the imaginable. As N. Stritzke and E. Scaramuzza argue, "procreation remains a gendered binary" in medicine, law, and culture, since queer pregnancy is rarely discussed in these realms and, further, "MTF (male-to-female) and FTM (female-to-male) people were (and still are in many countries) denied the right of reproduction altogether if they choose to aim for a change in civil status. They were, or still are, lawfully forced to submit to sterilization" (149). Stritzke and Scaramuzza acknowledge that the situation is improving in many countries (142). Yet trans pregnancy is still regularly ignored, lampooned, disparaged, or worse. I surmise that the unimaginability of trans pregnancy has similar etiologies as that of mannish pregnancy: in addition to trans- and homophobia, it stems from lack of familiarity with the history of reproduction—especially as concerns queer people—among academics and the general public alike.[8] Rather than pitting these varieties of reproductive embodiment against one another, or desiring finality in identity categorizations, *Masculine Pregnancies* recognizes the fluidity of identity and positions mannish pregnancy in a constellation of nonbinary, trans, and queer reproduction, historicizing its existence in interwar literature to contribute to a better understanding of the whole.

In the early years of the twentieth century, non-normative genders and sexualities were often combined under the umbrella of the same concept, inversion. Jana Funke explains that the term "'sexual inversion' conflates what we now describe as homosexual identity and trans or nonbinary identity" (Funke, "Radclyffe Hall," 6:25). To put it another way, sexologists had not yet separated sexual "deviancy" (same-sex attraction) from gender "deviancy" or comportment associated with the "opposite" sex, which could range from women smoking cigarettes and being savvy in business, to dressing in masculine clothing and living as a man (Doan 519).

Although *Masculine Pregnancies* is mostly concerned with mannish women who have relationships with men, the possibility of same-sex attraction nevertheless informs depictions of these characters. As such, a point Laura Doan makes with regard to the term *lesbian* provides important context: "while we should regard with circumspection any secure link between the masculine woman and the 'lesbian,' we need also to acknowledge a degree of association between the two" ("Topsy-Turveydom" 522). Doan argues that late 1920s England was a turning point after which *mannishness* was associated with sexuality; before then, however, "there was far more fluidity around notions of gender inversion, gender deviance, and sexuality" (522). Therefore, mannishness was not always perceived as an indicator of lesbianism, though it often lurks at the edges of depictions of mannish pregnancy, with characters hinting at, wondering about, or directly acknowledging the mannish woman in question having intimate relationships with women as well as men.

Lesbian, mannish, inverted: the variability among these terms begins to suggest just how fraught terminology is for scholars studying the history of queer identity. Among the challenges the scholar must navigate is presentism. As Doan contends, we should be cautious of applying modern terminology to interwar texts because they color our interpretive categories, "making it extremely difficult for us to differentiate between *what* was seen and read by *whom*; that is, how individuals were regarded by their own contemporaries and within their respective cultures, and how they regarded and presented themselves" ("Topsy-Turveydom" 526). In any case, it is impossible and unproductive for a scholar to attempt to say definitively that a character is *this* or *that* identity. They are, after all, fictional characters who do not have gender or sexual identities that exist off the page.

I have chosen to consider the masculine female characters in this book as mannish and inverted rather than trans (in the identitarian sense as opposed to trans as a theoretical framework or lens). First, the term transgender is anachronistic and, as Halberstam argues, applying current terminology to earlier iterations of queer lifestyles "denies them their historical specificity" when we should be "produc[ing] methodologies sensitive to historical change but influenced by current theoretical preoccupations" (*Female Masculinities* 46). Second, "inverted" is a much broader term than "transgender" in ways I explain in detail in chapter 3. The authors and audiences I study in this book understood non-normative genders and sexualities within the conceptual framework of inversion; as such, I find inversion to be an accurate framework from an identitarian perspective and a useful heuristic.

Although I do not read the characters in this book as trans in an identitarian sense, I readily acknowledge that it is possible to consider the forms of mannishness that I discuss here through a trans critical framework. Stryker and Currah describe this critical framework as "a conceptual space within which it becomes possible to (re)name, (dis)articulate, and (re) assemble the constituent elements of contemporary personhood in a manner that facilitates a deeply historical analysis of the utter contingency and fraught conditions of intelligibility of all embodied subjectivity" (8). More specifically, "transmasculinity" has proven to be a rich theoretical apparatus in recent modernist scholarship. Chris Coffman defines "transmasculinity" as "a broad range of masculine traits in persons assigned female at birth [and] encompasses not only those who embody what Halberstam calls 'female masculinity' but also those who consider themselves transgender or transexual" (2). Understood this way, it is entirely possible to situate the forms of masculinity that I consider here through this lens. Indeed, I hope to see scholarship that does just that. If, as Ato Quayson says, one of the chief purposes of criticism is that it "illuminates new ways of experiencing existence" (*Calibrations* xvi), we should welcome alternate approaches and readings rather than attempting to narrow the field of vision to a single "right" reading.

With regard to categories of gender, sex, and sexuality, a guiding principle of this book comes from Gayle Rubin. In the essay "Of Catamites and Kings" (1992), Rubin states:

> Our categories are important. We cannot organize a social life, a political movement, or our individual identities and desires without them. The fact that categories invariably leak and can never contain all the relevant "existing things" does not render them useless, only limited. Categories like "woman," "butch," "lesbian," or "transexual" are all imperfect, historical, temporary, and arbitrary. We use them, and they use us. We use them to construct meaningful lives, and they mold us into historically specific forms of personhood. Instead of fighting for immaculate classifications and impenetrable boundaries, let us strive to maintain a community that understands diversity as a gift, sees anomalies as precious, and treats all basic principles with a hefty dose of skepticism. (479)

Mindful of these many pitfalls and exigencies, I chose to rely on the texts themselves rather than my own, twenty-first century perceptions of masculinity exclusively. This book focuses on characters whose masculinity is a point of contention in the text itself. The pregnant characters I consider here are called "manly" by other characters, by a narrator, or in a self-description. For instance, the narrator of *Nightwood* tells us that parishioners in France perceive Robin Vote's body as man-like, while in Faulkner's *Jerusalem*, a man derisively notes that Charlotte Rittenmeyer wears "pants, man's pants" when pregnant (6). Some characters express the sentiment themselves, as when Ántonia Shimerda states, "I like to be like a man" while working on a farm in Nebraska (74).

I apply a similar logic with regard to the childbirth metaphor. In the examples considered throughout this book, the writers directly describe authorship in gendered terms and assert the legitimacy and superiority of what they call "manly" forms of creation. For instance, one of the characters in Faulkner's *Mosquitoes* states, "Women can [create] without art—old biology takes care of that. But men, men. . . . in art, a man can create without any assistance at all" (320). The texts I study therefore register manliness and masculinity as they were perceived in the interwar years. I will have much more to say about inversion and masculinity in chapters 1 and 3. For now it suffices to say that the conceptual overlap between "mannishness" and "trans" means that the study of mannish pregnancy is a necessary complement to both modernist studies of transmasculinity as well as studies of queer pregnancy in contemporary works such as *Pregnant Butch* and Maggie Nelson's *The Argonauts* (2015).

Bringing the figure of the masculine pregnant woman into focus as this book does has the significant potential to redefine the way modernist studies theorizes reproduction. The figure of the mannish woman in interwar literature has been the subject of a small but growing number of scholarly studies, yet the pregnant mannish woman has never, to my knowledge, received sustained critical attention by modernist scholars.[9] The unthinkability of masculine pregnant women is once again the culprit, preventing literary critics from recognizing the presence of these characters in interwar literature. This is, after all, an era in which the "mannish woman" was a figure of intense social, political, and medical debate since the suffrage movement and wartime labor demands increased her ranks to unprecedented numbers and salience. Reproduction, too, was at the forefront of American and European minds in the interwar years. Groups arguing for and against causes related to eugenics, access to birth control, and citizenship rights for immigrants fomented debate over reproduction. Was there literature, I wondered, that considered these two lightning rod subjects together? I quickly realized that depictions of masculine pregnant women in interwar literature are not uncommon, but criticism seldom recognizes them as such. Instead, the scholarly conversation tends to argue that pregnancy feminizes these characters despite textual evidence indicating that mannishness persists throughout gestation. Virtually all scholarship on reproduction in modernism centers on feminine women or assumes that femininity is a by-product of pregnancy, as in the common claim that pregnancy is "the most feminine of acts."[10] The title of my book refers to *masculine* rather than *male* pregnancy to reflect the central place of the mannish woman in my analysis. The following chapters take the persistence of masculinity throughout pregnancy seriously and examine it against attempts by fellow characters—and sometimes by authors and readers, also—to delegitimize masculine women who (pro)create.

When scholarship does address the confluence of masculinity and pregnancy, it tends to center male characters and authors.[11] In modernism, important work has been done on male writers who represent authorship as a kind of reproduction via the childbirth metaphor, wherein the literary text is the author's offspring. Yet most of this scholarship was written before the 1990s.[12] In the intervening years, queer and trans theorists have developed a multitude of conceptual frameworks for understanding the interlocking implications of gender, embodiment, and (pro)creation. In other words, scholarship on masculinity and pregnancy in modernism was largely written before such queer landmarks as Jack Halberstam's *Female Masculinity* (1998), which refuted the idea that masculinity is the property of men and demonstrated the diversity of forms that female masculinity has historically taken; and Lee Edelman's *No Future* (2004), a polemic that ignited debates in queer theory over the relationship between queer identity, kinship, and reproduction.[13] As a result, the intersection of masculinity and pregnancy in modernism is due for reconsideration.

Informed by queer theory, *Masculine Pregnancies* makes two major contributions to modernist scholarship. First, it draws critical attention to the figure of the mannish pregnant woman, as I have already discussed. These women exist outside modernism (and outside literature, of course), but depictions of her were newly salient in the interwar years because of the mannish woman's prevalence in political and social discourse.

Second, this book contributes to modernist scholarship by demonstrating that literary concerns about legitimacy pervaded the works of major modernist writers to a greater degree than previously acknowledged. *Legitimate* stems from *lex* and *leg*, roots meaning *law*.[14] To be illegitimate is to be outside the law and without state sanction. Reproductive illegitimacy, in the sense of bastardy, saturates Anglophone literature of the eighteenth and nineteenth centuries. *Tristram Shandy* (1759) and *The Scarlet Letter* (1850) are but two of the many familiar works treating the subject. By comparison, authors in the early years of the twentieth century seem to have turned their attention elsewhere because bastards appear less frequently, and plots are less likely to revolve around attendant issues. As Allen Johnson argues, modernism is better known for its depictions of castration, infertility, and impotence: "Again and again in modernist literature, it is the temporal logic of biology—of reproduction, lineage, and offspring—that is forcibly disrupted" (6). The relative dearth of plotlines related to bastardy in twentieth-century literature prompted Isobel Armstrong to ask, "what happens to the issues of genealogy and illegitimacy that preoccupy earlier novelists?" (254) at the end of her study of these issues in nineteenth-century literature, *Novel Politics*.

Close examination reveals that writers in the years between the World Wars were not so much quiet on the issue of illegitimacy as they were reimagining the terms of the discussion. Whereas authors of earlier eras tended to direct their attention to the biolegal status of the offspring (i.e., whether a child was a legitimate heir or a bastard), the authors I study expanded the scope of their attention to include the legitimacy of the pregnant person's gender. In sum, modernist engagement with legitimacy is marked by a thematic fascination with the gender of the (pro)creator.[15] I see this interwar expansion of attention to the gestator as an attempt by modernist authors to work out anxieties surrounding watershed sociohistorical events in the United States and Europe. These events include WWI and its disruptions to gender norms (particularly the perception that men were less manly as a result of physical injury and shell shock, and women more manly because of greater involvement in the workplace); the unprecedented inroads women and people of color were making in the literary realm as writers, editors, and publishers, thereby threatening the dominance of white male authorship; and, finally, the panoply of interwar attempts to control reproduction that included but were not limited to eugenics, the medicalization of pregnancy, restrictive immigration policies, and contested definitions of whiteness that raised questions about whose offspring were legitimate citizens.

Authors frequently combine masculinity and pregnancy to repressive ends—Pound and Faulkner do just that—but the combination is not *necessarily* repressive. Indeed, I show that the discursive combination of masculinity and pregnancy can facilitate the agency of women and queer people too. Scholarship on masculinity and reproduction in modernism overwhelmingly addresses the oppressive ends to which this combination of discourses was put. Nina Auerbach states flatly that the "metaphorical equation between literary creativity and childbirth" is both "timeless" and "oppressive" (506). Auerbach's assessment encapsulates how feminist critics have usually seen the relationship between masculinity and pregnancy.[16] There are plenty of examples of patriarchal oppression in the pages of this book; one of my goals is to follow a strand of discourse that uses depictions of pregnancy to disqualify women writers, and to unpack the effects of this disqualification on the development of literary modernism. But also, and crucially, this book contains examples of the opposite: female authors depicting female characters who embody masculinity for their own ends and desires. The texts studied here, especially *My Ántonia*, provide us with examples of characters for whom the combination of reproduction and masculinity is salutary.

These characters are reminders of the lessons Halberstam taught in *Female Masculinity*, chief among them that masculinity is not always a foreign trait imposed on women. Kaja Silverman's explanation of why she chose to consider male rather than female subjectivity in her influential book *Male Subjectivity at the Margins* (1992) is worth quoting here even though Silverman's book is not about reproduction. Her explanation sums up the imposition approach, which many feminist scholars still take toward masculinity studies: "It might seem surprising that I have chosen to pursue this project through male rather than female subjectivity, but I am motivated to do so in significant part because masculinity impinges with such force upon femininity. To effect a large-scale reconfiguration of male identification and desire would, at the very least, permit female subjectivity to be lived differently than it is at present" (2–3). I take no issue with Silverman's claim about reconfiguring male identification, and I agree that masculinity intersects with femininity with often violent results. Silverman nevertheless establishes a binary between masculinity and male subjectivity on one side, and femininity and female subjectivity on the other, making it difficult to see how masculine women fit into the analytical picture. For some women, masculinity is the authentic gender identity and femininity the impinging force. By reimagining the literary relationship between masculinity and pregnancy—and by imagining the figure of the masculine pregnant woman in modernism for the first time—this book maps out an alternative trajectory for both modernism and queer literature.

A reconsideration of masculinity and reproduction is underway in the critical conversations surrounding earlier literary periods. Scholars such as Alicia Andrzejewski and Melissa E. Sanchez have brought queer theory to bear on Early Modern British texts.[17] Andrzejewski notes that queer theory typically "positions queerness as antithetical to reproduction and futurity and therefore in opposition to the pregnant body," and notes that Shakespearean scholarship typically follows suit (106). She states in clear terms what is at stake when scholarship fails to consider the overlap between queerness and reproduction, a statement that applies equally well to modernist literature: "this [omission] contributes to the erasure of lesbian and bisexual women's and trans and nonbinary people's respective experiences as pregnant people. The assumptions that only women get pregnant; that every pregnancy ends in the birth of a child; and that pregnancy always reproduces the family in a recognizable form are inherent in definitions of heteronormativity, and these assumptions erase many people's lived experiences of pregnancy" (106–7). The work of Andrzejewski and others is beginning to inscribe queer reproduction in its rightful place in scholarly understandings of Anglophone literature. *Masculine Pregnancies* is aligned with this body of scholarship; I take a similar starting point, the assumption that reproduction and queerness are compatible, and apply it to the twentieth century. The representations of masculine pregnancy that I consider are not always queer in the sense of challenging heteronormativity, but many of them are. These depictions are part of a literary lineage that stretches back at least to the Early Modern period and forward to the trans parenthood memoirs of the twenty-first century.

In the interwar years, the written record of Black American writers tells a different story than that of white Americans. Childbirth metaphors appear with some regularly in the works of Black interwar writers, but mannish pregnancy does not.[18] Many interwar texts depict the vicissitudes of pregnancy for Black women, but these texts, such as Nella Larsen's *Quicksand* (1928), tend to emphasize the femininity of their protagonists. The reasons for this difference are many, but among them is undoubtedly the imbrication of race and gender as it existed in interwar America. This is not to say that mannishness had no purchase in Black women's lives or to suggest that Black authors had no interest in exploring such depictions in their writing. However, in the interwar era, "the grandchildren of the last generation of enslaved people were in the process of defining freedom in a society that held tightly to social and racial restrictions," explains Tara T. Green (15). Green argues that this milieu resulted in stark differences between "public depictions and the private strivings of Black women" (15). Furthermore, culturally, politically, and legally, Black women have been seen in the United States as more capable of hard work, of bearing the lash, of enduring rough lives than white women because of a false belief that they have a higher threshold of pain and greater muscle mass (Christian 7). In short, Black women have historically been construed as more masculine than white women. In the same way that privileged, rich men have more room to be feminine without risk—indeed, it asserts their power by showing how lightly they can throw some of it away (DuPlessis, "Virile" 20)—white women authors had relatively more room to be masculine themselves and to depict their white characters as mannish.

This dynamic was reflected in and exacerbated by issues connected to publication. Black writers were, from the very beginnings of the African American literary tradition, forced to contend with editors, publishers, and readers who questioned their very humanity. As Barbara Christian observes: "We must not forget that, by necessity, the first [Black] novelists were writing to white audiences. Few black people were literate at that time because of stringent laws against teaching slaves to read and write. The thrust of the black novel necessarily had to be a cry of protest directed at whites for their treatment of blacks. The problem was not whether black women were heroic, but whether they were women at all" (32). Black women had to write against the weight of centuries of history that characterized them and any Black female characters they might create as unwomanly or unhuman. In the words of Hazel Carby, they "had to confront the dominant domestic ideologies and literary conventions of womanhood which excluded them from the definition 'woman'" (6). This history helps us understand the dearth of mannish pregnant women in the literary tradition of Black writers in the United States. If, in the works of white authors, mannish pregnancy reads as a daring rejection of the idea that pregnancy is the pinnacle of femininity, the effect is the opposite for Black women authors and their Black characters. The femininity of Black women was already in question; depicting them as masculine would only amplify an existing stereotype rather than read as avant-garde rebelliousness. Conversely, the act of depicting a Black pregnant character as feminine and womanly, particularly texts that *emphasize* femininity such as Larsen's *Quicksand*, can be understood as attempts to inscribe the humanity of Black women.

Definitions: Male Pregnancy, Mannish Pregnancy, Masculine Pregnancy

The term "male pregnancy" and its synonyms "male maternity" and "male conception" have historically been used in literary criticism to refer to depictions of physical and metaphorical pregnancy in male *characters*, as well as the use of childbirth metaphors by male *authors*.[19] In keeping with this tradition, *Masculine Pregnancies* considers depictions of male pregnancy and childbirth metaphors in modernism. New to this tradition is my discussion of mannish women. By using the term "masculine pregnancy" instead of "male pregnancy," I expand the usual frame of reference to include depictions of mannish female characters who gestate human offspring.

This expansion requires some adjustments to the usual terminology. In this book, I use terms in the following ways. *Mannish pregnancy* refers to masculine women who are literally and/or metaphorically pregnant, as well as depictions of them in literature. In chapter 1, I provide historical background on the term "mannish" and its salience in the interwar years. *Male pregnancy* refers to men who are literally and/or metaphorically pregnant, as well as depictions of them in literature. Depictions of pregnant trans men are rare in literary texts before the twenty-first century.[20] Therefore, most of my references to "male pregnancy" indicate fictional depictions of pregnancy in cisgender men as a kind of fantasy or wish-fulfillment. *Childbirth metaphor* refers to comparisons between literary production and physical reproduction. Writers of all genders use this kind of metaphor, but in the pages of this book it most frequently occurs in the context of male-identified authors asserting a contrast between the creative "offspring" that male artists produce and the physical offspring women produce.[21] (The figure of the female artist who gestates is taken up most centrally in chapter 3.) *Masculine pregnancy* refers to the various ways that discourses of masculinity and pregnancy link up in literary imagination. As such, *masculine pregnancy* is an umbrella term covering all the above. The term furthermore conveys the fact that childbirth metaphors and depictions of pregnancy in men and mannish women occupied overlapping ideological territory for the authors I study. Barnes, Cather, Faulkner, and Pound almost always depict physical pregnancy in masculine women in texts that also thematically engage creative output. Therefore, when the discourses of masculinity and pregnancy intersect in the works of these authors, they do so in ways that invoke both metaphorical and physical pregnancies.

One of the most surprising revelations to emerge from my readings of mannish pregnancy is a concept I am calling "fictional kinship," which refers to literary constructions of genealogy that rely on storytelling and the imagination to rewrite biological kinship. The texts I study implicitly debate the role of the body in determinations about legitimacy. These texts pose the question, to what extent is genealogical legitimacy determined by biology? This question might seem an obvious or rhetorical one, since the illegitimacy of offspring rests on biological origins: are they genetically related to the father and mother? Yet in my readings of *Nightwood* and *My Ántonia*, a picture emerges wherein the stories we tell about reproduction and kinship matter just as much, if not more, than biology. Chapters 4 and 5 develop the trope of fictional kinship—a phrasing I adapt from the anthropological term *fictive kinship*—with reference to eugenic theories of race and historical concepts such as parental impression theory. Pound's and Faulkner's works, discussed in chapters 2 and 3, take a more traditional line. These works imply that legitimacy derives from masculinity, which men have supposedly easier access to by virtue of their embodiment (biology). I demonstrate that Pound and Faulkner leveraged the rhetorical force of scientific discourse around masculinity to legitimize their own claims to authorial greatness. Taken together, the representations of masculine pregnancy considered in these four chapters position legitimacy as a far more important shaping force in interwar literature than previously acknowledged.

Before discussing the works of Barnes, Cather, Faulkner, and Pound, I offer historical and cultural context that is necessary to understand the ways these authors engaged with and revised discourse surrounding masculinity and reproduction. Chapter 1, "A Cultural History of Gender and Reproduction," is a history of reproduction and gender in the years between the World Wars in the United States and England. This chapter considers threads of discourse not usually discussed together but that, when combined, demonstrate the multitude of ways that this book's keywords—masculinity, pregnancy, legitimacy, creativity—were picked up and deployed by fields as varying as medicine, anthropology, politics, and literature. The chapter surveys debates around eugenics, the medicalization of pregnancy, bastardy, and immigration (especially as informed by changing definitions of race). Many of the concerns that animated these debates have roots in earlier disputes over bastardy and inheritance in the eighteenth and nineteenth centuries, and modernist writers were responding, in part, to their literary precursors' depictions of bastardy. As such, this chapter also provides an overview of literary critical scholarship on bastardy in pre–twentieth-century Anglophone literature. Finally, this chapter takes up the figure of the "mannish woman" in the interwar years, enumerating the ways this newly salient figure exacerbated and complicated the period's reproductive debates.

After this survey of historical and literary context, *Masculine Pregnancies* moves into the heart of the book: analyses of modernist texts that register concerns surrounding masculinity, pregnancy, legitimacy, and creativity. In chapter 2, "Literary Obstetrics: Ezra Pound and the Midwives Act of 1902," I demonstrate that depictions of masculine pregnancy were an important part of the rhetoric Pound used to discredit female writers and editors, as well as to position himself and T. S. Eliot as legitimate artists. Central to my analysis is Pound's doggerel poem "SAGE HOMME," which he wrote to commemorate his collaboration with Eliot on *The Waste Land* (1922). This chapter details the various ways that Pound's depictions of masculine pregnancy were influenced by a contemporaneous medical debate between midwives and surgeons. This influence—hitherto unrecognized—reveals a flaw in the critical consensus that regards Pound as the intellectual "midwife" of *The Waste Land*. Situating Pound's poem in context with this medical debate provides a fitting introduction to one of the book's central claims: interwar writers began combining masculinity and pregnancy to delegitimize female writers and editors and to shore up their own claims to literary legitimacy.

Pound's work is emblematic of anxieties surrounding legitimacy for some creative types in the interwar years, as it manifests the desire to exclude anyone who does not inhabit a white masculine body. William Faulkner, the subject of chapter 3, "Pregnancy in Faulkner's Artist Novels: Masculinity, Sexology, and Creativity in Interwar America," was less dogmatic than Pound but nevertheless struggled to incorporate newly powerful female artists into old-fashioned models of gender and generation. I consider *Mosquitoes* (1927) and *If I Forget Thee, Jerusalem* (also known as *The Wild Palms*, 1939), arguing that Faulkner uses reproductive rhetoric to police the boundaries of "legitimate" art. I discuss these novels in context with the rise of sexology and the discourse of inversion, a concept thought to explain same-sex attraction. In doing so, I reveal surprising eruptions of sympathy for queer (pro)creation in the midst of the novels' more overt heteronormative plotlines. Faulkner's representations of masculine pregnancy sometimes function to assert the legitimacy of male authors only, as Pound's representations do. At other times, however, Faulkner's depictions of masculine pregnancy manifest identification with and admiration for masculine women who are both artists and pregnant people, and these depictions undermine the novels' otherwise misogynistic depictions of gender and creativity.

The queer interruptions in Faulkner's artist novels create a bridge with the final two chapters of this book, where I consider novels that grant cultural legitimacy to queer people and their offspring. While Pound and Faulkner combine discourses of masculinity and pregnancy to delegitimize queer bodies and their offspring, Cather and Barnes combine them to reject such exclusionary discourse. Chapter 4, "The Mannish Woman as Fertility Goddess: How Narrative Makes a Legitimate Mother Out of Ántonia Shimerda," focuses on *My Ántonia* (1918), the third novel in Willa Cather's prairie trilogy. In it, I discuss the aforementioned "fictional kinship" trope. I begin by considering the racial dynamics of whiteness in the United States, highlighting the ways they inform Cather's depiction of her protagonist as a mannish, Eastern European immigrant, as well as her depiction of Ántonia's neighbors' willingness to accept her as a legitimate American woman. I argue that Cather introduces a different version of creative legitimacy than the one espoused by Faulkner and Pound. Faulkner and Pound combine masculinity and pregnancy in attempts to argue for the legitimacy (and supposed superiority) of creations emanating from straight, white, masculine writers. *My Ántonia*, by contrast, implies that the biological offspring of queer individuals are not only legitimate but also inject much-needed variety into literature and genetics (this latter idea being distinctly and disturbingly eugenic). Ultimately, however, Cather undermines the centrality of biology to legitimacy. Whereas eighteenth- and nineteenth-century Anglo-American authors were preoccupied with heredity, inheritance, and other biology-based conceptions of legitimacy, Cather's novel suggests that narrative is just as important, if not more so, than biology because it is capable of revising people's ideas about who is and is not legitimate. Thereby, this chapter positions narrative as an alternative to biology-based notions of legitimacy.

As with chapter 4, the fifth chapter considers sympathetic representations of mannish pregnancy. In " 'Conceiving herself pregnant before she was': Parental Impressions and the Limits of Reproductive Legitimacy in *Nightwood*," I read Djuna Barnes's *Nightwood* (1936) through the lens of parental impressions. This ancient theory of reproduction persists into the twentieth century and holds that the imagination has the power to shape a fetus's physical form. I demonstrate that the Volkbein men in *Nightwood* attempt to erase their Jewish background by imaginatively shaping their offspring to be physically and emotionally suited for an aristocratic destiny in fascist countries. This chapter brings together strands of discourse from all previous chapters, including inversion, redefinitions of whiteness, the medicalization of pregnancy, and fictional kinship, weaving them together to reveal the limits of narrative to revise determinations of legitimacy. My reading of *Nightwood* demonstrates what narrative cannot do in the face of oppressive politics and furthermore questions the value of legitimacy in the first place.

Masculine Pregnancies concludes by suggesting avenues for further research. In the coda, I outline the ways mannish pregnancy complicates debates about queer kinship and what is commonly referred to as the antisocial thesis. Some of the energy animating these debates may have waned in recent years, but the totalizing negativity of Edelman's *No Future*—with its provocative positioning of queers as non-reproductive—and the utopic models of kinship that motivate José Esteban Muñoz's *Cruising Utopia* (2009) are still epistemic poles between which much of the conversation occurs. The mannish pregnant woman is a figure who is both queer and reproductive, by turns enveloped in discourses of normativity and futurity and rejected by proponents of the same. The coda suggests ideas for further analysis based on the ways this positionality troubles foundational assumptions of queer kinship debates.

Together, the chapters of this book widen the aperture on masculinity and pregnancy in modern literature. Modernists combined these discourses in ways that attempt to silence, diminish, and delegitimize anyone who is not the picture of the traditional artist. But so, too, did writers attempt to change what legitimacy in literature looks like, bringing mannish women, queer immigrants, and their biological and creative offspring into the fold. *Masculine Pregnancies* illustrates how some modernist texts are far queerer than usually assumed, while others use depictions of masculine pregnancy to shore up traditional notions of authorial and procreative legitimacy.

Chapter 1

A Cultural History of
Gender and Reproduction

This chapter offers a cultural history of gender and reproduction. The first section of this chapter deals with illegitimacy, especially in the sense of bastardy. I discuss some of the ways that writers before the interwar era engaged the concept of illegitimacy. These earlier engagements will set modernist ones in relief, helping the reader understand how interwar writers both built on and rejected traditional literary discourse about legitimacy. I then limn the history of the "mannish woman," her salience in the interwar years, and her disruption of reproductive assumptions.

From there, I shift my focus to discourse about men and masculinity. This section of the chapter discusses the outsize role that the supposed "crisis" of masculinity played in the development of literary modernism. I move then into a survey of some of the transatlantic racial politics that informed depictions of masculine pregnancy in the interwar period. Here, I pay particular attention to eugenics, contested definitions of whiteness, and Black American literary traditions. The chapter concludes with an overview of what is known as the "medicalization" of pregnancy, which altered how, where, and with whom people gave birth, as well as some of the conceptual connections between medicalization and disability discourse. All of the subjects covered in this chapter reappear throughout the book. The background provided here will give readers, especially those unfamiliar with the history of reproduction in the twentieth century, sufficient context to understand how discourses surrounding legitimacy, masculinity, mannishness, race, and medicine informed modernist depictions of masculine pregnancy.

Legitimacy

The depictions of masculine pregnancy considered in this book raise questions about legitimacy akin to those raised by Teek in A. K. Summers's *Pregnant Butch*, which I discuss in the introduction. Like Summers, modernist authors grappled with the public perception of masculine pregnant bodies. These authors depict characters who, upon encountering a mannish woman, wonder whether her masculinity will prevent conception; if masculinity will interfere with her ability to be a "good" mother; and if the masculine woman is due the same rights and courtesy as feminine pregnant people. These suppositions register the fact that mannish pregnancies raise questions for many people about legitimacy in the sense of genuineness or authorization: Are mannish women "real" women? Who gets to decide?

Genuineness and authorization were acute concerns for authors in the interwar years thanks to radically altered gender norms, the changing face of literary publishing, the increasing presence of queer people in the public sphere, and broad societal attempts to control reproduction. Faulkner and Pound, for instance, depict male characters who attempt to adjudicate creative legitimacy through childbirth metaphors, as I show in chapters 2 and 3. In the interwar years, women were making unprecedented gains in literature as writers, editors, and publishers. At the same time, queer people were more visible than ever. The salience—if not the existence (because it always existed)—of queerness resulted, in part, from the rapid growth of psychology and sexology, which drew the general public's attention to non-normative forms of sexuality and gender. Moreover, the trials of Oscar Wilde for homosexuality in 1895 and Radclyffe Hall's *The Well of Loneliness* for obscenity in 1928 increased awareness and attention. Even though these trials were intended to suppress knowledge of same-sex behaviors, the result was the opposite (Foster 150). Additionally, white women were gaining power and prominence in Anglophone literature in the early decades of the twentieth century,[1] and straight male writers often felt threatened by women's newfound power. As Rachel Blau DuPlessis argues, "the slow but inevitable opening of many professions to women evoked a craft-guild mentality on the part of some male writers—trying to limit access by titrating apprenticeships and also downgrading the 'masterworks' of those who did not learn in and from the exclusionary guild" ("Virile" 21). In *Masculine Pregnancies*, I consider several depictions of male characters who attempt to adjudicate legitimacy by co-opting (pro)creation and rhetorically positioning it as a masculine endeavor, thereby suggesting that creation of the literary and even the physical kind is best handled by men. This assertion is a fear response arising from the rapid social changes mentioned above, which disrupted the unquestioned dominance of white men in the literary realm; the need to make it suggests the author's anxiety over his own legitimacy, power, and cultural capital.

In a different vein, depictions of mannish pregnant women in works by Cather, Barnes, and, to an extent, Faulkner, Woolf, and Moore highlight the effect masculinity has on the reproductive experience. The effect is particularly noticeable with regard to the reactions of *other* characters, those who encounter mannish pregnant women. Many of them are depicted as questioning the legitimacy of mannish women as (pro)creators. This legitimacy is questioned in multiple ways in these texts: if she is eugenically "fit" to reproduce the nation's offspring; if her masculinity will render her an uncaring mother; and in the case of characters who are artists as well as reproducers, if pregnancy impedes her claim to legitimacy as a real artist, with "real" being a perpetually changing standard determined by the male artists in her milieu.

Legitimacy is a capacious term, constellating several concepts under a much broader one. As such, it is worth spending some time discussing its multiple denotations, the ways scholars have historically engaged with the concept, and how previous generations of authors contributed to discourses of legitimacy. Among the definitions of legitimacy in the *Oxford English Dictionary* is "conformity to the law, to rules, or to some recognized principle," "the fact of being a legitimate child. Also: the fact of a child's birth being legitimate," as well as "the fact of a thing's being what it appears to be; genuineness" ("legitimacy").[2] Common among all these definitions is a notion of gatekeeping, a line that separates the legitimate from the illegitimate. Any discussion of legitimacy, then, is also a discussion about power, in that we must consider who the gatekeepers are, what criteria they use, how permanent their decisions are, what benefits or punishments accrue from the decisions, who seeks legitimacy, and to what ends.

This kind of gatekeeping relies on an implicit spatialization wherein legitimacy becomes an ideological demarcation, a perimeter or dividing wall separating the legitimate from the illegitimate. Some discourse assumes a rather solid division between those who are legitimate and those not: you're either a bastard or you aren't. In the literary realm, this kind of thinking shows up in texts as well as criticism about them when writers implicitly assume that people lie but biology does not, leading to the erroneous notion that bastardy is a stable quality. Yet law and custom in Britain, the

Continent, and the United States manifest a great deal of permeability on this point. As Nancy Armstrong discusses, bastardy is an unsettled concept. For instance, in nineteenth-century England, the bastard was the responsibility of the mother according to the 1834 Poor Law, the responsibility of both parents by canon law, and *fillius nullius*—nobody's child—by other laws. Parents could choose to provide for illegitimate children through legal means, usually provisions in a will, though this was not required. Various Scottish and Continental laws "allowed children to be retrospectively legitimized by their parents' marriage, a practice not recognized by English common law" (38–39).

In the most formal of circumstances such as those above, the criteria for legitimacy are established by law, and decisions are made by individuals or governing bodies with legally vested authority. In extra-legal circumstances, however, the granting or withholding of legitimacy varies to a much greater extent. This variance is particularly apparent when we consider legitimacy in the sense of authenticity or belonging. When a determination of legitimacy is made by an individual or community, that determination may be subsequently withdrawn quite rapidly, without notice, and without logic. This fact does not mean that the determination is inconsequential. In the twenty-first century, for example, the elasticity of legitimacy has been weaponized against trans people. The care with which a trans person must approach public restrooms, lest someone decide they are not a legitimate man or woman and therefore an illegitimate user of the space who needs to be forcibly removed, exemplifies the violent repercussions that can arise from social determinations about legitimacy. The shifting winds of legitimacy can carry the force of a hurricane.

Legal and extra-legal power relations affect the way literary representations of legitimacy signify. As Marie Maclean argues, "representations of gender, reproduction and legitimacy change with changing power relations. As these representations change, so [tropes] arise, are recycled or are modified" (44). For instance, metaphors that compare writing to childbirth have historically signified differently when written by women rather than men. Susan Glover explains a paradigmatic case in her discussion of British women writers in the eighteenth century. She states that "children were under the legal authority of their fathers; married women had no rights to their children. For the woman writer, to figure one's literary output as offspring is to make a tenuous claim at best. . . . Issue from the womb without an identifiable father—production marked as female—could only be illegitimate" (97). In this case, the legal status of women and their off-spring shape the signification of the childbirth metaphor.

As the above examples attest, the concept of legitimacy raises questions with far-reaching consequences, many of them surrounding identity and gender. Margot Finn, Michael Lobban, and Jenny Bourne Taylor outline many of these questions, the following of which have the most bearing on the texts under consideration in *Masculine Pregnancies*: "What does it mean legitimately to belong—in a family, and in a place? What social and cultural tensions exist between different legal codes, between formal and informal, contractual and affective, concepts of legitimate relationships and identity, and how do these contribute to our understanding of the family? . . . Above all, what are the tensions among what contemporaries considered morally legitimate, what they considered legally legitimate, and what they considered as legitimate in social practice?" (3–4). Questions about legitimacy have long been negotiated in the public sphere, of which literature is an important part. Susan Glover argues that the eighteenth century begins to see theories that conceptualize legitimacy as "ascending from the people rather than descending from higher authority, a 'public sphere' (or an ideal of one) in which issues central to the national interest are subjected to critical, reasoned debate" (37–38). This kind of ascending legitimacy is not limited to eighteenth-century England; Maclean locates similar phenomena as early as the sixteenth century and as late as the twentieth (44). The questions asked by Finn et al. illustrate the wide variety of ways that discourses of legitimacy operate in Anglophone literature and related public spheres.

Nevertheless, scholarship on legitimacy in literature overwhelmingly focuses on a single facet, bastardy, and much of the scholarship on bastardy focuses on British novels from the eighteenth century. There is logic in this focus because these novels fairly overflow with "bastards and foundlings," to use Lisa Zunshine's phrase.[3] Susan Glover explains the prevalence of bastardy in the eighteenth century as a product of politics: "the questions raised by [the "exclusion crisis" related to James II] in England's politics were transposed to the domestic and literary spheres in the early decades of the 1700s . . . the role of property in law and culture became a founding preoccupation around which grew the imaginative prose fiction that would develop into the genre recognized by the end of the eighteenth century as the English novel" (15). The scarlet thread of bastardy winds its way through the nineteenth century too. As Margot Finn et al. say of novels in this era, a "preoccupation with the discovery of hidden kinship through illegitimate origins . . . pervades nineteenth-century literature" in part because "the idea of legitimacy in the broadest sense, its enactment, its ideological underpinning and its ultimate fragility, spanned a wide range of social and legal practices, cultural forms and institutions" (3). Bastards and foundlings appear less frequently in early twentieth-century literature. Consequently, scholars have paid less attention to it, and the critical conversation on illegitimacy is rather thin by comparison.

Concern with illegitimacy and its related issues persisted in twentieth-century literature, as a cursory look at almost any of Faulkner's major novels will attest. *Masculine Pregnancies* is concerned with discourses of legitimacy as they appear in early twentieth-century literature and nonfiction writing about literary craft. I discuss characters conferring social legitimacy on other characters, authors denying the legitimacy of competitors, and critics debating the legitimacy of characters, authors, texts, and scholarly approaches. I am arguing that the interwar years saw a shift in the rhetorical figurations that authors used to explore themes related to illegitimacy, including but not limited to bastardy. Central among these changes was a surge in depictions of masculine pregnancy that foreground the (il)legitimacy of the pregnant person's body.

The causes of this shift include world-historic events in the interwar era that undermined and altered traditional notions of kinship in the United States and Europe. Chief among these events was the Great War. Martha Vicinus explains that ideas surrounding "marriage and family" were by the 1920s "under new postwar pressures" that led to a loosening of norms surrounding white, middle-class kinship, which necessitated "a new vocabulary" to describe "new models of familiar intimate relations" (229). For instance, laws and social attitudes toward illegitimacy relaxed as out-of-wedlock pregnancy no longer seemed as scandalous as it used to in the wake of the Great War. Ruth Adam explains some of the context surrounding these changing attitudes among the British: "The 1914 War created a new and more merciful attitude towards the unmarried mother. All the pleading of individual reformers had never achieved for her what the massacre of young men did. Before it, society had stuck to the simple principle of deterrence. Having an illegitimate child was deliberately made so painful and humiliating that (so the theory ran) girls would avoid it at all costs. No one ever questioned whether this theory worked" (78). To be sure, illegitimacy still carried moral force before and after WWI, but that force was reduced by the horrors of war. Fewer people were willing to ostracize a woman who became pregnant by her beau while he was home on leave, especially when the death toll from the war was so high and handwringing over the need to replenish the British population had become commonplace. As Adam suggests, people were much more inclined to celebrate life, no matter the origins, after witnessing so much death. Interwar literature variously reflected, rejected, and amplified the dramatic changes to norms surrounding illegitimacy that the war brought about.

Some modernists revised symbolic figurations of legitimacy to reflect this new reality by shifting focus away from the offspring and toward the gender of gestators who were queer or simply did not fit an ideal of femininity. Threatened by the literary successes of women in the interwar years, these authors shored up their own credentials by adapting traditional representations of authorial legitimacy as male, that is, imaginative creation as the province of cis men. Depictions of masculine pregnancy in Pound's "SAGE HOMME" and Faulkner's artist novels use the childbirth metaphor in new ways that nevertheless serve an old purpose: to reinforce the idea that legitimate writers are heterosexual white men. Cather and Barnes, conversely, combined gender, reproduction, and legitimacy in new ways for new purposes: legitimizing the literary and biological offspring of queers and other outsiders.

Mannishness

Most of the authors under consideration in this book depict "mannish women" in their works. In the early years of the twentieth century, there was a widespread sense that white women from the United States and United Kingdom were becoming more masculine. These women were often labeled "mannish" in popular and scholarly documents. The flapper is one of the best-known examples of a woman who exhibited traits perceived as mannish, but she is only one of many types of women associated with masculinity in the late nineteenth and early twentieth centuries, including the New Woman and the suffragist.[4] Where the image of the flapper emphasized heterosexual attractiveness in spite of her masculinity (or perhaps because of it), the suffragist stirred controversy for her supposed lack of feminine sexuality and legitimacy as a "true" woman (Gorham Doss 105–13; Cohler 155–9).[5] The category of the "mannish woman" is not identical to any of these types but was sometimes used as an umbrella term that included flappers and suffragists. The traits that were perceived as masculine varied by time and place but usually included smoking, pants-wearing, decisiveness, and employment in traditionally male-dominated fields. What registers as masculine comportment changes depending on where, when, and who perceives it. Dressing in masculine clothing is perhaps the most frequently cited marker of masculinity because it is a highly visible indicator, but masculinity has historically included a range of traits and behaviors. As Vicinus argues, "mannishness" or masculinity in women has taken on many different meanings over time, ranging from "an estimable power of reasoning, or remarkable learning and knowledge, or an assertive patriotism in defense of one's country, or a dangerous aggressiveness in defying male privilege, or a too-overt interest in pursuing women as erotic objects" (xxiii). Havelock Ellis, writing in 1895, lists "direct speech" and "straightforwardness and sense of honor" as traits expressed by women who were masculine ("Sexual Inversion in Women" 153). What these traits have in common is an assertion of independence and autonomy; these assertions were, in turn, often interpreted as attempts by women to usurp privileges usually reserved for men. This interpretation helps explains why the figure of the mannish woman was so concerning for large portions of the transatlantic population. The mannish woman was a visible challenge to the gendered status quo. The category of "mannishness" fluctuated in the interwar years, and there was considerable disagreement among physicians, sexologists, and psychologists over how to label people who were assigned female at birth but exhibited masculine traits.[6] What *was* broadly agreed upon was that mannish women existed, and that their increased salience in transatlantic society and culture merited attention.

Public perception of masculinization was not universally critical. In fact, some commentators were favorably disposed toward mannish women. For instance, Laura Doan demonstrates that although the mannish woman was "hotly debated in most national newspapers and magazines," in wartime and postwar Britain, pundits "were less likely to regard her as unnatural or abnormal than to applaud her arrival and participation" in war work efforts ("Topsy-Turveydom" 518). Outside of wartime, however, criticism of mannish women prevailed, especially when these women were not obviously heterosexual. In the United States, participation in the suffrage movement was more of a catalyst for masculinization than the Great War, and, in contrast to British commentary, early reactions to the mannish woman in the United States were more likely to be critical than approving. As Behling puts it, "the U.S. woman suffrage movement's emphasis on securing social and political independence for women was translated by a fearful society, in American literature and the popular press, into a movement of women whose assumption of the prerogative to vote was perceived to have altered them into 'masculine women'" (102). On both sides of the Atlantic, critics of the mannish woman worried that she had become a "third sex."

They also worried that her masculine behaviors sapped her fertility, and that, if she managed to conceive, her masculinity would render her an unsuitable mother. The figure of the mannish pregnant woman therefore highlights the difference between what gendered and sexed bodies are "supposed" to do and what they actually do.[7] Realizing this highlights the importance of considering reproduction in analyses of mannishness, flappers, and the New Woman. All these figures raised similar questions about their legitimacy as "real" women, especially where womanly realness is defined by reproductive potential. As John D'Emilio and Estelle B. Friedman state, masculinity in women—especially educated women—was seen to spoil a woman's ability to be a good mother. They demonstrate that women's entrance into US colleges of higher education in the later decades of the nineteenth century "provoked an outpouring of polemical literature about the perils intellectual work held for women. A college education would ruin a woman's health, these writers argued, and especially make her unfit for motherhood, the noblest calling of womanhood" (190). It was not uncommon for intellectuals to speculate that female masculinity led to "shrunken wombs" and infertility (ibid.).

Like scientists and journalists, literary authors agreed that the mannish woman was worthy of attention—even if they did not all agree that she represented a threat—as evidenced by the increasingly frequent depictions of mannish women in the years surrounding the World Wars. Characters in interwar literature manifest this attention, from Radclyffe Hall's ambulance driver Stephen Gordon to Carson McCullers's defiant tomboy Mick Kelly.[8] Depictions of flappers often emphasized their exercise of masculine prerogatives; Hemingway's Lady Brett Ashley is perhaps the quintessential example in modernist literature. Hemingway depicts mannishness as incompatible with pregnancy, as when Lady Brett declares that she does not want to be a mother because "I'm not going to be one of these bitches that ruins children" (247). Many interwar literary depictions of mannish women hew to this line, implying that pregnancy is either impossible or a very bad idea for mannish women. Several of the texts I study suggest the same. Faulkner's *Jerusalem* ends with the death of a masculine female character from a botched abortion, and Barnes's mannish woman, Robin Vote, gives birth to a child who would have been considered degenerate by many of the book's original readers. Yet both of these stories contain ambivalences and disruptions to the notion that pregnancy and mannishness are incompatible, suggesting a nuance that rarely has been acknowledged in the critical conversation. Cather's depiction of Ántonia, meanwhile, is a complete rejection of the incompatibility thesis, as I demonstrate in chapter 4.

The perception of masculinity in the interwar period and the ways it is shaped by societal forces is central to my analysis of the mannish pregnant woman. In this regard, my work builds on that of Doan, whose careful analyses of WWI-era discourse surrounding masculinity make clear the importance of parsing the difference between perceptions of gender "deviance" and perceptions of sexual "deviance." Doan notes that historians often conflate the two by assuming that people in earlier eras perceived women who were deviant in terms of gender (masculine) as also and necessarily deviant in terms of sexuality (same-sex attraction) ("Topsy-Turveydom" 519). Evidence suggests, however, that "such cultural linkages were more elusive, particularly with regard to public speculation on the interrelatedness of gender inversion (traits, attitudes, or behaviors culturally associated with 'male' manifested in 'female' and vice versa) and sexual inversion" (521).[9] Interwar literature registers the mutable and subtle ways that mannishness was perceived as deviant or acceptable; sometimes fiction is a better register than nonfiction because authors could disclaim the ideas expressed therein, making these texts a rich source of information regarding the perception of gender and sexual deviancy.[10] Doan's work highlights a point I explore in depth in chapter 3, which is that inversion did not always signal same-sex attraction.

The assumption behind the category of "inversion" was the following: there are two sexes and these sexes are opposites of each other, where "sex" encompasses both anatomy and gender. People who were born with "male" anatomy but acted in ways associated with women, so the idea ran, must be at least partly inverted or opposite. Sexologists initially attempted to locate the source of inversion in the physical body but soon abandoned these efforts in favor of intangible sources such as the soul or spirit.[11] Hence, sexologists often claimed that an inverted woman has "the soul of a man in the body of a woman." Offensive as this idea strikes us today, it did have political expediency at the time. It allowed progressive sexologists to argue that queer people were not to blame for their behaviors and therefore should not be criminally punished. Sexologists attempted to further parse categories of mannishness with numerous sub-labels, many of which were ill-defined and short-lived in the sexological literature. The discourse changed frequently in the interwar years, as with any new field of study.

People whom sexologists labeled "female inverts" were often attracted to women, but same-sex attraction was not a necessary trait. Indeed, sexologists labeled many people—male and female alike—inverted despite being heterosexual (D'Emilio and Freedman 226). Comportment perceived to align with the "opposite" sex, such as dress and speech patterns, was often sufficient to earn the label "invert." Therefore, the mannish woman can be understood as a person who was inverted in terms of gender and sometimes—but not always—in terms of sexuality. For the female characters I study, this fact explains something that otherwise might seem contradictory, which is that they are both pregnant and inverted.

The female characters under consideration here do not pass as men, nor do they try to do so. It is for this reason that I do not argue that these characters are trans men, although I acknowledge that such distinctions are difficult to make and theoretically fraught. Emma Heaney explains that the categories of transmasculinity and transfemininity "emerged in sexological understanding as an extreme expression of this inverted condition" at the turn of the twentieth century (4). Early twentieth-century conceptions of mannishness and transmasculinity existed on a spectrum. Mannishness was thought to occupy the less threatening end of the spectrum because these women were not necessarily *sexually* inverted, whereas transmasculine people were understood to be inverted in terms of both sexuality and gender.

Further nuancing the picture of interwar female masculinity, Jaime Hovey cautions against assuming that non-normative gender is synonymous with anti-normativity. Hovey explains that many gender nonconforming people in the interwar years sought legitimacy and acceptance from mainstream communities. Their non-normative gender identities did not automatically lead them to reject or rebel against their gender-normative friends, families, and communities. Hovey focuses on transmasculine people, arguing: "Transmasculinity in the first part of the twentieth century is not anti-normative in the way queer in the post-Stonewall era is usually understood, associated with a progressive social agenda and rejection of sexual respectability, reproduction, and consumerism. Indeed, one finds the transmasculine in early twentieth-century modernist literary and film texts to be deeply invested in the social order" ("Joan of Arc" 116). Hovey's point is important because it shows us that in all the justly deserved praise of queer rebels, we risk skewing the desires and actions of queer people in the first decades of the twentieth century, and the critical conversation risks overstating the extent to which queer people rejected the traditional, family-centered social order. For instance, Cather's Ántonia is a mannish woman for whom social legitimacy is crucial to her well-being; the same could be said of Cather herself.

Authors who create queer characters that seek legitimacy or ultimately renounce their queerness have sometimes been charged with rationalization. Jack Halberstam describes these "projects of rationalization" as narratives that find "reasonable explanations for behavior that may seem dangerous and outrageous at first glance" (*In a Queer Time & Place* 55). For example, a cross-dressing female character may be "assigned an economic motive for her masquerade" (ibid.), or poverty is made to account for her lack of finery and frills. A project of rationalization, states Halberstam, "placates mainstream viewers by returning the temporarily transgender subject to the comforting and seemingly inevitable matrix of hetero-domesticity" (55). Although Halberstam's focus is transgender characters in late-twentieth and early twenty-first century texts, Behling has demonstrated that a similar phenomenon occurred with mannish female characters in texts from a century earlier. According to Behling, a spate of popular fiction in the 1910s depicts masculine women, especially suffragists, who are "rescued" into heterosexuality. "Having staked a claim in the masculine worlds of business or education and having renounced a dependent heterosexual existence or, in some cases, embraced sexual inversion," states Behling, "these fictionalized masculine women drew as much fear and ire as the real-life suffragists did" (86). She continues, explaining that authors devised literary strategies to discredit these masculine women by depicting them as "organically aberrant and behaviorally criminal" (5), or else by "demasculinizing them and then seducing them with heterosexuality" by the end of the text (83). Authorial motives for projects of rationalization vary and range from disapproval of mannishness as a threatening or degenerate pose, to self-censorship on the part of authors who were fearful of the reaction their works might receive if they depicted mannish women positively.[12]

One often finds projects of rationalization in scholarly criticism of mannish female characters. This is true despite Halberstam's *Female Masculinity* making waves when it was first published in 1998 and continuing to have tremendous influence in the fields of literary criticism and gender studies today. Despite this influence, too few critics read masculine female characters as simply that, masculine women, and instead assign to them economic or power motives. Terence Martin, for instance, explains Ántonia's masculinity as a product of economic necessity, stating that Ántonia "grows coarse and muscular doing the work of a man on the farm" (306).

Martin's reading is correct but incomplete because it negates Ántonia's direct, emphatic declaration: "I like to be like a man" (74). In another vein, critics sometimes imply that masculinity is a sign of repressed or unacknowledged same-sex attraction. This is not a rationalization, per se, because it does not return a queer character to comforting hetero-domesticity. Yet these readings nevertheless position masculinity as a screen or symptom rather than a genuine expression of identity. Sometimes masculinity *is* a screen and sometimes economic necessity drives behaviors, but not always. I am arguing that we need to make more room for female masculinity as an authentic gender identity, especially where the female characters in question are involved in reproductive processes. Even in texts that return masculine women to the aforementioned matrix of hetero-domesticity, or in texts where an economic or power motive is also present, critics need not rationalize female masculinity. *Masculine Pregnancies* holds space for female masculinity in texts that feature reproductive plot lines, which has the potential to upend received critical wisdom about familiar texts. In the case of *My Ántonia*, for example, such an approach demonstrates that the ending of the novel is far less conservative than the critical consensus would have it. In my reading of Cather's novel, the ending is a continuation of—not a break with—the queerness that defines the first third of it.

Eugenics

Many of the interwar arguments against mannishness were fueled by eugenic theories of reproductive fitness. Critics often expressed the idea that mannishness was anti-social, a term that suggested condemnation for comportment that was thought to damage society by setting an immoral precedent that threatened the nuclear family's gender divisions, or else by endangering the future of society through a refusal of heteronormative reproduction. (The nexus of reproduction, queerness, and supposedly anti-social behavior returns in a new guise in the twenty-first century in the "anti-social thesis" debates in the field of queer theory; I take up this line of discussion in the coda.) One such detractor to female masculinity on anti-social grounds was the American physician and writer William Howard Lee. To Lee, the idea of a pregnant mannish woman was far more troublesome than a woman who was infertile or chose not to reproduce. A character in his 1901 novel *The Perverts* gives voice to the author's views, stating: "When a woman neglects her maternal instincts, when her sentiment and dainty feminine characteristics are boldly and ostentatiously kept submerged, we can see an anti-social creature more amusing than dangerous. . . . [But] should this female be unfortunate enough to become a mother, she ceases to be merely amusing, and is an anti-social being. She is then a menace to civilizations, a producer of non-entities, the mother of mental and physical monstrosities" (qtd. in Behling 56). Women who failed to conform to standards of femininity and maternity, whether through childlessness or masculinity or both, were shirking their duties to the nation according to critics of Lee's ilk. Lee assumes that masculinity is a choice, something similar to a fashion statement, but that nevertheless has biological ramifications that reverberate down a family line. Sentiments such as these were not confined to the United States. Deborah Cohler argues that the "ideological and material production of the British 'race'" depended on "bourgeois English women as mothers of the nation" (xii). Similarly, Jane Garrity states that white British women were seen as "national assets" during the interwar years because of their capacity to bear white citizens: "these select Englishwomen would both stabilize the imaginary borders of the nation and contribute to the expansion of its empire. Women's identification with nation was thus submerged in their identification with race" (*Step-Daughters* 1). Discourse around this figure of the "race mother" highlights the fact that fears about mannishness in the early years of the twentieth century were less about same-sex attraction and more about eugenic nationalism, as Cohler argues (xii). To put it another way, there was more worry that these illegitimate women would pollute the national body than that they were sexually inverted, in part because same-sex intercourse is non-reproductive. Black and brown women were typically excluded from this nationalistic discourse; instead, they were discouraged or prevented from reproducing through efforts known as "negative eugenics." The centrality of race motherhood did not shift until the late 1920s (Doan, "Topsy-Turveydom," 522). Given that the texts I study here span the years 1918–1939, they represent an important archive of changing attitudes toward gender, reproduction, and legitimacy. The modernist authors in the following chapters take advantage of the elasticity of the concept of "legitimacy" to work out anxieties about changing gender, authorial, racial, and community norms.

Race and Reproductive Legitimacy

The First World War accelerated a major epistemological shift in which race—including whiteness—was negotiated politically, culturally, and scientifically.[13] Urmila Seshagiri explains that "race" in the period from 1750 to 1900 "described biological, national, religious, linguistic, and character differences" (8). In the interwar years, however, the signifiers of "race" narrowed. Increasingly, the term referred to skin color. A consideration of race is essential to any study of reproduction in the interwar years because, as Seshagiri argues, the idea of race "invoked the consistent transfer of traits from one generation to the next" (8). As a result, reproduction was at the very center of debates about race in the period leading up to the First World War and beyond. The scientific racism of eugenics and cognate disciplines focused attention on "what was lost, gained, or permanently altered in this transfer" of traits through generational lines (Seshagiri 8). Although Seshagiri's focus is Europe and Great Britain, her point applies similarly to the United States. She continues, stating that "disruptions in the continuity of racial identity—through miscegenation, geographical displacement, religious conversion, or political upheaval, for example—engendered scientific as well as cultural anxieties about hybridity, contamination, and degeneration" (8). Scientific racism in the interwar years often took the form of eugenic policies aimed at controlling the continuity of racial identities by prohibiting "unfit" people from reproducing, anti-miscegenation laws that criminalized racial mixing, and immigration policies that curtailed geographic displacement. Many people attempted to define the number of races. They produced widely varying answers—some as low as 4 and others as high as 29—suggesting the faulty ground on which these attempts were built (Frye Jacobson xi). The qualifications for inclusion in a particular racial group often depended more on the cataloger's own interests than any kind of scientific principles. As Frye Jacobson argues, race was often defined, negotiated, and rewritten to suit political ends (140).

Eugenic nationalism was a driving force behind American efforts to redefine race, and these efforts show up in the literature of the day. White Americans often justified racist policies on the grounds that citizenship should be extended to only those people deemed fit for self-government, and white European stock was typically held up as the paragon of fitness (Frye Jacobson 140). Yet, as Frye Jacobson argues, whiteness was not a monolithic category of privileged persons but rather a hierarchical category that determined privileges according to nationality and immigration status as well as skin color. The whiteness of "Celts, Slavs, Hebrews, Iberics, and Saracens, among others" was a matter of heated debate that centered on fitness for self-government (7–8). The people granted the stamp of legitimacy as white expanded between the 1840s and the 1920s, a change catalyzed by the restrictive immigration policies enacted by the 1924 Johnson-Reed

Immigration Act. Frye Jacobson explains the shift as resulting from the perception that the Johnson Act "solved" the problem of inferior immigrants: "in the 1920s and after, partly because the [perceived] crisis of over-inclusive whiteness had been solved by restrictive legislation and partly in response to a new racial alchemy generated by African-American migrations to the North and West, whiteness was reconsolidated: the late nineteenth century's probationary white groups were now remade and granted the scientific stamp of authenticity as the unitary Caucasian race" (7–8). The Johnson-Reed Act was considered a triumph of the United States eugenic movement (87). The changes it wrought in prevailing attitudes toward race can be seen in the written record produced by native-born white Americans. When these writers discussed "Celts, Teutons, and Slavs" before the 1920s, they tended to distinguish these groups as racially distinct from Anglo-Saxons; thereafter, these groups were increasingly included in the Caucasian "race" (91). As a result of the Johnson-Reed Act, the flow of immigrant populations decreased. At the same time, the Great Migration of Black populations to northern, midwestern, and western states gave new charge to old antagonisms between white and Black Americans, leading many whites to focus on the "Negroid" race as more threatening than "Celts, Teutons, and Slavs" (8–9). Reproduction was at the heart of this revisionist wave because the pregnant body is the site for the "transfer of traits from one generation to the next" that Seshagiri discusses. The legitimacy of children—as citizens, as racially "superior" types, or as inheritors of a nation's future—hinged on the national, racial, and gendered legitimacy of the people who conceived and gestated them.

Masculinity and Modernism

Where white women writers often saw opportunity in the changing gender norms of the era, these changes stirred up feelings of fear—with an undercurrent of envy—in many white male writers who feared losing their status at the pinnacle of authorial legitimacy. Anxiety over masculinity and the compensatory strategies that developed as a result of this anxiety contributed to what critics traditionally call "high" modernism. From Wyndham Lewis calling modern art "rough and masculine work" (qtd. in Tickner 42) to Eliot thanking Pound for cleaning up the chaotic "menstrual fluid" that was *The Waste Land* before Pound got his hands on it (Koestenbaum 118), modernist writers often asserted a relationship between masculinity and modern art.

As Julian Murphet notes, male modernists frequently "relate[d] the work of genius to the literal phallic processes of erection and insemination" (57). Feminist critics typically see this masculine posturing as 1) a symptom of misogynistic fears over women gaining increasing rights, 2), eugenic worries over an increasingly "effeminate" population, or 3) aesthetic reactions against the Dandy, that nineteenth-century man of letters most commonly represented by Oscar Wilde. Rachel Blau DuPlessis cautions us to remember that modernist masculinism is at least as much a product of anxiety as it is of misogyny: for every sentiment expressing hatred of women or desire to exclude them, it is possible to find one expressing envy or appropriation of traits stereotypically thought of as womanly, including those connected to reproduction and maternity ("Virile" 21).

Anxiety over masculinity was not unique to authors and artists. Indeed, similar anxieties swirled in scientific communities in the early twentieth century. G. J. Barker-Benfield credits worry over waning male power with initiating the growth of obstetrics as a medical field, stating, "it was men's anxieties about themselves, their fear of the changing status of women, and their desire to conquer and control the innermost power of nature that explains the overturning—in the controlled, medical sphere—of the traditional shibboleth" that barred men from examining women's privates in an era when white women were viewed as untouchable (58). Anxieties of the kind experienced by writers and medical professionals are not specific to the early twentieth century either. Historians of masculinity tell us that anxieties of this kind have always existed because people have always felt that they were living through a period when masculinity was in crisis. This fact leads to the conclusion that "the very term 'crisis' is simply inadequate," as historian Christopher J. Forth argues. Forth explains, "if there is no stable or non-critical period to be found prior to the disturbance in question (and historians have not found one), then the very idea of a crisis makes little sense" (3). Yet the rhetoric of "crisis" surrounding masculinity persists, and, as Natalya Lusty notes, "the concept of crisis is rarely applied to femininity" (1). Whether or not masculinity was in crisis in the early years of the twentieth century, modernist writers certainly believed it was. It is this fact that leads Gerald N. Izenberg to make the compelling claim that the arts are an ideal place to look for evidence that people *felt* masculinity to be in crisis (8).

Scholarship over the last thirty years or so has done much to solidify our understanding of how canonical modernist authors crafted a mythos of modernism as a virile, cis-masculine endeavor.[14] The masculine mythos dominated modernist criticism until the 1990s. Since then, scholars have demonstrated that modernism is much queerer and more diverse than traditional accounts suggest. My study of masculine pregnancy contributes to this critical reevaluation. If assertions of masculine virility in modernism are common knowledge, what is less well-known is the extent to which these assertions exist cheek-by-jowl in modernist oeuvres with pregnancy, childbirth, and reproductive control. Even a cursory search yields a long list of male modernists who connected literary creation to metaphorical and literal reproductive processes. For instance, Joyce's *Ulysses* describes Mina Purefoy's long labor and delivery in language that surveys the history of British literary style, and Yeats had a vasectomy in the hopes of rerouting that "vital" energy to his poetry (T. Armstrong 133–58). This says nothing of the artists whose work is suffused with depictions of pregnancy and childbearing. William Carlos Williams is an obvious example. He often delivered babies as part of his medical practice, and reproductive imagery appears throughout his writing and para-literary texts. His self-designed cover for *Kora in Hell*, for instance, depicts "ovum in the act of penetration by sperm" (40).[15]

Critical interpretations of male authors who compare literary creation to physical procreation are remarkably homogenous. The usual argument runs thus: male writers, regardless of the era or genre in which they are writing, use the metaphor to co-opt the affordances of pregnancy. These affordances include the physicality of it, as when authors trade on the assumption that motherhood is indisputable (the physicality of pregnancy and birth leaving no doubt who the mother is). By positioning himself as a mother rather than a father, a male author asserts ownership over a creation. David D. Leitao argues that use of the metaphor in Classical Greek literature was primarily a way to claim ownership against plagiarists, against co-collaborators when the relationship soured, and against the idea that poets merely transcribe ideas from muses (127). Womb envy is often detectable in the use of childbirth metaphors by male authors, instances of which usually imply that physical reproduction and artistic production are incompatible while still expressing respect, awe, or envy toward physical reproduction.

Whether authors saw the affordances of pregnancy as benefits or hindrances changed over time in at least one respect. The perceived naturalness of pregnancy was variously thought of as an affordance to be claimed or, conversely, forced on one's rivals. In the seventeenth century, as Terry Castle notes, Anglophone writers embraced childbirth metaphors as a way to describe their own writing processes, but by the eighteenth century they were more likely to use the metaphor to disparage their competition. The pendulum swung back toward embrace in the nineteenth century, as the Romantics reclaimed the metaphor for themselves. These alterations were driven, Castle argues, by changing conceptualizations of the writing process. When writers preferred to think of writing as a natural, automatic process—inspiration from the muses, and so forth—they tended to claim the metaphor to describe their own writing; when prevailing notions held that writing was a rational, scientific, controlled process, writers tended to reject the metaphor for their own works and apply it instead to their competitors (202–6). All of the above rests on the assumption that pregnancy is easy and automatic, which female writers have forcefully rejected. Castle speculates provisionally on modernist use of the childbirth metaphor, noting that writers in the early twentieth century unwillingly or unthinkingly employ the metaphor in the Romantic vein (that is, accepting the idea that writing is a natural process like pregnancy), despite the fact that their aesthetic strives to make writing mechanical (206–7).

Yet some modernists did craft pregnancy metaphors that fused together notions of reproduction and writing as a technical process. They did so through rhetoric that "masculinizes" pregnancy by remaking it into a hard, clean, mechanical, and bloodless process.[16] For instance, the protagonist of F. T. Marinetti's *Mafarka, The Futurist* (1909) gives birth to a mechanical "son." Mafarka is both father and mother, using his own "creative energy" to "impregnate" himself and bring to "birth" to a giant, sentient airplane (195). The son has all of Mafarka's masculinist traits but none of the weaknesses that come with human embodiment. *Mafarka* thus depicts reproduction without women, a manifestation of Marinetti's particular brand of misogyny. Carol Diethe explains that Marinetti believed women wanted sex constantly because of a Nietzschean will to pregnancy, and for that reason were dangerous to men and their creativity (xvii). Marinetti's novel imagines a world in which this threat is neutralized because reproduction is entirely masculine and mechanical. Even in instances less overtly misogynistic, masculinized reproductive discourse has exclusionary force. As Emma E. L. Rees states, the discourse of reproduction is frequently "appropriated by men to apply to industrial or technological processes from which women, by virtue of a lack of opportunity, are for the most part excluded" (47). Pound and Faulkner crafted metaphors that are remarkably similar in purpose. They trade on the social import of pregnancy to reimagine childbirth metaphors in ways that close ranks around authorial legitimacy, positioning women—especially mannish women—outside the realm of legitimacy as (pro)creators.

This kind of delegitimizing move is familiar to feminist modernist scholars. Critics have long recognized the role of masculine posturing in the development of modernist aesthetics, and important work on child-birth metaphors in modernism has been done by Susan Stanford Friedman, Sandra M. Gilbert and Susan Gubar, Patricia Yaeger, and others.[17] While Castle's essay focuses on male writers, Friedman's classic study of childbirth metaphors gives equal weight to male and female authors. She argues that the use of childbirth metaphors by a male artist is necessarily different from a female artist's use of it. "Confined to 'headbirths,'" Friedman states, "men *cannot* literally conceive and birth babies. The reader's awareness of this biological collision contributes to a perpetual tension in the metaphor" (55). Friedman goes on to state that "history and biology combine to make [male use of the childbirth metaphor] a form of literary *couvade*, male appropriation of procreative labor to which women have been confined" by virtue of cultural norms establishing writing as the province of men (56). As mentioned in the introduction, the vast majority of this scholarship was written before the boom in queer theory in the 1990s and 2000s.

Masculine Pregnancies reconsiders the ground paved by Friedman in light of trans and queer critiques of biologically based notions of gender and reproduction. I begin from the opposite assumption, that men *can* literally conceive and birth babies (in literature as well as real life, in the form of fictional characters and trans men). And, pressing the idea further, I assume that femininity is not a by-product of pregnancy. Doing so allows me to build on this earlier scholarship by expanding the frame of reference to include masculine women and nonbinary characters. I demonstrate that critics' assumptions surrounding masculinity and pregnancy have led to two misconceptions: 1) masculinity and reproduction can only combine in ways that are oppressive, and 2) queer pregnancy is a literary concern that arose in the twenty-first century. I want to stress that I do not disagree with critics who argue that deployments of masculinity and reproduction can lead to oppressive outcomes; rather, I am arguing that these outcomes are not the only ones possible. Further, I agree with Friedman's claim that *readers* usually assume men cannot literally conceive and that masculinity is incompatible with pregnancy. These assumptions are still common. It is logical for critics to build on this foundation when considering reader responses to depic-tions of masculine pregnancy. It does not follow, however, that critics need to assume the same. I am arguing that the texts themselves are often far queerer with regard to reproduction than critics have acknowledged, and that recognizing this queerness expands the critical landscape.

The Medicalization of Pregnancy and Disability Discourse

The interwar years in England and the United States witnessed what historians refer to as the medicalization of pregnancy, which was a shift in medical discourse that moved pregnancy physically out of the home and into medical facilities, and moved it rhetorically from an event that occurred in the life of a healthy person and to an illness that required medical intervention. Several recent studies of literature depicting male pregnancy, a close cousin to mannish pregnancy and childbirth metaphors, have done so within a disability studies framework. The most influential of these is Michael Davidson's "Pregnant Men: Modernism, Disability, and Biofuturity in Djuna Barnes" (later revised as a chapter in *Invalid Modernism*). This essay is an important exception to the dearth of recent scholarship on masculinity and pregnancy in modernism. Davidson reads male pregnancy as "a form of disability" that facilitates considerations of "repro-futurity outside of its heteronormative frame" (120).[18] Davidson's focus is expressly pregnant men rather than the broader category of masculine pregnancy that I consider in this book. He considers "what happens when reproduction is removed from female biology and shifted discursively onto other bodies" (120). I find Davidson's work enormously productive for thinking through the relationship between gender and embodiment in modernism, and I reference his arguments with some frequency in the pages of this book. Like Davidson, I reject the assumption that femininity inheres in pregnancy. Nevertheless, my approach to the relationship between masculinity and pregnancy differs from Davidson's in ways that are important to address because they intersect with key events in the history of reproduction and the medicalization of pregnancy.

Classifying pregnancy as a disability aligns with medical and legal discourse that has been oppressive to pregnant people. Decades of feminist scholarship have documented this oppression. Legal scholar Jeanette Cox summarizes a major strand of feminist opposition to pregnancy as disability discourse: "gestation should not be characterized as a disability because it represents heightened rather than diminished biological functioning . . . [and reinforces] the outdated view that women's physical differences from men are deficiencies rather than merely differences" (448–49).[19] Therefore, classifying male pregnancy as a disability further reinforces the idea that pregnancy is an abnormal deficiency; according to this line of thought, pregnancy moves an otherwise "normal" body into a category of embodiment defined (legally, at least) by diminished capacity.

Feminists in the twentieth century have been relatively uniform in their resistance to discourse that establishes the cis male body as the medical norm, but debates surrounding the classification of pregnancy as disability are more divisive. Workplace protection is one such arena of debate. In the United States, pregnant people are legally protected against workplace discrimination but are not automatically covered under the federal Americans with Disabilities Act (ADA).[20] Cox argues that the "reluctance to associate pregnancy with disability . . . has resulted in a legal regime in which many pregnant workers currently have less legal standing to workplace accommodations than other persons with comparable physical limitations" (448–49).[21] In the legal realm, classifying pregnancy as a disability makes sense on realpolitik grounds to mitigate discrimination in the workplace, but it is a stop-gap measure, not an ideal permanent solution to the problem of discrimination against pregnant people. Judith G. Greenberg argues that even the legal expedient is questionable: "bringing pregnancy under the ADA would reinvigorate the stereotype of pregnant women as disabled and not fit for work" (qtd. in Cox 225). Where such stop-gap measures are not necessary, the risks of reinvigorating pregnancy as disability discourse outweigh the theoretical or conceptual benefits.

Furthermore, the idea of pregnancy as disability shares ideological space with the medicalization of pregnancy that occurred in England and the United States in the first half of the twentieth century. I discuss this process in depth in chapter 2. In sum, the medicalization of pregnancy refers to the fact that pregnancy was historically thought to be normal and healthy, but in the late nineteenth and early twentieth centuries, medical professionals increasingly characterized it as an abnormal condition requiring management by physicians. Barbara Katz Rothman notes that in the United States, "the transition from almost all births taking place at home to almost all births taking place in the hospital took just over two generations. In those two generations, birth changed from being an event in the life of a family to being a medical procedure" (29). The transition took longer and was never so complete in the United Kingdom, but the broad strokes of the shift are the same. Some of the changes in health care that came along with medicalization led to better outcomes for pregnant people and their babies. However, medicalization also led to procedures and environments that many experience as dehumanizing. As Rothman puts it, "the early hospitalization and medicalization of childbirth was extreme. Pregnant women were indeed treated as sick, and childbirth became very much a surgical procedure. General anesthesia was the norm. The delivery room was an operating room and the obstetrician was a surgeon" (29–30). Some of the ways that the medicalization of pregnancy manifested in the interwar years echo eugenic approaches to the treatment of people with disabilities, including forcible sterilization and shackling to exam tables.[22] Pregnant people and their allies fought hard against the classification of pregnancy as an abnormal condition in efforts to ameliorate the dehumanizing aspects of medicalized pregnancy. By the 1980s medical practitioners had largely ceased to talk about pregnancy as an illness or disability (Rothman 30, 37). Reading masculine pregnancies within the framework of illegitimacy rather than disability allows me to theorize depictions of masculine pregnancy in modernism without reinvigorating the historical and ideological associations between pregnancy and disability discourse that activists fought against.[23]

My analyses in the following chapters demonstrate that Pound, Faulkner, Cather, and Barnes manipulated the elastic concept of illegitimacy in ways that both reflect and expand interwar discourse surrounding pregnancy and masculinity. The social and cultural tensions that inform determinations of illegitimacy get the most attention in the pages of this book, but the concept of illegitimacy appears in many more forms. This chapter focused on social legitimacy among the Anglophone literati and their notions of authorial legitimacy, especially as shaped by scientific discourse. In chapter 2, I focus on the medicalization of pregnancy, especially a British debate between midwives and medical doctors, as they informed Ezra Pound's attitude toward his role in the editing of *The Waste Land*; in chapter 3, the role of eugenics in social and legal determinations of legitimacy inform my reading of Faulkner's artist novels. Questions of legal and moral legitimacy surface in my analysis of *My Ántonia* in chapter 4. In this novel, the title character has a child out of wedlock. This baby is therefore legally illegitimate but, I argue, gains moral legitimacy over the course of the novel through the words and stories of other characters. Kinship—familial belonging—is taken up most directly in my discussion of *Nightwood* in chapter 5, but also figures in the coda.

Chapter 2

Literary Obstetrics

Ezra Pound and the Midwives Act of 1902

If the previous chapter looked at the concept of legitimacy with a wide-angle lens, this chapter is a close-up examination of a specific kind of legitimacy—cultural authenticity or belonging—among the Anglophone literati in the interwar years. I focus on Ezra Pound and T. S. Eliot and their notions of authorial legitimacy as they were shaped by medical discourses of the day. The benefit of this narrowing of focus is twofold. First, it provides a defined example of one of the ways modernist authors used the trope of masculine pregnancy to adjudicate legitimacy in the literary realm. Second, this chapter analyzes a key aspect of the trope of masculine pregnancy. The reader will recall from the introduction that I define "masculine pregnancies" as depictions of masculine pregnant women and metaphorical male pregnancy. This chapter considers metaphorical male pregnancy; specifically, it considers Pound's depiction of Eliot as pregnant with *The Waste Land* (1922) and himself as the supposed "midwife" who delivered the child. A large strand of the scholarship on masculinity and pregnancy concerns depictions of men who are pregnant with literary "offspring." As such, this chapter puts *Masculine Pregnancies* in conversation with this tradition of scholarship while offering a new and nuanced take on a canonical text, demonstrating that modernists adapted traditional tropes for the twentieth century by shifting attention to the gender of the gestator.

Ezra Pound's role as the "midwife" of *The Waste Land* is something of a modernist legend. As Hugh Kenner tells it, T. S. Eliot's poem was long and sprawling before Pound's keen editorial eye shaped it into the masterpiece we know today (7–12). In a letter to Eliot, Pound memorialized their collaboration with an obscene poem titled "SAGE HOMME." The title is a twist on the French "sage femme," which literally translates as "wise woman" but is an old-fashioned name for a midwife. In "SAGE HOMME," Eliot is pregnant with the verses that will become *The Waste Land*, but his labor is unsuccessful until Pound, the "wise man" of the title, steps in to perform a caesarean section on Eliot, thereby delivering Eliot's poetic offspring. In the decades since Pound wrote "SAGE HOMME," scholars have frequently referred to Pound as the midwife of *The Waste Land* or modernism in general. Yet Pound's self-declaration as "sage homme" and its relationship to the heated political and social climate surrounding midwifery in the WWI era has not, to my knowledge, received scholarly attention.[1] Pound wrote "SAGE HOMME" at a time when doctors (predominately male) and midwives (overwhelmingly female) had distinct roles, especially regarding surgery (including C-sections). This chapter considers Pound's self-assigned role in modernism in light of a medical debate about the regulation and licensure of English midwives, in which many doctors characterized midwives as ignorant, unskilled, and slovenly.

Attending to this history leads to a provocative claim: Pound is not the "midwife" of *The Waste Land*. I do not dispute his role in editing the poem but the assignation of the title "midwife." Pound neither uses this word nor describes his activities as those of midwifery. Rather, he uses the masculine pregnancy trope to figure Eliot as a legitimate creator, and he adapts the midwifery metaphor to position himself in the masculine image of the obstetric surgeon. This figurative language allows Pound to distance his own work from that of midwifery by engaging the same rhetoric as doctors who sought to delegitimize midwives in the licensure debates. As such, calling Pound the "midwife" of *The Waste Land* misrepresents his self-assigned role in modern literature. Finally, by turning a feminist lens on the scholarly conversation, this chapter highlights the importance of feminist attention to our received stories about modernism, particularly the metaphors we use to discuss the processes of writing, editing, and publication.

I argue that the term "surgeon" is a more accurate translation of "sage homme," as it both reflects the historical context and Pound's engagement with it. For Pound's use of doctors' rhetoric is best understood as part of his well-known pattern of delegitimizing female writers and editors. At the time, doctors were achieving some success in their efforts to push female professionals out of the delivery room. Pound, I am arguing, used reproductive language to leverage the rhetorical force of doctors' arguments for modern literature. In characteristic fashion, then, Pound took the old intellectual midwifery metaphor and "made it new" by associating it with the knowledge ("sage") and masculinity of surgeons. Therefore, this chapter is concerned with *labor*—in the sense of parturition as well as work—and the counterintuitive use of reproductive rhetoric to position women as unsuited to involvement in (pro)creation.

Situating Pound's poem in context with a contemporaneous medical debate provides a fitting introduction to one of this book's central claims, that certain interwar writers put the masculine pregnancy trope—of which the male childbirth metaphor is one iteration—to different use than previous generations of writers. These earlier writers typically constructed metaphors comparing writing processes with reproductive ones for two purposes: to deny outside help, whether that be from the muses or an erstwhile collaborator; or, conversely, to signal the ease with which they write, as though the muses' whispered ideas impregnate the poet's mind, and the mind then gives "birth" as naturally, inevitably, and easily as women do (literal childbirth is none of these things).[2] Pound, we will see in this chapter, and William Faulkner, as we will see in the next, went in a different direction. They used representations of masculine pregnancy to delegitimize female writers and editors, and to shore up their own claims to literary legitimacy in the face of changing literary demographics. And, unlike earlier writers, Pound's reproductive metaphors strengthen rather than deny his collaboration with Eliot. To further elucidate interwar authors' use of masculine pregnancy tropes, specifically the male childbirth metaphor, I conclude this chapter with a comparative reading of Jean Toomer's *Cane* (1923). This brief analysis shows how another interwar writer adapted the childbirth metaphor for the twentieth century. Toomer's use of the metaphor is aligned with the second of the two traditional uses of it—demonstrating creative inspiration from the natural world—but is adapted for the condition of a modern Black man whose creativity is thwarted by racist violence. In Pound's and Toomer's texts, the challenges of the modern world (specious in Pound's text and harrowingly real in Toomer's) are a crucible that forges a new kind of writer, but this writer is still, inevitably, male.

"SAGE HOMME" in the Critical Conversation

Eliot wrote most of *The Waste Land* in 1921.[3] Between November of that year and January 1922, Pound reviewed various drafts of the poem, recommending excision of nearly half of the original lines and substantive revisions for the remainder (Ricks and McCue 549–54). Throughout the writing and revision process, Eliot relied on his first wife, Vivien, for editorial feedback; her role in shaping the poem is most evident in "A Game of Chess."[4] When the poem was nearing completion, Pound offered spiteful congratulations to Eliot, writing in a letter on January 24, 1922, "Complimenti, you bitch. I am wracked by the seven jealousies, and cogitating an excuse for always exuding my deformative secretions in my own stuff . . . Some day I shall lose my temper, blaspheme Flaubert, lie like a shit-arse and say 'Art shd. embellish the umbilicus'" (qtd. in Ricks and McCue 550). The relationship between art and reproduction introduced in this statement is further elaborated upon in the poem "SAGE HOMME," which immediately follows in the letter. In "SAGE HOMME," Pound invokes long-standing tropes of creativity: the poet pregnant with verse and the intellectual midwife who aids the development of ideas (though the latter of these tropes, I am arguing, Pound revised for the modern era). Early lines of "SAGE HOMME" read:

> These are the Poems of Eliot
> By the Uranian Muse begot;
> A Man their Mother was,
> A Muse their sire.
>
> How did the printed Infancies result
> From Nuptials thus doubly difficult?
> [. . .]
> Ezra performed the caesarean Operation. (Qtd. in Koestenbaum, 122–23)

Note here that Pound initially aligns Eliot with one of the traditional uses of the male childbirth metaphor, that of birth resulting from inspiration from the muses. But whereas most older uses of the metaphor in this vein signal easy delivery—suggesting that the poet's writing process is as natural and inevitable as childbirth—"SAGE HOMME" tells a story of a difficult delivery. The reason for the difference is in the first stanza: "A Man their Mother was, / A Muse their sire." In traditional childbirth metaphors, muses are female and poets male. Eliot here depicts parents whose genders are inverted. In this queer modern coupling, the poem suggests, professional help is needed to bring about a successful delivery. Enter Pound as the surgeon performing the "caesarean Operation." As I will explain, Pound's use of a male pregnancy metaphor to describe Eliot delegitimizes feminine authors, and his adaptation of the midwifery metaphor legitimizes manly men as authors. In previous eras, the bastard was the key figure for authorial explorations of legitimacy. By the interwar years, however, many writers had shifted their attention elsewhere. The idea of bastardy figures nowhere in "SAGE HOMME." Instead, Pound focuses on the gender of the gestator and "midwife" to make his claims about legitimacy.

References to Pound as the "midwife" of *The Waste Land* or modernism in general are common. While many of these references mention "SAGE HOMME" directly, the idea of Pound-as-midwife has become such a critical commonplace that scholars frequently make no mention of Pound's poem. Jean-Michel Rabaté says of "SAGE HOMME" that it "leaves no doubt as to the role Pound has chosen: he is only the midwife ('Ezra performed the caesarean operation' [sic]) and not the impregnator of his friend" (198). In saying that Pound is "only" the midwife, Rabaté is commenting on the frequently discussed homosexual overtones in the poem. Many critics, including Rabaté, Wayne Koestenbaum, and Rachel Blau DuPlessis ("Propounding"), have interrogated the gender and sexual politics of Pound and Eliot's collaboration, as well as Pound's arrogation of conception, pregnancy, and childbirth to the male poetic realm.

I am less concerned here with the sexual politics of the poem and more with the slippage between "midwife" and "surgeon" manifest in Rabaté's phrasing, which is quite common in discussions of *The Waste Land*'s composition. Mark Ford similarly conflates midwives and medical men, stating that Pound "figured himself as the male midwife . . . who had performed a 'caesarean Operation' on Eliot's poem" (par. 11). Michael K. Gold extends the medical metaphor in his discussion of Roger Vittoz, the Swiss doctor who treated Eliot for the nervous breakdown he suffered while writing the poem. Gold argues that Vittoz's role in the composition of *The Waste Land* "is comparable to Ezra Pound's famous 'caesarean Operation.' If Pound was the midwife of the poem, as Wayne Koestenbaum and others (including Pound himself) have claimed, then Dr. Vittoz was the anesthesiologist on call during the delivery, guiding Eliot through the birthing process and slipping him an epidural when the pain became too great" (519). James E. Miller Jr. even goes so far as to characterize Pound's work as "using the editorial knife to bring to birth the poem published in 1922" (4). The language of Gold and Miller places Pound's editorial work firmly in the surgical theater, yet neither notes the disparity between this setting and the label "midwife."[5]

The difference is significant because midwives could not legally wield knives or perform surgeries at this time, of which Pound was very likely aware.

That Pound's role in the composition of *The Waste Land* should be so frequently discussed, and the difference between midwives and surgeons remain unnoticed for so long, is a telling reminder that the history of reproduction is not well-known by scholars and the general public alike, although this history quite literally involves every human being. Only in the last 65 years or so has "women's history" been considered a legitimate area of historical study in academia. As Jean H. Baker stated in 2004, "Women have always considered their past, often through genealogies, storytelling, oral histories, and even quilts. But in the last half-century women's history in books and articles has come of age" (66). The social histories of pregnancy, childbirth, midwifery, and related subjects are slowly making their way into other fields, including literary criticism.[6]

Conversely, reproductive metaphors have long been recognized and discussed within literary circles. More specifically, intellectual midwifery—both the practice and the terminology describing it—dates back at least to Socrates and has been used regularly by writers since.[7] Given this long history, some may argue that critics' use of the term "midwife" to describe Pound is less a reference to "SAGE HOMME" than a reference to Pound's place in the tradition of intellectual midwives. Yet Pound was a poet obsessed with *le mot juste*, the "word that did justice to the thing" (qtd. in Moody 278). Ignoring or glossing over the differences between midwife, surgeon, and "sage homme" in favor of a stock metaphor presents a skewed picture of Pound's self-assigned role in Anglo-American modernism, as well as his conception of the relationship between literature, childbirth, and masculinity.

Pound, as I will show, masculinized the midwifery metaphor in an attempt to shore up the boundary between legitimate and illegitimate art, and to position women's creations outside that boundary. One of the ways Pound makes this old metaphor new is by transferring to it some of the rhetorical energy that used to surround the figure of bastard. In the eighteenth and nineteenth centuries, the bastard was transatlantic writers' preferred figure for representing illegitimacy. Yet even during this period, writers used bastardy to raise questions about legitimacy that go beyond bastardy, questions such as: "What are the cultural reactions to fraud and imposture, whether used for economic gain or social advantage? How might self-consciously illegitimate behaviour operate as a form of opposition to the dominant codes of legitimate society and what kinds of political agendas does this open up? Above all, what are the tensions among what contemporaries considered morally legitimate, what they considered legally legitimate, and what they considered as legitimate in social practice?" (Finn 3–4). Questions like these were still urgent in twentieth-century England because of numerous factors that include rising tides of nationalism, eugenic population control measures, and the increasing presence of women in the workplace. However, in the wake of World War I, the figure of the bastard simply did not carry the anxiety and emotional intensity it used to. As Ruth Adam states, "The 1914 War created a new and more merciful attitude towards the unmarried mother [in England]. All the pleading of individual reformers had never achieved for her what the massacre of young men did" (78). The more permissive postwar atmosphere came with changing attitudes about premarital sex, especially for soldiers and their girlfriends: "In this emotional climate of snatching at straws of comfort in an otherwise unbearable bereavement, it became excusable for a girl to 'give all' to a man on the last night before he went back to the Front" (Adam 76). These changes led writers to seek out ways of representing illegitimacy that did not revolve around bastardy exclusively. For most of the authors under consideration in *Masculine Pregnancies*, that meant focusing on the legitimacy of the pregnant person's body. Pound revised the old intellectual midwifery model by inverting the genders of the procreative couple, and yoked the male childbirth metaphor to the masculinity of surgeons. Doing so allowed him to position educated white men as the legitimate practitioners of poetry.

I am sympathetic to DuPlessis's argument that many male modernists, including Pound, were ambivalent about women's increasing literary power, and that their manifestos and nonfiction statements about writing were often more misogynistic than their poems written for publication, where far more nuance is present ("Virile" 22). I also agree with Calvin Thomas's assertion that the "conventional account" of modernist gender politics is "a portrait of the artist as a young (or old) misogynist" (259–60). In other words, pointing out Pound's misogyny is hardly tide-turning. Nevertheless, we have not yet abolished the lingering effects of attitudes such as Pound's in the critical conversation. The frequency of references to Pound as the midwife of *The Waste Land*, and the absence of discussion about actual midwives, is a case in point. I am not suggesting that references to Pound-as-midwife always imply attitudes similar to Pound's, but that the field of modernist literary scholarship remains largely organized around patriarchal values.

When I say this, I have in mind Kate Manne's definition of misogyny. Manne argues that misogyny is not the property of a single individual who harbors hate for all women; rather, misogyny is "the system that operates within a patriarchal social order to police and enforce women's subordination and to uphold male dominance" (33). Manne's definition is particularly apt in the context of this chapter because it dovetails with the delegitimizing purpose to which Pound put the masculine pregnancy trope and connects it to broader social contexts. Pound's attempt to position women outside the boundary of legitimate (pro)creators was influenced by a similar endeavor in medical communities to delegitimize midwives; both efforts are instantiations of the system of misogyny, which crosses disciplinary, temporal, and geographical boundaries.

Misogyny against Midwives at the Turn of the Twentieth Century

In the years preceding WWI, efforts were underway in the United States and England to "professionalize" medicine. Professionalization meant many things in practice, including the creation of medical organizations. One result of these efforts was a very public dispute in England over the licensing and registration of midwives. Midwives advocated for these regulations as a way to professionalize the field and improve the public's perception of it.[8] They eventually prevailed with the passage of the Midwives Act of 1902, though not without vigorous opposition from a sizeable number of doctors. At this time, the term "doctor" referred to physicians, surgeons, and apothecaries, professions which banded together in 1858 as part of an attempt to differentiate themselves from quacks—with whom they associated midwives—and to justify higher fees. The medical specialization of obstetrics emerged in the mid-nineteenth century, a development that intensified the dispute between midwives and medical men. Because women were largely barred from medical schools, they were mostly barred from obstetrics (Cahill 336).

Some doctors supported midwives in their licensure efforts, seeing midwifery as a profession that relieved doctors of work that required long and irregular hours. As Jean Donnison demonstrates, however, many other doctors viewed midwives as competition for work that was an important component in a financially viable career, particularly for young doctors who were still building their practices (45). The strongest opposition came from general practitioners and doctors in rural locations, where parturient women tended to be a larger share of doctors' patients than in urban locations (120, 132). Some of the arguments against licensing midwives were self-serving, though not all. Many of the doctors' reservations stemmed from a genuine conviction that the English public would be better off if midwives were put out of business entirely. The reputation of midwives was quite poor at the turn of the century, and people such as R. R. Rentoul, one of the most vocal critics, tried to leverage midwives' reputation to doctors' advantage. The general public tended to think of midwives as untrained, sloppy, immoral women similar to "Sairey Gamp" of Dickens's imagination (102).[9] In some regards, these characterizations were justified. Several prominent legal cases in the second half of the nineteenth century concerned midwives who ran lying-in homes, places where women could conceal pregnancy and give birth in secret. As Donnison explains, "the unwanted children of these women were then put out to nurse, many being placed with [women known as "baby-farmers"], under whose regime of neglect, starvation and slow poisoning they soon died" (80). In general, however, evidence suggests that midwives had better outcomes than medical men. In 1936, for instance, the maternal mortality rate among women attended by midwives was significantly lower than the national average, despite the fact that their clientele generally came from lower socioeconomic classes and were therefore more likely to suffer from malnutrition and overwork (184). Nevertheless, midwives had a poor reputation, and doctors took advantage of it in their efforts to delegitimize their competition.

Midwives employed a number of strategies to improve their reputation. Among these strategies was a campaign to establish a government-backed system of licensing and registration based on similar models in place on the Continent. No such system existed in England, Donnison notes, although religious bodies had previously exerted loose control over midwives' behavior—requiring them to christen infants, to prevent false attribution of paternity, and so forth—but did not regulate their skills in any meaningful way (6–7). Prominent midwives and even some nurses (including Florence Nightingale) pushed for registration for decades before seeing results. Efforts became more organized and vocal in the mid-1800s as women gained political organizing skills in suffrage campaigns (65). The largest organizations representing midwives considered licensing and registration essential to stamping out the stereotype of midwives as unprofessional and uneducated, and agitated for legislation to that effect throughout the closing decades of the nineteenth century.

Although several proposals failed, midwives' persistence paid off, and in 1902 they won an important victory. The Midwives Act of 1902 is a landmark piece of legislation that established the Central Midwives Board.

The Board served as a mechanism for training and certifying midwives; as Robert Stevens observes, after the Act's passage, "a woman could not call herself, nor practise as a midwife, unless she was certified under the Act" (par. 4). Practicing without certification was a criminal offense. The Central Midwives Board was responsible for creating exams to determine eligibility, issuing certifications, and maintaining the roll of certified midwives (par. 9–10).

Throughout the years leading up to the 1902 Act, many doctors and organizations representing them worked to heighten the public's perception of the difference between doctors and midwives. Several influential doctors' organizations, such as the British Medical Association and the Obstetrical Society, objected to proposals to license and register midwives (Donnison 80–83). Arguments against the bill that would eventually become law often relied on hyperbole, fear-mongering, and paternalism. For instance, in an 1895 letter to the editor published in *The Times* of London, M. Greenwood, MD, argued that the proposed law would create a class of medical professionals who lacked the education and skills of doctors but, by virtue of their credentials, would be considered by pregnant women as equally trustworthy. In Greenwood's estimation, the bill would create an "Inferior Order" of midwives, "than which I can conceive no greater public evil" (13). Robert Barnes, also a medical doctor, similarly argued that midwives were uneducated, and even implied that they were immoral. The bill, he said, would "fail in providing security against the many criminal malpractices to which pregnant women are exposed" (14). Finally, George Brown, a member of the General Medical Council, argued that "the evil" caused by "ignorant and untrained midwives . . . is admitted by all members of the medical profession," and that "the vast majority of the profession throughout the country are opposed" to licensure and registration (6). As these examples attest, much of the rhetoric stressed the assumed need to protect pregnant women from midwives' injurious presence.

These arguments were complemented by the simultaneous medicalization of pregnancy. Medicalization describes a rhetorical shift in language used by medical practitioners that, over time, expands "medical jurisdiction into the realms of other previously nonmedically defined problems" (Gabe and Calnan 223). With regard to pregnancy, an event traditionally thought to be normal and healthy was increasingly characterized as an illness requiring management by skilled medical professionals. J. H. Keay, for instance, argued in the pages of the *British Medical Journal* in 1901 that doctors have a responsibility to attend poor women in labor, because no woman should have to "entrus[t] her life to an unskilled person" for lack of ability to pay a doctor's fee (1506). Keay implies that all pregnancies are life-threatening events and, because Keay seems to assume doctors are uniformly better skilled, midwives are unfit to attend childbirths. Discourse such as this contributed to a significant change in labor and delivery trends. Whereas midwives had once attended all births, by 1909 medical men were attending half of them in England (Donnison 185).[10]

Even the passage of the 1902 Act was a victory that came with many compromises. Medical men made up the majority of the board established by the Act to certify midwives, and the Act prohibited midwives from becoming a majority of the membership (Donnison 178–79). Furthermore, the Act made it illegal for midwives to use instruments, such as forceps, or to attend complicated births. When midwives recognized complications, they were obliged to send for a doctor. In this regard, the law formalized longstanding tradition (McIntosh, "Profession" 29). Donnison explains that this tradition arose in the thirteenth century with the creation of surgeons' guilds: "under the guild system the right to use surgical instruments belonged officially only to the surgeon. The surgeon was therefore considered the appropriate person to send for in labours where natural delivery was not possible" (2). When surgeons joined forces with physicians and apothecaries in the aforementioned 1858 union, this right transferred to the new group known as doctors (Donnison 2). After the 1902 Act, midwives could not legally attend complicated births, much less perform caesarean operations.

Pound and Midwifery

Was Pound aware of this dispute between midwives and medical men? A preponderance of evidence indicates he was. Pound moved from the United States to England in 1908 and lived there until 1920 (Moody xiv-xv). During this period, newspapers regularly covered events related to continuing disputes between midwives and doctors. For example, in 1910 *The Times* ran several Letters to the Editor regarding matters of payment when midwives sent for doctors in complicated cases (Fremantle 9). The issue came to public notice again in 1913, when a medical-ethical society in Cheshunt launched a protest against midwives by refusing to respond to their emergency calls "without immediate payment of a higher fee than usual," claiming that emergency calls resulted in many unpaid bills. A parturient woman died when her midwife called on three doctors, and all refused because payment was not immediately given (Donnison 185). Other issues related to the licensure dispute appeared in the news thereafter, including in 1918 when a law finally passed to clarify payment questions in emergency cases, placing the burden of responsibility on local authorities (McIntosh, *Social History* 160).

A publication with close ties to Pound discussed this medical dispute multiple times. Pound published reviews, articles, and poetry in *The New Age* while it ran under A. R. Orage's editorship (1907–1922). Pound was, for a time, the magazine's London editor. *The New Age* billed itself as "a weekly review of politics, literature and art" (Scholes). In its review of politics, the magazine covered the dispute between midwives and surgeons directly. Most prominently, the lead article in the August 4, 1910, issue provides a surprising amount of detail on a bill under consideration by the House of Commons. Fully one-quarter of the page is dedicated to "the second reading of the Government's Midwives (No. 2) Bill," which would, if passed, require "that where the qualified medical practitioner is called in upon the advice of a certified midwife, he shall be entitled to recover his fees from the *Guardians*" (italics original, "Notes of the Week" 314). Moreover, an article from the January 20, 1910, issue gives considerable space to a related issue. The anonymous author comments wryly on one of the exclusionary effects of the Midwives Act: "With all the talk about the proper sphere of women, it is amusing to find they are scarcely allowed to have a voice at the birth of children. The editors remind us that 'When a Departmental Committee was appointed to consider the working of the Midwives' Act, the Privy Council did not place upon it a single certified midwife, while in only seventeen English counties and seven county boroughs have women been appointed to a Midwives' Committee'" (Dukes 282). This note registers the success doctors were then having in their attempts to delegitimize midwives by positioning these female professionals as less qualified than their male counterparts in the realm of labor and delivery. Elsewhere in the same issue, Alfred E. Randall's poem "Promethius Re-Bound" satirizes Pound or, to be more specific, F. S. Flint's review of Pound's "Personae" ("How many Flints weigh a Pound? / Sacre nom de Dieu!" [p. 268]). Therefore, it is more likely than not that Pound read this issue of the magazine.

In addition to the salience of the midwives-doctors dispute in periodicals, several of Pound's friendships were likely to have brought him into contact with contemporary pregnancy-related issues. Pound's friendship with William Carlos Williams might have afforded one source of such information. Williams frequently attended births in his medical practice and occasionally mentioned these cases in letters to Pound (*Pound/Williams*). More relevant still are H. D.'s two pregnancies. H. D. and Pound were, of course, young lovers and briefly engaged to be married. In 1915, H. D. was pregnant by another man. She endured a traumatic parturition that resulted in stillbirth. She was attended by a female obstetrician (one of the first) at a maternity clinic in London (Caloyeras 6). Significantly, H. D. did not blame the obstetrician for the stillbirth and opted for one again when she gave birth to Perdita in 1919 (62). Pound was emotionally distraught over Perdita's birth.[11] He visited H. D. in the maternity ward and, in her recollection, Pound said, "my only real criticism is that this is not my child [while] pounding *(Pounding)*" on a wall with a walking stick (italics original, *End to Torment* 9). Besides "SAGE HOMME," one of the few texts in Pound's oeuvre discussing midwifery is Canto V, a poem about fertility and marriage. Later I discuss the poem in more detail, but now I want to touch on its composition history.[12] For it is plausible that H. D.'s parturitions spurred Pound's thinking about obstetrics. Pound began drafting Canto V in 1915 (the same year as H. D.'s stillbirth) but quickly abandoned the work, leaving it untouched for the next four years. H. D. gave birth to Perdita on March 31, 1919; by April, Pound was once again working on Canto V. If accurate, this composition history would help solidify the intellectual trajectory that connects Canto V to Pound's self-appellation as "sage homme." Both H. D.'s pregnancies and Williams's obstetric experience are personal avenues by which Pound might have learned about the differences between midwives and doctors.

In the years surrounding Canto V, H. D.'s pregnancies, and Eliot's composition of *The Waste Land*, Pound's theories of art manifest awareness of key reproductive debates of the day. When describing the process of artistic creation, he used terminology drawn from biology, eugenics, and Malthusianism, demonstrating he paid more than passing attention to these issues. For example, he called Marianne Moore a "Malthusian of the intellect" ("Doggerel" 364) and castigated the United States Comstock Act for "lump[ing] literature and instruments for abortion into one clause" (qtd. in Moody 334).[13] Pound also developed a theory of artistic creation in biological terms. In 1914 he argued for the idea of the artist "as DIRECTING a certain fluid force against circumstance, as CONCEIVING instead of merely observing and reflecting" (qtd. in Moody 257). And in the 1922 postscript to Remy de Gourmont's *The Natural Philosophy of Love*, Pound notoriously surmised that the brain is a "great clot of genital fluid" and London a "passive vulva" into which he was driving new poetic ideas ("Translator's Postscript" 206).

Drawing the connection between Pound and medical issues even closer, Pound makes a case for literature as a pursuit requiring the same habits of mind as medicine. In a review of Joyce's *Ulysses* that was published in *The Dial* in May 1922, Pound writes: "*a great literary masterwork is made for minds quite as serious as those engaged in the science of medicine.* The anthropologist and sociologist have a right to equally accurate documents, to equally succinct reports and generalizations, which they seldom get, considering the complexity of the matter in hand" ("Paris Letter: Ulysses" 638, italics original). In another review of *Ulysses* from August of the same year, Pound refers to literature as a discipline that steps in where science fails or falters ("Paris Letter" 337). Pound published these reviews four and seven months, respectively, after writing "SAGE HOMME."

That Pound was thinking of science and medicine while writing about *Ulysses* brings me to another possible reason for his revision of the intellectual midwifery metaphor, particularly his association of himself with surgeons. *Ulysses* is, of course, full of reproductive imagery. The serialized episodes that appeared in the months leading up to the "SAGE HOMME" letter include the following: a midwife whose bag contains "a misbirth with a trailing navelcord, hushed in ruddy wool" (Episode III 32); reference to Socrates, who "had a midwife to mother as he had a shrew to wife" (Episode IX 21); and reappearance of the midwife, whose bag now contains "eleven cockles" rolling around (Episode X 36). Given the frequency of references to midwifery in *Ulysses*, Pound's adaptation of the old intellectual midwifery metaphor seems as though it could be calculated to lampoon Joyce. Modernizing the metaphor would imply that Eliot and Pound did one better than Joyce with *The Waste Land*. Put bluntly, Joyce can have his Sairey Gamps; Pound and Eliot have surgeons. The prevalence of surgical metaphors, combined with Pound's use of language affiliated with reproductive debates, makes Pound's awareness of the dispute between surgeons and midwives almost certain, and leads to the conclusion that he coined the term "sage homme" to align himself with doctors rather than midwives.[14]

Pound's Masculine Pregnancy Metaphor

Contra Rabaté, then, "SAGE HOMME" leaves little doubt that Pound chose the role of surgeon, not midwife, to describe his intervention into Eliot's metaphorical male pregnancy. The line "Ezra performed the caesarean

Operation" is the most obvious evidence, characterizing his own editorial activities as those of a surgeon. This characterization makes sense in the context of a pregnancy Pound describes as "doubly difficult" because of the inverted genders of the parents. C-sections were done, then as now, for high-risk pregnancies. As such, Pound's poem implies that Eliot's delivery of *The Waste Land* would not have been a success without Pound's intervention; the poem, Eliot-as-Poet, or both, would have metaphorically died without the operation. And Eliot was, indeed, on the verge of a nervous breakdown while composing the poem, particularly before giving the drafts to Pound for review (Koestenbaum 112–17).[15]

Pound had ready alternatives to the term "sage homme," though neither affords the same figurative possibilities. Both "man-midwife" and "accoucheur" were in use at the time as names for men who attended women in childbirth. Pound would have been aware of both terms, as they appear in *Tristram Shandy*, a novel he considered required reading (T. Gioia par. 9).[16] Instead of using "accoucheur" or "man-midwife," however, Pound coined a term by adapting the French "sage femme." This adaptation aligns with a familiar, sexist epistemology of embodiment. As Alicia Ostriker describes this epistemology, "the body is base and the mind is exalted. . . . As to woman: woman in our mythology *is* the flesh" (248). Pound correspondingly coined a term that emphasizes intelligence ("sage") and distances himself from a profession associated with women. He amplifies that connotation by discarding the part of the term with links to the body ("femme"), replacing it with a word long-associated with the mind ("homme"). The poem then confirms these associations by connecting Pound with doctors, a profession, as we saw, that prided itself on knowledge, skill, and technical precision. These associations and connotations map directly onto the rhetoric employed by doctors in the licensure debates to discredit midwives and burnish their own reputations. Significantly, both Pound and Eliot reiterated the obstetric imagery elsewhere when referring to *The Waste Land*, with Eliot calling the poem Pound's "caesarean operation" and Pound referring to it as "my obstetric effort" (qtd. in Ricks and McCue 553–54). As mentioned earlier, obstetrics was a relatively new specialization almost exclusively composed of medical men.

Reading the first stanzas of "SAGE HOMME" through the lens of obstetrics opens new interpretive possibilities for the remainder of the poem. Consider the following lines, which immediately follow Pound's claim to have performed the caesarean operation:

Cauls and grave clothes he [Pound] brings ,
Fortune's outrageous stings,
About which odour clings,
Of putrifaction [. . .]

He writes of A.B.C.s. [. . .]
    Sans satisfaction;
Breeding of animals
Humans and cannibals,
But above all else of smells
    Without attraction

Vates cum fistula

Critics typically translate "*Vates cum fistula*" as "poet/singer with a pan pipe"
or "poet/singer with an ulcer" (*fistula* referring to a hole of some sort).[17]
Pound ended an earlier collection, *A Lume Spento*, with a series of nine
poems titled *Fistulae*. Unlike "SAGE HOMME," the tone of the *Fistulae*
poems is youthful desire and joy (Moody 53–54). The distinct differences
in tone imply that a different approach to the word "fistula" in "SAGE
HOMME" is in order.

The reproductive theme in "SAGE HOMME" leads to an alternative
translation, an obstetric fistula. Reading the line as such shows symmetry
between the first section of the poem, which figures Eliot-as-parturient-poet,
and these stanzas, which figure Pound-as-parturient poet through the references to cauls, breeding, and unsatisfactory writing. An obstetric fistula,
also sometimes referred to as a vesico-vaginal fistula, is a medical condition
that develops during childbirth, particularly prolonged labor. A hole torn
in the vaginal wall leads to urinary and sometimes fecal incontinence. The
condition is associated with strong, unpleasant smells (Morantz-Sanchez 93).
It is not an exaggeration to say that obstetric fistulae often destroyed lives
before successful methods of repair were discovered. John Dieffenbach, a
German physician, explained the side effects in the *Lancet* in 1836:

> The constant passage of the urine into the vagina must necessarily
> produce considerable irritation, and even inflammation . . . the
> skin assumes a bright-red colour, and is partially covered with
> [boils]. The patients complain of a most disagreeable burning
> and itching sensation, which often compels them to scratch

themselves until the blood comes forth . . . washing with cold water is of little avail, since the linen is quickly saturated with the fluid which escapes. . . . The air in the chambers of such patients acts injuriously on their lungs, and wherever they go they taint the atmosphere. . . . This unhappy accident breaks through all family ties. . . . Some of these unhappy patients . . . would willingly resign their lives to get rid of the misery which surrounds them. (757–58)

Sixteen years later, in 1852, the American physician J. Marion Sims published the results of his experiments on three enslaved women that led to the discovery of the first successful method for surgical repair. This discovery resulted in worldwide fame for Sims and the now-discredited title as "the father of American gynaecology" (Morantz-Sanchez 94).[18] Obstetric fistulae were thereafter repairable by surgeons. Between Pound's emphasis on disagreeable smells and rotting fabrics, as well as the reproductive theme carried throughout "SAGE HOMME," an obstetric fistula is a logical referent for the line *Vates cum fistula*.[19]

Read as such, the stanzas immediately preceding the *vates* line imply Pound's need for a surgeon to clean up and masculinize his poetry, in the same way Eliot needed Pound's surgical editing.[20] While the first section of "SAGE HOMME" celebrates Pound-as-editor, these later lines focus on Pound's own poetic output and find it lacking. As a result, the poem implies that Pound is a more successful surgeon than poet. He describes his own writing as animalistic, primitive, and unclean ("breeding of animals / Humans and cannibals / But above all else of smells / Without attraction"). His poetry, then, is characterized by traits diametrically opposed to the technical precision, civilization, and intellectual mastery Pound associated with modern poetry and surgery. Descriptions of the female body as leaky and animalistic have a long history of gendered associations extending far beyond Pound, but to which his metaphors hew closely. Indeed, Pound's frequent use of bodily excretions, particularly urine, to denigrate women led Koestenbaum to argue that sexism of this sort "probably served as common ground" for his friendship with Eliot and the lawyer/agent John Quinn, all three of whom used similar language in letters exchanged between one another (174). For example, Quinn said about Margaret Anderson and Jane Heap of *The Little Review*, "I think of female literary excrement; washy, urinacious menstruations. . . . These people seem to sweat urine and probably urinate sweat . . . by God! I don't like the thought of women who seem to exude as well as bathe in piss, if not drink it, or each other's" (qtd. in Koestenbaum 174). The parallels between Quinn's rhetoric and the aforementioned medical description of women suffering from obstetric fistulae—"wherever they go they taint the atmosphere" with the smell of urine—do not need belaboring.

Pound's association of wateriness and excess with women is consistent in this period of his career, even when he ascribes these traits to himself. Consider, for instance, Pound's "Portrait d'une Femme," which includes the lines "Your mind and you are our Sargasso Sea, / London has swept about you this score years / [. . .] and yet / For all this sea-hoard of deciduous things, [. . .] There is nothing!" (qtd. in Ben-Merre 125–26). The idea that the woman of the title is a failed poet is familiar; many critics have argued that this poem transforms the female artist into a muse in an attempt to neutralize her feminist and artistic potential.[21] David Ben-Merre, however, convincingly reads Pound himself as the failed female poet. The accretion that characterizes this woman is associated, in Ben-Merre's reading, with Pound's interest in anthology, juxtaposition, and parataxis. He states, "I tend to think of Pound's 'Portrait d'une Femme' as a self-portrait. It is difficult to overlook the similarities between the lady's (dishonestly gendered) 'sea-hoard' and Pound's anthological model of collection, later on full display in his salon—*The Cantos*" (129). If we read the poem as Ben-Merre does, as self-portraiture, the description of the "femme" as "pregnant with man-drakes" becomes decidedly queer.[22] Not quite a male pregnancy because of the unambiguous labeling of the poet as a woman, neither is the poem representing a heteronormative pregnancy. This pregnancy is as unsuccessful as the one Pound depicts for himself in "SAGE HOMME." In "Portrait," the (pro)creation "never proves" (125). Here, then, watery excess is associated with women, and both with poetic failure.

As Ronald Bush explains, these associations align with "a theme that runs through Pound's middle and later work: that 'the female is a chaos,' the male a principle of form and order" (353). The latter, of course, he associated with modern poetry. A less damning—though still misogynistic—example can be found in a letter Pound wrote to Marianne Moore in 1919:

The female is a chaos,
the male
is a fixed point of stupidity
[. . .]

You, my dear correspondent,
are a stabilized female,
I am a male who has attained the chaotic fluidities. ("Doggerel" 362)

Pound admired Moore's poetry, and, as such, the passage above is best read as praise for Moore's masculine qualities. Pound's gender-bending claim bears comparison with Virginia Woolf's more famous one of the androgynous mind in *A Room of One's Own*. Woolf, too, argues that female artists ideally have some masculine traits (94–103). Yet, unlike Pound, Woolf argues that the reverse also is true, that male artists benefit from feminine traits. Pound, conversely, devalues them. Immediately after stating "the male / is a fixed point of stupidity," he writes, "only the female / can content itself with prolonged conversation / with but one sole other creature of its own sex and / of its own unavoidable specie / the male / is more expansive" ("Doggerel" 362).

That Pound laments the female traits he sees in himself is only made clearer in "SAGE HOMME." The reference to cauls ("cauls and grave clothes he brings") continues the reproductive theme into the second section of the poem. Instead of Eliot pregnant with verse, here Pound is the parturient poet, and his childbirth is far less successful because he does not have the masculinizing influence of a surgeon-editor. In rare instances, infants are born with a portion of the caul, the amniotic membrane that encloses fetuses in the womb, still attached. The caul is easily removed and generally harmless. The condition is often considered good luck (Forbes 495). Nevertheless, "SAGE HOMME" connects cauls with the "outrageous stings" of "fortune," which suggests it be read as another example of female leakiness, of biological material exceeding the boundaries of the body. That Pound carries with him "cauls and grave clothes" implies that he, like Eliot, recently gave birth, but that Pound's childbirth experience was less successful than Eliot's, resulting in an obstetric fistula, clothes that smell of death and decay, and possibly a stillborn poetic child. Given Pound's and Eliot's frequent use of smells and bodily excretions to describe women, these lines would have signaled to Eliot, the intended reader of "SAGE HOMME," that Pound aligned his own poetry with that written by the literary women they so often maligned. This portrait of Pound-as-poet thus exemplifies what would have happened to Eliot if Pound-as-surgeon had not performed the caesarean operation. Pound's poetry, "SAGE HOMME" implies, needs a male surgeon to sanitize and modernize it as Pound did for Eliot's.

Pound began experimenting with the old trope of intellectual mid-wifery at least three years prior to writing "SAGE HOMME." Images of childbirth and fertility suffuse Canto V, a poem first published in *The Dial* in 1921. As mentioned earlier, Pound began the poem in 1915 but quickly abandoned this early draft, leaving it unfinished until 1919 (Preda). The version published in 1921 includes the line "Fracastor (lightning was mid-wife)" (*Cantos of Ezra Pound* 20). Pound's 1954 revision of the poem makes the lightning allusion clearer: "Fracastor had Zeus for midwife, / Lightning served as his tweezers" (qtd. in Bacigalupo 114). Girolamo Fracastoro was a sixteenth-century physician and poet whose mother was killed by light-ning while holding the infant Fracastoro shortly after his birth (Terrell 21). Pound's lines imply that although Fracastoro's mother may have given birth to the physical infant, the birth of the poet/doctor was facilitated by Zeus. This dual role as poet/doctor is precisely that which I am arguing Pound claims for himself in "SAGE HOMME."

The connection between Pound and Fracastoro hinted at in Canto V is reinforced by an allusion Pound made in a 1916 letter. In response to a fan, Pound composed a short autobiography in which he directly compares his life with Fracastoro's:

> Born in Hailey, Idaho. First connection with vorticist movement during the blizzard of '87 when I came East, having decided that the position of Hailey was not sufficiently central for my activities—came East behind the first rotary snow plough [sic], the inventor of which vortex saved me from death by croup by feeding me with lumps of sugar saturated with kerosene. (Parallels in the life of Fracastorius.) After that period, life gets too complicated to be treated coherently in a hurried epistle. (*Letters* 120)

In this passage, Pound likens himself to a baby by implying that he was incapable of feeding himself and by reference to croup, an illness com-mon in children. The connection of the snow plow to vorticism, in turn, implies that this journey facilitated the birth of Pound-as-poet just as light-ning (here, kerosene) facilitated Fracastoro's birth. Science and technology implicitly figure into both passages via the inventor of the snow plow and Fracastoro's profession.

Taken together, this letter and Canto V indicate that Pound under-stood his poetic career to be facilitated by science and technology, a point not surprising to those familiar with Pound's biography. But the childbirth references in both this letter and Canto V suggest he was playing with metaphors for the birth of the artist at the same time that he was thinking through the relationship between poetry and science. Because midwives were in disrepute among the general public in the early decades of the twentieth century, the old trope of intellectual midwifery ill-fit Pound's idea of modern poetry as scientific, intellectual, and masculine.

The term "sage homme" offers a resolution to the conundrum. It connects Pound to the long tradition of intellectual midwives while eschewing associations with the profession of midwifery. The line stating that Pound performs the "caesarean Operation" emphasizes his connection with medical men, linking Pound's editorial work to surgeons. The exclusionary rhetoric of surgeons was, with some success, pushing female professionals out of business and positioning surgeons as the only legitimate medical practitioners for attendance at childbirth. At the time Pound was writing, then, labor and delivery was a realm in which misogyny was on the rise, with increasing numbers of the general public believing that attendance by a medical man led to better outcomes. Whereas women were slowly gaining rights and power (in literary realms as elsewhere), with respect to childbirth, women were paradoxically losing ground.

Pound, of course, made no secret of his desire to stem the unprecedented growth of women's power and prominence in literature; he even attempted to start a magazine for which "no woman shall be allowed to write" (qtd. in Moody 317). It is telling that Pound marked his own editorial work as masculine, since this is an area in which women's newfound legitimacy was particularly conspicuous. Margaret Anderson and Jane Heap, castigated by John Quinn in the aforementioned letter as "women who seem to bathe in piss," were undeniably influential in modern letters. And at a time when Pound was financially strapped and keen to establish his reputation in literary circles, he found himself beholden to the judgment of women editors such as Dora Marsden of *The Freewoman* and Harriet Monroe of *Poetry*. Evidence therefore leads to the conclusion that Pound felt a need to distance his editorial efforts from those of women by coining a term that masculinizes editorial work.

The language of ownership in childbirth parallels that of editorial work in a way that further illuminates Pound's rhetoric. The interventions of an editor usually go unnamed and unremarked in the text itself. Credit for the textual creation goes to the author. In childbirth, midwives typically say that the woman delivers the baby while the midwife assists. Credit for the delivery goes to the parturient person. Conversely, the language used in conjunction with doctors and surgeons asserts ownership over the childbirth process. The doctor, rather than the gestator, is said to deliver the baby. Pound similarly claims his stake in *The Waste Land* by insisting that "the printed Infancies result[ed]" from his operation on them. Eliot's dedication of *The Waste Land* to Pound ("il miglior fabbro") affirms Pound's right to claim a degree of ownership over the poem. Therefore, unlike earlier generations of writers who used reproductive metaphors to deny collaboration, Pound uses them to strengthen his connection with Eliot.

In 1922, the language of surgery carried rhetorical force, and all evidence indicates that Pound engaged that force for his own efforts. His desire to "masculinize" literature is consistent with doctors' efforts to delegitimize midwives by emphasizing doctors' supposedly superior training and knowledge. *Le mot juste* for Pound, therefore, is not "midwife." Neither, however, is "sage homme" for critics committed to feminist principles. By replacing "femme" with "homme," this term recapitulates the erasure of women that doctors sought to enact, without reference to those historical circumstances. "Surgeon" is a far more accurate reflection of Pound's chosen role *and* of the historical moment. As the surgeon of *The Waste Land*, Pound literally cut into the body of the poem with his editorial revisions and metaphorically distanced himself from women's work by figuring himself as a male medical professional. Recognizing the difference between "midwife," "surgeon," and "sage homme" acknowledges reproductive language as an important part of the rhetoric Pound used to delegitimize female authors.

Much of Pound's metaphorics of creation is posturing, part of the many outrageous personae Pound constructed throughout his life. My reading of "SAGE HOMME" is consistent with this posturing: in the first four stanzas, Pound adopts the role of the wise man, the trained, educated surgeon who performs a "caesarean Operation" on a feminized Eliot. In later stanzas, Pound becomes the leaky, uneducated, feminized writer who needs a surgeon to deliver his poetry. Since midwives were, at the time, thought to be sloppy, unskilled, old-fashioned women, calling on an intellectual midwife to deliver his and Eliot's modern poetry would hardly serve the figurative purpose. In this context, the sanitation, intelligence, and skill then associated with surgeons made this profession a better fit. The poem thereby implies that legitimacy in the realms of poetry and reproduction rests on masculinity. This figuration thereby provides insight into the ways that reproductive language was used by an influential modernist writer to position women as illegitimate (pro)creators in the realm of modern letters.

Male Childbirth Metaphor in *Cane*

An illustrative comparison can be found in Jean Toomer's *Cane* (1923). In this book, Toomer uses reproductive language to similar effect—to suggest that a new kind of literature will be written by male artists—albeit in a dramatically different context. The male childbirth metaphor appears at the end of the book, wherein Toomer represents *Cane* as the first in a generation of modern Black literature. Unlike the artist imagined in Pound's depiction of a pregnant man, however, the artist imagined by Toomer is thwarted by the threat and reality of racist violence. Even though Toomer preferred to think of himself as American rather than Black or biracial, *Cane* is undeniably focused on the lives of Black people (Robles 28). *Cane* is composed of vignettes of multiple genres, including short narratives, poems, and a closet drama. The first half of the book is set in rural Georgia. The second half is set in urban locations in Washington, DC, and, in one instance, Chicago. The final vignette, the closet drama, returns to Georgia and focuses on a Black man who moved there from the North in an attempt to connect with his Southern roots. The book ends with a childbirth metaphor that suggests a circumscribed kind of hope for renewal that comes through the artist drawing inspiration from the natural world.

Cane does not depict mannish pregnant women. There is a mannish woman (Carma), and there are pregnant/parturient women (Becky and Karintha; Esther, who is never physically pregnant, is defined by her desire for pregnancy), but nowhere is a mannish woman pregnant. Instead, this book subtly suggests that masculinity and pregnancy are not compatible.[23] For instance, the character most directly described as mannish is Carma. The narrative voice introduces her this way: "Carma, in overalls, and strong as any man, stands behind the old brown mule, driving the wagon home" (12). The phrase "strong as a/any man" is repeated in the vignette and is echoed by other descriptors that suggest mannishness (masculine clothing, performing work traditionally done by men, sexual freedom typically only seen in men, and so forth). Even though Carma is depicted as sexually active, there is no mention of children in her tale.

Where *Cane* does engage masculine pregnancies is in its use of a childbirth metaphor at the close of the book. The final lines read: "Outside, the sun arises from its cradle in the tree-tops of the forest. Shadows of pines are dreams the sun shakes from its eyes. The sun arises. Gold-glowing child, it steps into the sky and sends a birth-song slanting down gray dust streets and sleepy windows of the southern town" (117). Janet M. Whyde reads this metaphor as directly relating to artists and artistic creation. Kabnis, the protagonist of the final vignette (in which the metaphor appears), is a thwarted poet who hails from a line of orators and whose goal is to "shap[e] words t fit m soul" (sic 111). At the end of the vignette, he rises from a basement in which he passed the night in a drunken stupor, sloughing off some of the illusions that have held him back (52). Kabnis rises at the same moment as the gold-glowing sun/son and is bathed in its light. Whyde thereby argues that the metaphor suggests renewal for both Kabnis and the South: "The southern town is transformed into a blank slate waiting to be populated" by Black Southern artists (96). *Cane* is both the harbinger and the first instantiation of that renewal.

I stated earlier that the book ends on a note of circumscribed hope. The kind of circumscription I have in mind is described by Lucinda H. MacKethan in "*Cane:* A Pastoral Problem":

> *Cane* begins with sunset scenes. There is, then, from the very beginning, a realization that the life represented in the South-ern scenes is a dying thing which might be captured in art but not preserved as an escape from or a cure for modern ills. The sunrise at the end of *Cane*, then, is a symbol of hope, but not hope based on the simpler rural existence that is given lyrical treatment throughout the book. Rather, because of the sunrise we are able to hope for a sort of reconnection or rerooting process through which Kabnis, a modern black man, might find renewal through an acceptance of the land and the past that have molded his racial identity. We see Kabnis first in the dead of night, waiting for daylight. At the end he is bathed in sunlight, after a night which presents a dramatic possibility of catharsis. (434)

In addition to closing out the book, this childbirth metaphor also echoes sun, sunrise, and sunset imagery that repeats throughout the vignettes. As such, the metaphor takes on heightened significance as it reverberates with previous references. These previous references are frequently connected to scenes of violence against Southern Black bodies. The echoes of this earlier imagery in the final childbirth metaphor therefore dramatically limit the extent to which hope and renewal are possible.

Nevertheless, hope for renewal is there. Indeed, I read it in the very existence of *Cane* itself. *Cane's* design is circular. Of the book, Toomer said, "CANE's design is a circle. Aesthetically, from simple forms to complex ones, and back to simple forms. Regionally, from the South up into the North, and back into the South again" ("To Waldo Frank" 152). From this design principle, I see the final lines of *Cane* as self-referential; the book that the reader holds in their hands is the product of this promised artistic renewal. And *Cane* is at least partly autobiographical. Mary Battenfeld demonstrates that "the final section of Cane draws its power and its inspiration from the racial violence Toomer witnessed or learned of in Sparta [Georgia]. As Toomer wrote to Waldo Frank, 'Kabnis sprang up almost in a day, . . . It is the direct result of a trip I made down into Georgia'" (Battenfeld 1239). Toomer found the kind of artistic and spiritual renewal in Georgia that is promised in the childbirth metaphor that ends the book. I therefore read *Cane* as the "gold-glowing child" whose existence will renew Black literature, and Toomer/Kabnis as a writer pregnant with literary offspring. Like "SAGE HOMME," the body from which this new literature will come is inevitably male; for Toomer, this new storyteller will be a son/sun of the Southern soil.

Toomer's use of the male childbirth metaphor aligns with an older tradition of its use, even as his deployment of the metaphor is necessarily changed by virtue of circumstance, especially modernity and Blackness. Terry Castle explains that writers of earlier generations often used the childbirth metaphor to deny outside help or to signal the naturalness of their inspiration (196–97). As many critics have shown, Toomer embraces the idea of creativity as connected to spontaneous action, organic processes, and animal impulses.[24] It therefore makes sense in Castle's framework that Cane would embrace the childbirth metaphor and use it to signal the beginning of a new literary aesthetic.

Although *Cane*'s deployment of the childbirth metaphor is similar to that of Renaissance poets' use of it, there are distinct differences that result from the fact that Toomer was writing of Black people in modernity. Where earlier generations of white authors leveraged this metaphor to suggest the ease and spontaneity of composition, Toomer's book stresses the opposite.[25] Inspiration might come through the natural world, but it is anything but easy because the relationship of Black Americans to the soil is laced with blood. Toomer's references to this legacy of violence address both the past of slavery and the present of Jim Crow in which he was writing. Lynchings and murders of Black men, women, and children appear throughout the book. Therefore, (pro)creation in *Cane* carries with it the potential for physical and psychic destruction. To create *Cane*, Toomer had to connect with Southern soil; to connect with Southern soil is to court danger. Creation in the logic of this book is tied to the bloody Southern soil.

Both Pound and Toomer used male pregnancy metaphors to associate the process of artistic creation with a particular intellectual tradition. For Pound, that tradition was medical men. For Toomer, it was the long lineage of writers who believed that artistic inspiration came from connection to the natural world, particularly the soil. Toomer and Pound also adapted the male pregnancy trope to reflect the modern condition. Pound's coinage of *sage homme* attempted to distance himself from the old-fashioned mid-wives conjured by the term *sage femme*. Toomer created an iteration of the childbirth metaphor that registers the role of racist violence in the Black artist's life. Toomer's metaphor is also a reflection of modernity because *Cane* is an elegy for a Southern way of life that was dying, as MacKethan's reading illuminates. The only way to recapture this life is through art. The gold-glowing child of the metaphor is a tenuously hopeful harbinger of modern Black art.

By paying attention to reproductive metaphors in modernism, we can better appreciate the importance of figurative language that circulates in critical discourse. An instructive example can be found in L. D. Burnett's survey of verbs that historians use to discuss their subjects. Burnett points out the gendered connotations that verbs carry, stating that historians frequently describe women's intellectual endeavors with those connected to the material world, such as " 'fashioned,' 'crafted,' [and] 'shaped' " (par. 3). These terms, Burnett argues, are a reminder that the lives of women were often "relegated to the realm of materiality; to men alone belonged significant ideation" (par. 5).

The term "midwife," too, carries with it a gendered history that merits consideration in contexts beyond "SAGE HOMME." How, for example, does the intellectual midwifery metaphor construct the relationship between mind and body, male and female, and how does it vary depending on context? Does it recapitulate stereotypes and reinforce biases? What about other metaphors for writing, editing, and creation? Critics have done this kind of feminist work on literary devices and figures of speech, notably Barbara Johnson on apostrophe and Susan Stanford Friedman on the childbirth metaphor. Yet the need for such work persists, in part because figurative language is easy to overlook when it is a critical commonplace. For instance, in my 2013 article "Modernism, Monsters, and Margaret Sanger," I compared Sanger to "the system builder, the modernist idea of the artist as an architect who builds frames to organize the chaos of modern life" (456). I concluded that Sanger's "system," the birth control movement in the United States, failed to control the complicated political and cultural climate of reproduction, just as other modernist system builders like Yeats, Eliot, and Pound could not make the center hold. Although my article addressed Sanger's sometimes narcissistic dominance over the birth control movement in the United States, I did not consider the implications of my architecture metaphor. This metaphor suggests that Sanger was a lone figure, drawing out blueprints and raising the birth control movement from the ground up. In fact, Sanger built on decades of work done by other activists and medical workers and relied on huge numbers of volunteers to drive the movement. The "system builder" was a metaphor that the essay left unexamined. As George Lakoff and Mark Johnson argue in *Metaphors We Live By*, human conceptual systems are "fundamentally metaphorical in nature," with the result that metaphors "govern our everyday functioning down to the most mundane details. Our concepts structure what we perceive, how we get around in the world, and how we relate to other people" (3). For this reason, metaphors are deeply imbricated with systems of inequality.

Earlier, I asked how childbirth metaphors construct the relationship between mind and body. All of the texts under consideration in this book examine that relationship in one way or another. In the following chapter, I focus on William Faulkner's artist novels: *Mosquitoes* (1927) and *If I Forget Thee, Jerusalem/The Wild Palms* (1939). Pound and Faulkner similarly conceptualize masculine men as uniquely able to generate legitimate art. As such, these texts have ideological similarities to eighteenth- and nineteenth-century depictions of bastardy, wherein biology is the lodestar in determinations of legitimacy. Interestingly, however, we can trace a change in Faulkner's thinking between the first artist novel and the second. His later novel moves away from the realm of metaphor and into the realm of literal reproduction, featuring depictions of mannish pregnancy. As I will discuss, these depictions of mannish pregnancy hint at the possibility of legitimate female artists (albeit a misogynistic possibility: her art can be legitimate only if she is masculine-identified). The presence of this possibility in *Jerusalem* makes Faulkner a logical bridge to my analyses of Willa Cather's *My Ántonia* (1918) and Djuna Barnes's *Nightwood* (1936) in the second half of this book. There I show that these novels employ depictions of masculine pregnancy to quite different effect than Pound's "SAGE HOMME": to affirm the legitimacy of female and queer (pro)creation and to show how the stories we tell about offspring matter just as much, if not more, than biology.

Chapter 3

Pregnancy in Faulkner's Artist Novels

Masculinity, Sexology, and Creativity in Interwar America

In 1934, William Faulkner was struggling to write the book that would become *Absalom! Absalom!* (1936). He chalked up his difficulties to the book's incomplete gestation, stating, "I believe that the book is not quite ripe yet; that I have not gone my nine months, you might say" (*Selected Letters* 83–84). Faulkner links pregnancy with male creativity by implying that *Absalom* gestated in the body of a male author, a notion that both affirms and rebuffs his perception of writing as a womanly pursuit. For this is an author who claimed that creative pursuits were "really no manly business" but rather "a polite painting of china by gentlewomen" (ibid., 216). Faulkner was intensely anxious about his self-perceived femininity, which stemmed in part from his profession. The ways in which artistic creation is and is not like procreation, especially when informed by discourses of masculinity, was a sustained interest of Faulkner's. This interest appears both before and after Faulkner's use of the male childbirth metaphor to describe *Absalom*, most notably in his artist novels, *Mosquitoes* (1927) and *If I Forget Thee, Jerusalem* (also known as *The Wild Palms*, 1939).

These novels, indeed all the texts I consider in this book, draw on a theory that shaped interwar understandings of gender and sexuality: inversion. The term "inversion," in its non-theoretical sense, denotes "a reversal of position, orders, sequence, or relation" ("inversion"). Sexologists yoked this term to what we today think of as gender, sex, and sexuality. The result was a corpus of ideas based implicitly on the binaries of male/female, masculine/feminine, attracted to women/attracted to men, even as these theorists were, in other ways, developing more fluid and flexible notions of embodiment. In the zero-sum accounting of inversion, a gain in one place results in a loss elsewhere; if masculinity is the inverse of femininity, for example, any loss of masculinity equates to an increase in femininity.

Because *Mosquitoes* and *Jerusalem* draw on the theory of inversion but do so on either side of the Great Depression (1927 and 1939, respectively), and because the Great Depression hastened a dramatic shift in cultural norms related to masculinity, Faulkner's artist novels are a particularly rich source for any consideration of sexuality and gender in the interwar period. Critics generally agree that these novels are misogynistic and aesthetically unsuccessful, and I do not disagree.[1] Nevertheless, I see considerable insight to be gained by studying *Mosquitoes* and *Jerusalem* in light of changing attitudes about gender, reproduction, and art. The discourse of inversion frames my reading of masculine pregnancies in Faulkner's artist novels. Such a reading reveals, I argue, parallels between Faulkner's and Pound's use of reproductive rhetoric to police the boundaries of legitimate art; it also, more surprisingly, illuminates eruptions of queer knowledge in the midst of the novels' heteronormative plotlines.

The stakes of my argument are twofold. On one hand, this argument brings us to familiar, sexist terrain: *Mosquitoes* and *Jerusalem* position femininity as incompatible with "real" art and masculine women as inferior, inauthentic artists because their bodily drives toward procreation inevitably interrupt aesthetic creation. (There are some interwar writers who implied that procreation and artistic creation are incompatible because of societal constraints around procreation rather than biological inevitabilities; in this chapter, I offer a brief consideration of Virginia Woolf's *Orlando* [1928] to exemplify this point.) *Mosquitoes*, especially, implies that women evolved for procreation, while men evolved for artistic creation. In the interwar period, as discussed in chapter 1, white female authors gained power and prominence in literature. The works of many male artists manifest anxiety over the need to compete with female authors. Ezra Pound's "SAGE HOMME" is one such example. As we saw in the previous chapter, Pound metaphorically positions (pro)creative labor and delivery as events better handled by masculine men. He describes T. S. Eliot as a feminized poet giving birth to *The Waste Land*'s verses, claiming "A Man their Mother was." The success of *The Waste Land*, Pound implies, rests on Pound's own masculine, surgical editing skills to deliver the "offspring" safely. Whereas Pound's "SAGE HOMME" relegates actual women to the background, Faulkner's novels foreground the female body. Faulkner uses the sexological theory of inversion to suggest that the ability to get pregnant is the very thing that makes women inferior artists. Therefore, although the means may be different, the end is the same in both Faulkner and Pound: "legitimate" artists are masculine, and men have easier access to masculinity by virtue of their embodiment. Further, Faulkner's novels suggest that women artists who are masculine will eventually be thwarted by the female body's drive to reproduce; therefore, women are inferior artists because of their bodies.

On the other hand, my reading of Faulkner's artist novels takes us to unexpected territory precisely because *Mosquitoes* and *Jerusalem* foreground the reproductive female body. Jaime Harker argues that Faulkner's novels are full of "eruptions of alternative knowledge and communities" ("Queer Faulkner" 117). Harker defines these eruptions as surprising implications that become apparent by reading against the grain (ibid.). They emerge in the midst of the main narrative and "threaten to undo the mainstream voice of Southern patriarchy. Attention to these counter-narratives rescues Faulkner from his own planter class pretentions and outs the queer heart of his narrative genius" (ibid.). I use Harker's concept of queer eruptions for my reading of *Mosquitoes* and *Jerusalem*, novels in which eruptions often occur around depictions of mannish or inverted women. The surprising implications occasioned by the bodies of inverted women unsettle Faulkner's main narratives, making claims of male artistic superiority less convincing and introducing a kind of queer knowledge that affirms the power of mannish women as (pro)creators and patriarchal masculinity as damaging to men. The main narratives in both artist novels imply that legitimate art is the province of men and reproduction the province of women. However, reading against the grain reveals counter-narratives suggesting that art—the putative male version of pregnancy—is not as the main narrative depicts it to be, and that mannish women can be successful, productive artists. Finally, counter-narratives in Faulkner's artist novels imply that hegemonic masculinity is psychologically harmful to men themselves.

These counter-narratives allow us a glimpse of the confusion and ambivalence that some writers felt when confronted with queer and/or female artists. This glimpse, in turn, gives us a fuller understanding of the ways modernists deployed the trope of masculine pregnancy. Pound was defiant in his use of the trope for exclusionary purposes, but the queer eruptions in Faulkner's novels show a male writer who was less dogmatic and far more conflicted over the legitimacy of women artists. In my reading, Faulkner's artist novels deploy pregnancy as a sort of trump card to delegitimize mannish women artists, suggesting that their artistic careers are short-lived because the reproductive drive of the female body will put an end to it. Nevertheless, the implication that mannish women are capable of making legitimate art is present in these novels. The fact that this idea coexists with misogyny toward female artists is a testament to the mixed reactions occasioned by this era's rapidly changing gender norms.

Gender and Sexuality in Interwar America

Biological essentialism tends to haunt conversations about reproduction. A case in point is the persistent association between femininity and pregnancy, which I discuss in detail in the introduction. Even if we resist this discourse, we cannot escape the fact that many people still make essentialist assumptions about gender and gender differences when thinking about pregnancy, which makes gender differences real in sociopolitical terms. These assumptions affect how writers, characters, and readers interact with discourses of reproduction. As Joanna Bourke puts it, "Anatomy may not be destiny, but the belief that it is moulds most lives" (11). Further, terms such as "masculinity" and "femininity" carry social meaning, even when "masculinity" is divorced from the male body. The field of sexology, which was burgeoning in the interwar years, began to think about masculinity as separable from the male body, but it was a slow and halting process.

John Duvall and others have shown that Faulkner was well-read in sexology and wrote characters who voice or are motivated by its theories.[2] Sexology is a discipline concerned with "sexual behaviors, identities, and relations" that emerged in Western modernity in the last decades of the nineteenth century (Bland and Doan 1). The term "inversion," when employed in the context of sexology, is often used as a synonym for homosexuality. Yet George Chauncey has demonstrated that the term was more capacious, especially when the discipline was in its earliest years (121). Many behaviors in addition to homosexuality could result in being labeled "inverted." John D'Emilio and Estelle B. Freedman explain that many of the early sexologists who studied same-sex attraction "tended to define it not as homosexuality, but as 'sexual inversion,' a complete exchange of gender identity of which erotic behavior was but one small part" (226). In the logic of inversion, Chauncey notes, "a woman could not invert any aspect of her gender role without inverting her complete role" (121). The result was that people were often labeled inverted even if they were heterosexual, by virtue of behaviors and traits typically associated with the "opposite" sex.

Women who engaged in behaviors coded masculine, such as reading books, smoking cigars, and wearing pants, were often labeled inverts.[3] Many early feminists were labeled inverts because they were perceived to be aggressive and independent; likewise men who were passive and nurturing (Bauer 99). That sexologists and the general public alike considered some heterosexual individuals to be inverted is key to my analysis of *Mosquitoes* and *Jerusalem* because several of the characters on whom I focus are depicted as both heterosexual and inverted.[4]

In the interwar years, sexologists were attempting to develop models that could encompass the diversity of human gender and sexuality. Despite these attempts, most sexologists nevertheless adhered to the binaries of male/female (biology), masculine/feminine (gender presentation and personality, which sexologists often conflated and referred to as "the mind"), and attracted to women/attracted to men (sexuality). Further, the first terms in these binaries were thought to "go with" or be linked to each other, and vice versa, such that "male" was assumed to go with "masculine" and "attracted to women." Any deviation could earn the label "inverted." A homosexual man was often referred to as a woman living in a man's body, or a person born with a man's body but a woman's mind. Today, the idea that a homosexual man is a woman living in a man's body is broadly recognized as offensive, but at the time this idea was thought progressive by many people, including some gay individuals (Doan and Waters 42–43). Inversion was a way of conceptualizing identity and embodiment that did not involve culpability. Rather than seeing homosexuals as people deserving criminal punishment for making immoral choices, as was the norm, inversion positions them as people deserving pity and empathy for being born in the "wrong" body (Chauncey 114).

Medical understanding of sexuality changed rapidly in the first three decades of the twentieth century, and by the 1920s, sexological models of inversion had begun to move away from theories influenced by nineteenth-century notions of binaries and sex roles (Chauncey 146). Nevertheless, binary thinking of this sort is powerful and continues to shape lay and medical opinions about gender and sexuality today. The older, binary-based ideas of inversion had hardly begun to dissipate in the popular imagination by the interwar years.[5] At that time, Americans learned about the theory of inversion through the works of Havelock Ellis, Edward Carpenter, Ellen Key, and other writers on sex whose ideas were, at least in the short term, more influential than those of Freud (D'Emilio and Freedman 224–25). This means that, for Faulkner as for most of his contemporaries, sexuality and gender were linked in such a way that a lack of masculinity implied femininity and potentially homosexuality, and vice versa.

What counted as "masculinity" in the interwar period? The Great Depression altered the predominant notion of masculinity in the United States, and Faulkner's novels reflect this shift. To understand inversion and the binaries on which it is based, we have to understand what constituted masculinity as it was understood in the interwar years. First, race underwrote American notions of gender. Indeed, Kyla Schuller argues that "binary sex does not exist in a parallel or intersecting dimension with race. Rather, the rhetoric of distinct sexes of male and female consolidated as a *function* of race" (introduction). Second, a particularly salient version of masculinity in the first two decades of the century emphasized traits particular to the self rather than a man's inherited place in society. Smiler et al., explain that in the last decades of the nineteenth century, "status and prestige came from 'old' money, education, reason, and class privilege, but in the modern era, the iconic self-made man obtained his position, power and money through skill, cunning, luck and emotion—following his 'gut'" (268). Masculinity in 1920s America entailed autonomy and the agency and wherewithal to forge a path based on one's own talents and abilities rather than family ties. The self-made man superseded family connections. Furthermore, "gender differences were routinely attributed to men's superior evolution" in the 1920s (more later on this idea of gendered evolution); as such, biology was the foundation on which this particular definition of masculinity was built (Smiler 266).[6]

Even within marriage, the satisfaction of individual desires began to take precedence over familial needs. For instance, sociologist Ernest Groves used the rise of companionate marriage in the 1920s as evidence of this trend in his 1928 book *The Marriage Crisis*. He argued that companionate marriage shifted the focus from the family unit to the individual: "Family life ceases to be a means of economic production, and is an end in itself that is required to furnish individual satisfaction to outweigh the cost it imposes" (qtd. in D'Emilio and Freedman 266). Although Groves refers to changes that affected both men and women, this new emphasis on the individual within marriage aligns with the decade's focus on autonomy as a key factor of masculinity.

The Great Depression changed all this. The emphasis shifted back to the family over the individual. Whereas breadwinning was one aspect of masculinity among many in the 1920s, it became the central trait in the 1930s. This is not to suggest that autonomy and the self-made man ceased to be relevant, but that the Great Depression pushed economic issues to the forefront of discourse. The term "breadwinning" is important here because it expresses the financial as well as familial obligations (Warren 319). Breadwinning was so important in the 1930s that it was "required to obtain status, participate in consumer culture, acquire a mate, and maintain appropriate appearance" (Smiler 275). The most masculine man, in this logic, acquires a mate, begins a family, and provides financially for that family. This logic led to an obvious corollary: many men who lived during the Great Depression felt emasculated by their inability to find work.

The shift in focus from autonomy to breadwinning and its concomitant familial obligations means that Americans defined and related to masculinity in different ways when Faulkner penned his first artist novel, *Mosquitoes*, in 1927, as compared to when he wrote the second artist novel, *Jerusalem*, in 1939. The novels reflect this shift in their depiction of masculinity as it relates to the artist. Despite the differences, both novels are rooted in inversion theory. They depict masculinity as the inverse of femininity and masculinity as a necessary trait for "real" artists, thereby implying that feminine people are only ever illegitimate artists. Importantly, these novels foreground the female artist rather than erasing her (the latter of which Pound does, as we saw in the previous chapter). These foregrounded depictions provide the opportunity for counter-narratives about (pro)creation and gender to erupt in the midst of the main narratives. These counter-narratives imply that women who are inverted—that is, women with a female body and male "mind"—can be legitimate artists. The novels eventually shut down this queer potentiality, however. They do so through depictions of masculine pregnancies that suggest artistic creation is incompatible with a pregnant body.

Mosquitoes and the Self-Making Man

Mosquitoes is a product of the 1920s in the sense that it engages the then-prevalent idea of masculinity as self-making. It is, on the surface, a novel endorsing a masculinist vision of the artist: an independent, male figure whose creative process eschews women, money, and outside support. Yet the relationship that the novel develops between the self-made man and artistic creation, particularly the use of the masculine pregnancy trope to forge this connection, creates space for eruptions that unsettle the dominant narrative.

The action in *Mosquitoes* revolves around a party of artists aboard the Nausikaa, a yacht owned by Mrs. Patricia Maurier. Maurier is a generous if unsophisticated patron of the arts who brings together painters, sculptors, and writers for a four-day cruise on Lake Ponchartrain. Much of the novel consists of various characters, almost always male, pontificating about art. Dawson Fairchild (a writer modeled on Sherwood Anderson) frequently debates aesthetics with Julius Kauffman, an art critic. Other artists on board include Gordon, a muscular, taciturn sculptor (one of the few who produces art rather than just talking about it); Dorothy Jameson, an unsuccessful painter; and Eva Kauffman Wiseman, a poet and sister to Julius. Also on board are Maurier's niece and nephew, college-aged twins named Pat (female) and Josh Robyn. The cruise is punctuated by difficulties from the mundane to the serious: the guests dislike the food, several of the men are unsociable, Pat sneaks off the yacht with a deckhand only to get lost in a swamp on the way to town, and the yacht is marooned for more than a day before a tugboat can free it. The characters are plagued throughout by heat, stagnation, and mosquitoes.

During one of many monologues, Dawson Fairchild lays out a theory of artistic creation that aligns masculinity with self-sufficiency. In a stunningly sexist passage devoted to art and reproduction, Fairchild muses that the purpose of art is:

> Getting into life, getting into it and wrapping it around you, becoming a part of it. Women can do it without art—old biology takes care of that. But men, men . . . A woman conceives: does she care afterward whose seed it was? Not she. And bears, and all the rest of her life—her young troubling years, that is—is filled. Of course the father can look at it occasionally. But in art, a man can create without any assistance at all: what he does is his. A perversion, I grant you, but a perversion that builds Chartres and invents Lear is a pretty good thing. (320; ellipses original)

This passage is key to my reading of *Mosquitoes* and is one to which I will return, for it encapsulates both the main narrative's depiction of the artist as a self-sufficient man as well as a queer eruption that unsettles this narrative. For now, however, the important point to note is Fairchild's insistence on the artist's self-sufficiency and the superiority of male creative faculties. For despite Fairchild's label of "perversion," he clearly values artistic creation (which he labels male) above female reproductive creation. After all, Chartres and Lear get names; a child is an "it." Although the novel regularly lampoons

Fairchild, his conception of the artist as an independent man is sustained in the only depiction of a successful artist, Gordon. Gordon eschews the company of other artists and is indifferent to Mrs. Maurier's money. Other traits of his align with the dominant mode of masculinity of the day: he is physically strong, decisive, and emotionally closed-off.

This theory of the artist as a self-sufficient man squares with Faulkner's vision of his own creative process. Faulkner characterized the creation of legitimate art—as opposed to gentlewomen's china painting—as a masculine pursuit involving a hard body and difficult physical labor. For instance, his introduction to *As I Lay Dying* compares his writing process on the novel to shoveling coal and stoking fires (Guttman 17–18). Moreover, Faulkner saw self-sufficiency as equally important to hardness for the creation of art. He credits the former as the key to his ability to write *The Sound and the Fury* (1929), saying, "One day I seemed to shut a door between me and all publishers' addresses and book lists. I said to myself, Now I can write" (qtd. in Blotner 212). Authorial independence, for Faulkner, requires disregarding the wants of publishers and instead writing without concern for what will sell; authentic art is untainted by commercialism.

That Faulkner should insist on the artist's distance from both femininity and commercialism is no coincidence. Like many of his modernist contemporaries, Faulkner characterized consumerism and the marketplace as feminine. He saw writing as a pursuit that feminizes men, but thought writing with the goal of making money was worse.[7] As Sondra Guttman argues, Faulkner needed the money that came from sales of his popular novels such as *Sanctuary* (1931), but he despised the "softness" it inspired (17). For example, he reflected on the moment when he started to experience commercial success with the comment, "I began to get a little soft . . . I began to think about making money by writing" (introduction to *Sanctuary* v). By this logic, the artist must constantly resist the feminization supposedly caused by commercialism because he must retain masculine hardness to create legitimate art. This stance of Faulkner's suggests that even if the novel lampoons the character of Fairchild, the theory of art that Fairchild espouses cannot be dismissed. The relationship between masculinity and art that Fairchild describes is corroborated elsewhere in the novel and in Faulkner's personal theory of art. Much like the prevailing idea of masculinity in the 1920s, Fairchild's comment figures the artist as male, and his maleness is manifest in a version of masculinity that emphasizes autonomy.

Fairchild's monologue suggests something of the push-and-pull of masculinity and femininity generated by the artist's mind in competition with the feminizing effects of the marketplace. The idea is raised most directly in the notion that male minds are capable of self-fertilization ("a man can create without any assistance at all"). Fairchild calls this process a "perversion," which Lisa Rado reads as hermaphroditism. Her position is that Faulkner "imagines his creative consciousness as itself both 'male' and 'female' in response to modern changes in the cultural constructions of gender" brought on by the field of sexology (15). Rado's interpretation is reinforced by a later reference to a poem titled "Hermaphroditus." The novel credits this poem to the character Eva Kauffman Wiseman, but it was published earlier by Faulkner himself under his own name. Rado reads this poem as evidence that Faulkner applied the concept of hermaphroditism to his own creative process, and that it appealed to him because the concept allowed him to explain the aspects of his personality and behaviors—including his penchant for writing—that he perceived as disturbingly feminine (22).

While I find Rado's argument compelling, I do not agree that it is the most accurate label for the "perversion" of male artistic creation as described by Fairchild. Instead, I suggest self-fertilization is a more accurate label for this theory of artistic creation. Self-fertilization refers to animals capable of impregnation without a partner. The vast majority of hermaphroditic animals, by contrast, require a partner for fertilization.[8] Fairchild even refers to art as "reproduction from within" at another point in the novel (320). The difference between hermaphroditism and self-fertilization may seem slight, but it carries multiple implications.

First, it squares with the novel's depiction of masculinity as autonomous and self-making. Second, reading Fairchild's theory as one of self-fertilization reveals one of the "eruptions of alternative knowledge and communities"—to recall Harker's words—that destabilize the main narrative's implication that male creative faculties are superior to female ones. To explain, first consider the argument made by Smiler et al. that in the 1920s, gender differences were typically attributed to the "superior evolution" of men. This notion is given voice in Fairchild's quote if we read his theory of artistic creation as self-fertilizing. He claims that men do not need women to find fulfillment—"getting into life" as he calls it—because men are capable of conceiving, gestating, and delivering artistic offspring on their own. Superior evolution, indeed—with a healthy dose of sexism, to boot. The idea that male creation is evolutionarily superior to female procreation gains further support from an earlier scene in the novel. Faulkner's description of the swamp in which Pat (the niece of Mrs. Patricia Maurier) and David, a ship steward, become lost connects female fecundity to pre-human times. Pat and David leave the Nausikaa for some fun in a nearby town but quickly find themselves lost in a swamp on the way. The mist enveloping them "might have been the first prehistoric morning of time itself; it might have been the very substance in which the seed of the beginning of things fecundated; and these huge and silent trees might have been the first of living things, too recently born to know either fear or astonishment, dragging their sluggish umbilical cords from out the old miasmic womb of a nothingness latent and dreadful" (169). The passage directly links female procreation with reproductive processes so old they predate humanity. In addition to being associated with the pre-human world, female procreation is distinctly threatening. Umbilical cords and wombs are supposed to nourish the beings attached to/within them, but the swamp in which David and Pat wander withholds nourishment—they are unable to find even potable water—and, further, the swamp attacks them with a plague of mosquitoes. Less an example of womb envy than fear of women's reproductive capacities, "miasmic" is a particularly apt description of the environment as Faulkner depicts it. Through this figurative language, the novel underscores Fairchild's implication that male creation (read: art) is preferable to female procreation because it is more evolved and less harmful. This, then, is the dominant narrative of *Mosquitoes* as concerns artistic creation.

Yet by reading against the grain, we can detect a counter-narrative in which the male, self-fertilizing mind is less evolved than the dominant narrative implies. Humans are not, of course, self-fertilizing, and the vast majority of self-fertilizing organisms are plants and invertebrates (Avise xi). This fact undercuts the dominant narrative by rhetorically associating these self-fertilizing men with creatures low on the evolutionary scale. This kind of "ladder of nature" thinking is obsolete in biological sciences today, but in Faulkner's day many people thought it axiomatic that humans occupied the top rung of the evolutionary ladder.[9] Therefore, reading Fairchild's theory of art as self-fertilization instead of hermaphroditism reveals an eruption that unsettles an otherwise misogynistic depiction of male minds as more evolved and civilized than women's. To be sure, female reproduction still reads as a threatening force in *Mosquitoes*, yet Faulkner's use of biological and evolutionary metaphors complicates his favorable depiction of male creation by aligning it with forms of reproduction that would have been considered less evolved at the time of the novel's publication.

A similar eruption occurs in context with Faulkner's portrait of the female artist. The counter-narrative here suggests that inverted women can create legitimate art: in the binaristic logic of sexology that Faulkner employs, inverted women might have a female body but they have a male mind, and it is this male mind that makes them capable of producing art. *Mosquitoes*, when read with the grain, puts forth the essentialist idea that feminine women cannot be artists because they do not possess the self-fertilizing (male) mind necessary for the creation of authentic art. Fairchild, for instance, positions childbearing as the chief occupation of the female mind. He claims women need an other, a child, to be biologically satisfied: "A woman conceives: does she care afterward whose seed it was? Not she. And bears, and all the rest of her life—her young troubling years, that is—is filled" (320). In other words, women do not care about the partner or the art; only the child matters. (And, apparently, the only part of women's lives worth discussing is the childbearing years.) Julius Kauffman, the art critic aboard the Nausikaa, similarly states that women "bear geniuses. But do you think they care anything about the pictures and music their children produce? That they have any other emotion than a fierce tolerance of the vagaries of the child?" (248). The implication is that, unlike male minds that are evolved for artistic creation, the minds of women are evolved for biological reproduction. This idea is generally in accord with Faulkner's professed theory of art as well as prevailing gender norms of the day, in that biological reproduction and caregiving were assumed to be the most important elements in a woman's life. For male artists in the interwar years who were concerned about the gains women were making in literature and art, this idea was a convenient rationalization. Claiming that women were evolved for reproduction assuaged fears by suggesting that these gains were short-lived and illegitimate; the Sylvia Beaches and Margaret Andersons would go away once their reproductive drives kicked in.

Nevertheless, *Mosquitoes* contains an eruption in the midst of this heteronormative, misogynistic logic. The artist character Eva Kauffman Wiseman represents the possibility of legitimate female artists. That Eva is female is never in doubt, but Faulkner plainly wrote her as a mannish, inverted woman. Several critics have noted Eva's masculinity and sexual fluidity. Frann Michel further comments on her "ambiguously gendered name," Eva Kauff*man* Wise*man*, and argues that she "fits [Havelock] Ellis's account of the female invert as a masculine woman by virtue of her sharing of the male character's profession [writing], conversation, and desire" (12). Furthermore, the typescript version of *Mosquitoes* makes it clear that Faulkner wrote Eva as someone who is sexually attracted to women.[10] This earlier version of the novel includes a scene in which Eva watches, longingly, as two women embrace passionately (McHaney xvii). Recall the binaristic logic of sexology, wherein attraction to women is usually assumed to go with masculinity.

Yet surprisingly, given the sexism discussed above, Faulkner also attributed some of his own poetry to Eva (the aforementioned "Hermaphroditus"), and she is more closely aligned with the "real" artists on the Nausikaa than with the unsuccessful, unproductive ones. The novel's logic runs thus: if male minds are capable of self-fertilization, and if inverted women have male minds in female bodies, it follows that Eva would be capable of creating legitimate art. This character therefore lends unexpected support to Fairchild's comment that artists create with "the ultimate intention of impressing some woman" (250), since Eva is also attracted to women. Fairchild here expresses the notion, common in Faulkner's oeuvre, that sexual desire inspires art.[11] Even though Fairchild's example is that of heterosexual desire of a male artist for a woman, the presence of Eva suggests that a woman's desire for another woman can be just as inspirational, and that *this* woman's mind, at least, is attuned to artistic creation instead of biological procreation. There is still a great deal of misogyny in this depiction of female artists. For one thing, it excludes the possibility of legitimate art being created by anyone with a "female mind." Nevertheless, the counter-narrative involving Eva unsettles Faulkner's attempt to use reproductive rhetoric to position legitimate art as the province of men alone.

Like Pound's "SAGE HOMME," with its masculine surgical editing, Faulkner's *Mosquitoes* locates the origins of legitimate art in the masculine mind and denigrates the female mind as incapable of such creation. Pound's gender-bending is limited to depictions of himself and Eliot as feminized poets; the poetry they produce in this mode is leaky, messy, and dirty. The possibility of legitimate art produced by female or feminine people never enters "SAGE HOMME." Faulkner's Eva therefore represents a key difference between Pound's and Faulkner's works because the presence of this character hints at the possibility of legitimate female artists.

Masculine Women and Feminine Men in *If I Forget Thee, Jerusalem*

The hint that is Eva Wiseman in *Mosquitoes* becomes overt characterization in a novel Faulkner published twelve years later. In *If I Forget Thee, Jerusalem*, Faulkner considers the figure of the mannish female artist directly. In my reading of this novel, legitimate art can be created by women, but the reproductive drive of the female body ultimately curtails her success. Reproductive rhetoric thereby reinforces the supposed superiority of male artists. Just as inversion is the tool by which *Mosquitoes* rationalizes Eva's artistic abilities, inversion similarly explains why *Jerusalem's* Charlotte Rittenmeyer can be an artist who produces legitimate art, and why her feminized lover, Harry Wilbourne, finds success writing formulaic short stories for mass-market publications. Finally, the logic of inversion underpins one of the most confusing and disturbing scenes in the novel, Harry performing an abortion on Charlotte. Unlike *Mosquitoes*, however, *Jerusalem* privileges breadwinning rather than independence as the defining trait of masculinity, a change in tune with prevailing attitudes in the United States in the wake of the Great Depression.

When Charlotte and Harry meet, she is a frustrated artist whose life in New Orleans with a husband and two children is a bore. Harry is a medical resident just months away from completing his training. Charlotte quickly persuades him to leave school and run away with her to Chicago. Her affection for Harry is genuine, but the affair allows her access to something just as important to her as love: space, time, and inspiration for art (recall my earlier point about Faulkner believing that sexual desire inspires art). The couple struggles for money because Harry did not complete his medical degree. They eventually move to a remote mining community in Utah where his lack of credentials is irrelevant. The isolation of the community presents unforeseen difficulties, however. Charlotte's contraceptive douche bag ruptures in the extreme cold of Utah in winter, but she is unable to replace it because the community is too remote to have stores or medical services beyond those Harry provides. Soon pregnant, she asks Harry to perform an abortion on her. He has the technical knowledge and experience to perform the procedure successfully but resists for months on the grounds that he loves her too much. When Charlotte eventually prevails, Harry makes a mistake, and the wound gets infected. In the end, she dies and he is sentenced to fifty years of hard labor.[12]

Although Charlotte is never mistaken for a man, her actions would read as masculine to audiences in the 1930s and would, in truth, signal masculinity to many readers today. She is a more successful breadwinner than Harry, initiates their first sexual encounter, abandons her children (an act thought to be unnatural or actually impossible for women), finds housing for herself and Harry, and wears men's clothing. The novel provides enough information about her early life to indicate that her masculinity is a consistent trait rather than a recent reaction or a power grab enabling the affair. Early in their courtship, Charlotte explains that she arranged her marriage to her husband, a man nicknamed Rat. She states, "All my family were brothers except me. I liked my oldest brother the best but you cant [sic] sleep with your brother and he and Rat roomed together in school so I married Rat" (35). This statement's suggestion of incest begs for commentary, which I provide later. Charlotte indicates that she took the lead in her marriage: stating "I married Rat" implies that Charlotte arranged it rather than he. Second, Charlotte reveals her desire to fit in with her all-male siblings, and perhaps even a yearning to be masculine herself. Her oldest brother, presumably the fullest embodiment of adult masculinity among the siblings, is the one to attract her attention. This early affinity for masculinity, combined with her later masculine behaviors, makes her an inverted woman along the lines of Eva, with the added trait of successful breadwinning.

Also like Eva, Charlotte is capable of creating art that is legitimate in Faulkner's terms. She does not seek out commercial success, which, as we saw earlier, is central to Faulkner's logic. The narrator consistently aligns Charlotte's sculptures with masculinity and the "hardness" that characterizes Faulkner's ideal of art. Her sculptures are durable and heavy, "something with weight in your hand . . . that displaces air and displaces water and when you drop it, it's your foot that breaks and not the shape" (35). Some of her figures are "fantastic and perverse" with a "lean epicene" quality that is "sophisticated and bizarre" (74). Her art is, then, unexpected and experimental (such as *As I Lay Dying*) rather than formulaic like the works that brought Faulkner money but not creative fulfillment. By depicting both Charlotte and her art as masculine, the main narrative suggests the possibility of a legitimate female artist. This depiction is still misogynistic—Charlotte may be a woman, but her hard, experimental art is the product of an inverted woman's male mind—yet the presence of this legitimate female artist in *Jerusalem* presents far more and far queerer possibilities than *Mosquitoes*.

Harry is Charlotte's foil, an inverted man whose female mind enables him to successfully participate in the supposedly feminized marketplace of pseudo-art. Charlotte's masculinity causes Harry to feel more acutely the lack of his own. Indeed, he frequently thinks, "She's a better man than I am" (113). This statement is both an indication of Charlotte's gender and an indicator of Harry's frame of mind regarding his own gender. Harry doubts his masculinity, an assessment that was likely echoed by the novel's original audience because of his inability to get a job. Throughout the affair, he anxiously tries to figure out his role in the relationship. He is confused in part because Charlotte tells him she does not want a traditional husband. She tells him, "if it was just a successful husband and food and a bed I wanted, why the hell do you think I am here instead of back there [in

New Orleans] where I had them?" (89). But the ideological linkage between masculinity and breadwinning is not easily abandoned for Harry. At the beginning of the affair, he struggles to find work because he failed to finish his medical degree. He eventually gives up, spending his days sitting on park benches while calculating the couple's insufficient budget and blaming it on his lack of manliness. He "shift[s] the various components of the sum and their bought equivalents here and there like a jigsaw puzzle, knowing that this was a form of masturbation (thinking, *because I am still, and probably will always be, in the puberty of money*)" (80; italics original). The narrator here implies that Harry cannot think of himself as a fully adult man if he is poor and jobless. Instead, he figures himself as a child playing games when he should be working. Shifting the puzzle pieces of his finances will not change the budget any more than it will increase his sense of masculinity.

The narrator continues to equate masculinity with finances in a way that manifests Harry's anxiety about both. After Charlotte's death from the botched abortion, Harry considers his role in it, thinking, "A miser would probably bungle the blowing of his own safe too. Should have called a professional, a cracksman who didn't care, didn't love the very iron flanks that held the money" (250). The verb "bungle" denotes confused, clumsy mistakes suggestive of anxiety and nervousness. (Harry is here echoing Charlotte's assessment; she calls Harry several variations of "bloody bungling bastard" while on her deathbed [17].) Furthermore, the safe metaphor subtly refers to Charlotte's masculinity in the connection forged between her body, which is lean, muscular, and hard, and the "iron flanks" of the safe. Earlier in the novel, Harry calls her leg a "flank" in a tender moment. After a swim, Charlotte walks by a dozing Harry, who wakes to kiss her "sun-impacted flank" (94). Similarly, Faulkner wrote a love poem to Helen Baird, the woman on whom Charlotte's character is based, praising "her boy's breast and the plain flanks of a boy" (qtd. in Blotner 151). Taken together, the language suggests that part of what Harry loves about Charlotte is her masculinity, and the safe metaphor captures this aspect of his affection for her. But her masculinity also seems to exacerbate his anxiety because it calls his own into question. If, as John Duvall argues, masculinity in Faulkner "is the power to feminize the other" (55), Charlotte is indeed masculine.

In keeping with the binaristic logic of inversion, Harry's lack of masculinity manifests as an excess of femininity. At one point he manages to find work writing short stories for mass market publications, despite having no professional training for this work. The stories he writes are formulaic and mildly scandalous, generally told from the first-person perspective of a female narrator. He, like Faulkner, is derisive toward this kind of work, dismissing the idea that the stories might have artistic value. Harry calls his stories "sexual gumdrops" (104), a term that implies both their sensationalized subject matter as well as a squishiness that recalls Faulkner's comment about "get[ting] soft" when he began thinking about making money off his writing. In this novel, writing for pay is a femininizing endeavor; this positioning underscores the depiction of Harry as an inverted man. Harry, already feminized by his struggles to find work and by Charlotte's masculinity, takes to commercial writing easily. His soft, formulaic stories stand in stark contrast to Charlotte's hard, heavy, experimental sculptures. Whereas the most legitimate artist in *Mosquitoes* is the hyperbolically masculine Gordon, *Jerusalem*'s most legitimate artist is a woman, while the man creates insubstantial fluff. When read through the lens of inversion, however, this dynamic actually supports the idea put forward by Fairchild, the idea that only the male mind is evolved for the creation of legitimate art. Charlotte has a masculine mind and Harry a feminine one. Thus, the novel devalues the female mind as unsuited to artistic creation.

Jerusalem eventually shies away from the queer possibilities suggested by this legitimate female artist. In the end, the novel condemns Charlotte as a trespasser in the male realm of legitimate art through the use of a well-worn misogynistic trope, that of the uncontrollable female body. Yet this condemnation also contains within it the novel's most surprising eruption of alternative knowledge. Charlotte's insistence that Harry perform the abortion gives rise to a reading that reveals the dominant, misogynistic narrative as hypocritical and cruel. This dominant narrative implies that Charlotte may have been able to create legitimate art for a while (thanks to her male mind), but the reproductive drive of her female body overwhelms everything else and kills her in a flood of female blood. The main narrative blames Charlotte's death on her supposedly unnatural creative desires; the counter-narrative, however, implicates patriarchal gender norms in her death.

To explain, we need first to consider the novel's depiction of procreation as incompatible with the creation of legitimate art. The first such depiction occurs early in the novel, before Charlotte has left her husband and children for Harry. Charlotte's relationship with Rat is procreatively fertile (they have two daughters together), but artistically sterile (Charlotte is uninspired to create). Throughout his career, Faulkner was preoccupied with the sterility that results from incest. We can understand Charlotte's marriage as an example in this vein.[13] As is clear in the aforementioned quote about Charlotte arranging her marriage to Rat, their relationship is akin to incest since she chooses Rat as a substitute for her brother. That their marriage is marked by a kind of sterility, albeit creative rather than biological, aligns with this preoccupation and furthermore suggests that physical reproduction is a block to artistic fertility.

Later events in the novel amplify the suggestion that art and reproduction are incompatible. Charlotte's affair with Harry is creatively fertile, as evidenced by her outpouring of art in various mediums. She makes sure that her relationship with Harry is procreatively sterile though the practice of contraceptive douching. After her douche bag breaks and she is unable to replace it, Charlotte quickly becomes pregnant. This pregnancy brings a swift end to her art and eventually a painful, bloody end to her life. The final time she engages in an artistic endeavor of any kind takes place several weeks after the douche bag breaks but just before she realizes she is pregnant. She and Harry attempt to communicate with the Polish-speaking miners with whom they live in Utah. Harry is unable to convey any messages, but Charlotte overcomes the language barrier through her drawings (169–70). A week later she misses her period and realizes she is pregnant, then two weeks later asks Harry to perform the abortion (171–73). He resists for several months, during which time she does not create art of any kind.[14] The novel thereby makes the misogynistic argument that pregnancy is incompatible with artistic creation; even inverted women cannot overcome the female body's drive to procreate, which Fairchild calls "old biology." *Jerusalem* deploys the trope of masculine pregnancy to kill off its mannish woman artist, thereby neutralizing the supposed threat of inverted women as legitimate creators. This novel thereby allows us to better understand the multifaceted ends to which interwar writers put the masculine pregnancy trope: for male writers who were unnerved by women's successes in the literary and artistic realms, masculine pregnancy could be a tool to assuage fears.

It is important to note that some interwar texts suggest that pregnancy and creativity are incompatible but to a very different end. For instance, Virginia Woolf's mock biography *Orlando* also depicts a character for whom pregnancy and creativity are incompatible in order to critique social norms surrounding pregnancy rather than pinning the blame on biology. *Orlando* points a finger at society's treatment of pregnant people. In this fantastic romp of a novel, the titular character is a writer and aristocrat who lives for four hundred years and changes gender at thirty years of age. Orlando is living as a woman in the Victorian Era when she becomes pregnant. Passive voice is appropriate here: as the novel depicts it, Orlando's impregnation is a kind of immaculate conception initiated by Queen Victoria. Her reign was defined by imperial expansion and abundant fertility. As many scholars have noted, these were twinned enterprises. By encouraging the British people to emulate her large family, Queen Victoria supported imperial expansion: the health of the empire depends on large families to staff imperial outposts, or so the logic ran (*Conceived* 80). Orlando's conception is immediately preceded by a scene in which she gazes upon a statue of Queen Victoria that is covered with "widow's weeds and bridal veils . . . crystal palaces, bassinettes, military helmets, memorial wreaths, trousers, whiskers, wedding cakes, cannon [sic], Christmas trees, telescopes, extinct monsters, globes, maps, elephants and mathematical-instruments" (232). As I argue in *Conceived in Modernism: The Aesthetics and Politics of Birth Control*, the statue "is overburdened with material objects while the narrator's description is encrusted with nouns and adjectives describing the trappings of empire—military, familial, and exotic alike" (85). While gazing upon this statue, Orlando is "forced by a superior power" to look upon her body (233)—a woman's body, at this point in the novel—and immediately thereafter returns home; once there, she realizes she is pregnant (235).

Orlando struggles to write at various points in their life, but never does her writing suffer so much as it does in the Victorian era while pregnant. As with the "superior power" that forces Orlando to focus on her body, a foreign force takes over when Orlando begins to write: "the pen began to curve and caracole with the smoothest possible fluency. Her page was written in the neatest sloping Italian hand with the most insipid verse she had ever read in her life" (238). The narrator then recounts that Orlando "was all of a quiver, all of a stew. Nothing more repulsive could be imagined than to feel the ink flowing thus in cascades of involuntary inspiration" (239). The "superior power" is something that the narrator elsewhere calls "the spirit of the age" (236). The spirit of the Victorian age is pronatalism in service of the empire. The pronatalism of the era demands strict adherence to binary, hegemonic gender roles in which there is no room for gender variability and a woman's purpose is procreation, not creation. For Orlando, a person defined by their gender fluidity and artistic drive, "the spirit of the nineteenth century was antipathetic to her in the extreme, and thus it took her and broke her, and she was aware of her defeat at its hands as she had never been before" (244). Thereby, Woolf's novel implies that if procreation and creation are incompatible, it is because societal constructs make it so. Woolf's and Faulkner's novels both suggest that pregnancy and creativity are incompatible, but the cause of the incompatibility is quite different. *Jerusalem's* main narrative makes an essentialist argument about (pro)creativity; *Orlando* makes a constructionist one.

Abortion, Misogyny, and Masculinity

Where Pound depicts himself as a skillful manipulator of the knife/phallus in his editing of *The Waste Land,* Faulkner depicts his literal surgeon character as lacking the requisite masculinity to be successful in his endeavors. Most critics see Charlotte's death as a punishment for the abortion; my reading of the novel through the lens of masculine pregnancy necessitates a reconsideration of it as resulting from more complex circumstances. Indeed, the novel does not condemn abortion in general. Harry performs one in Utah for a neighbor, and this woman suffers no ill effects.[15] While punishment of a kind is legible in the bloody manner of Charlotte's death, I read it as punishment for her masculinity or, to be more precise, her ventures into the masculine realm of art. As I will explain, however, a counter-narrative is legible in the abortion scene, which also implicates hegemonic masculinity in Charlotte's death.

In the abortion scene, Harry's failure to meet the norms of masculinity manifests as an inability to wield the phallus. When preparing to perform the abortion on Charlotte after months of her insistence, Harry is visibly nervous, with hands that shake uncontrollably (185–86). Charlotte attempts a joke to calm him down, metaphorically turning Harry's penis into a surgical knife: "We've done this lots of ways but not with knives, have we?" (186). She then encourages him to "ride me down" with the knife (186).[16] Despite the best of intentions and careful preparation, Harry wounds her in the process. The connection between the phallus and the surgical knife leads to the conclusion that Harry's indecision, nervousness, and shaking are due to his lack of masculinity. Charlotte eventually dies in an outpouring of blood from between her legs, a liquid excess reminiscent of menstruation and evocative of the long-standing trope of the female body as leaky, unruly, and uncontrollable.[17] The dominant narrative here is alarmingly heteronormative: Harry failed to be a real man by giving in to the woman's demands and doing the abortion, and Charlotte failed to be a real woman by controlling her man and trying to deny her biological destiny. Charlotte may have the mind of a man—a mind that drives her assertive behaviors and facilitates legitimate artistic creation for a while—but her body is female, and this body's biological drive to reproduce catches up with her. Moreover, in the binaristic thinking of sexology, Harry cannot simply choose to "be a man" when he needs to. He may have the body of a man (he did impregnate Charlotte, after all), but he has the mind of a woman. His female mind is the cause of his failure in this crucial scene.

By reading against the grain, however, we can detect a counter-narrative that implicates society's demands on men to live up to gender norms and illuminates the psychological damage these norms can cause for people who fail to fulfill them. In the abortion scene, Faulkner emphasizes Harry's anxiety over his inability to perform, and it is this anxiety, manifest in his uncontrollably shaking hands, that causes him to wound Charlotte. He is anxious because he doubts his own ability to wield the phallus. Therefore, his failure to fulfill the sociocultural norms of masculinity ultimately leads to his mistake during the abortion. The idea that hegemonic masculinity is psychologically harmful runs directly counter to the "mainstream voice of Southern patriarchy" that, as Harker explains, characterizes the main narratives in most of Faulkner's novels. As we have seen, the main narrative of *Jerusalem* is no exception. Yet this novel also contains a counter-narrative depicting the psychological wounds inflicted on men who fail to meet the demands of hegemonic gender norms.

It is easy to dismiss both *Mosquitoes* and *Jerusalem* as misogynistic and outdated, especially since they are some of Faulkner's least successful novels in aesthetic terms. Yet reading them through the lens of masculine pregnancy reveals eruptions that destabilize the patriarchal main narratives. These eruptions recuperate neither the sexism nor the aesthetic shortcomings of the novels, but their presence create a richly textured picture of gender, sexuality, and reproductive discourse as they were understood in the interwar period. The idea that female minds are evolved for biological creation is a classic example of essentialism; Faulkner doubles down on it by adding to it the notion that the feminine mind is incapable of creating legitimate art while the male mind is evolved for artistic creation. In this chapter, as with the previous one, we saw how authors combine essentialist ideas of gender with masculine pregnancies to police the borders of art, demarcating who is and who is not capable of creative legitimacy, and how long that creativity will last. Yet in the midst of these misogynistic main narratives, counter-narratives in Faulkner's novels erupt, illuminating gender nonconforming characters who hint at alternative queer futures. The next two chapters take us to novels that use the trope of masculine pregnancy to explore in much more detail queer potentialities and realities. Willa Cather's *My Ántonia*, the focus of chapter 4, and Djuna Barnes's *Nightwood*, the subject of chapter 5, move out of the realm of metaphorical pregnancy and into depictions of literal pregnancies. These novels refuse the misogynistic logic of gender and reproduction that we see in Pound and Faulkner. Instead, they take seriously the reality of queer (pro)creation.

Chapter 4

The Mannish Woman as Fertility Goddess

How Narrative Makes a Legitimate Mother
Out of Ántonia Shimerda

In this chapter, I focus on *My Ántonia* (1918), the third novel in Willa Cather's prairie trilogy that begins with *O Pioneers!* in 1913 and continues with *Song of the Lark* in 1915. I argue that Cather introduces a different model of creative legitimacy than the metaphorical one espoused by Faulkner and Pound. As we saw in chapters 2 and 3, those authors combine masculinity and pregnancy to argue for the legitimacy (and supposed superiority) of creations emanating from the masculine mind and body. In contrast to Faulkner and Pound, Cather's *My Ántonia* deals in literal and metaphorical pregnancy, to suggest that the offspring of queer individuals are not only legitimate but can inject variety into exhausted forms of literature and—more troublingly—genetic stock. Her novel moreover implies that, important as the body is to determinations of legitimacy, narrative is more important because it can overturn those determinations. In other words, this novel turns an illegitimate child—in the sense of born out of wedlock—into a legitimate one, and an illegitimate mother—in the sense of not authorized or acceptable—into one whose mothering will enrich the nation; these changes are accomplished through the power of narrative. *My Ántonia* thereby offers an alternative to biology-based conceptions of legitimacy.

Cather wrote the novel at a time when non-normative modes of sex and gender occupied a central position in American discourse. As C. Susan Wiesenthal argues, "medical tropes of the 'Mannish Lesbian' or the 'unsexed' woman had been . . . pervasively disseminated throughout the cultural imagination" by the time Cather wrote the prairie trilogy (45). From mainstream to niche media outlets, commentators frequently discussed "mannish women" in terms that raised doubts about their legitimacy as mothers and even as "true" women, as I note in chapter 1. It must be said, however, that not everyone took issue with mannish women, especially if their behaviors fit into virtuous narratives. For example, women filling in for men during wartime were often perceived as doing a patriotic duty.[1] Cather herself was a mannish woman. She wore men's clothing and went by the name Will or Willie at various points in her life. Blanche Gelfant explains that "all accounts of her [by people who knew Cather] refer to her 'masculine personality'—her mannish dress, her deep voice, her energetic stride" (380).[2] Moreover, mannish female characters permeate Cather's writing. For instance, Wiesenthal convincingly reads Alexandra Bergson, the protagonist of O Pioneers!, as a " 'mannish' woman who appears to combine certain traditional aspects of masculinity and femininity" (49). Yet except for a reference to Alexandra wearing a man's coat, Cather conveys this character's masculinity through implication.

By comparison, Cather's portrayal of Ántonia as masculine is overt. The narrator, Jim Burden, calls her manly or masculine multiple times, and Ántonia states directly, "I like to be like a man" (74). Jim and Ántonia are childhood friends who meet when both are newly arrived in Nebraska. Jim, who is then 10 years old, moves from Virginia to live with his grand-parents after his parents pass away. Ántonia, just a few years older than Jim, emigrates with her family from Bohemia (now the Czech Republic). Ántonia grows into a strong, capable farmhand who wears men's clothing and boasts about how much she can plow. Her masculine comportment leads to concerns among her neighbors that she needs help assimilating to American gender norms. Jim's grandmother and a few other matriarchs of the community devise a plan to "save" her by arranging for a job in the nearby town of Black Hawk. She works in this job for several years, then falls in love and runs away with a man who abandons her when she even-tually gets pregnant. Unmarried and penniless, she returns home to work the family farm. She wears men's clothing while farming, up to and includ-ing the day she gives birth. These scenes suggest parallels with Faulkner's heterosexual invert, Charlotte Rittenmeyer of If I Forget Thee, Jerusalem, a novel I discuss in depth in the previous chapter and to which I return at the close of this chapter. Ántonia eventually marries Anton Cuzak, another Bohemian immigrant, who treats the baby as his own. Ántonia and Anton go on to have nine more children and live on a large, successful farm. Jim has been away for most of this time, only hearing about Ántonia's life from neighbors. When he visits her some twenty years later, Ántonia's masculinity no longer troubles him. Instead, Jim is overcome by her vitality, describing Ántonia as the matriarch of a healthy family whose farmland is as fertile as her body. In the novel's concluding pages, Jim thinks of his childhood friend as "a rich mine of life, like the founders of early races" (171).

Ántonia's phrasing with regard to her gender—"I like to be like a man" (74)—is worth pausing on. The fact that she says "like a man" weighs heavily in my decision to read her as a mannish woman rather than a trans man. She enjoys the attributes of masculinity without identifying as a man. Furthermore, using *transgender* as a label for historical figures is anachronistic, as Susan Stryker and Paisley Currah write (6). Nevertheless, my reading of Ántonia as a masculine woman is not intended to foreclose the possibility of other readings that consider Antonia within other categories of identity and other conceptual frameworks, including those that use, for example, transmasculinity as a critical concept. Allison K. Hammer's study of Cather draws on the work of Stryker and Currah to define *transmasculinity* as a term that "map[s] a 'conceptual space' where contemporary scholars can more broadly question the intelligibility, and legibility, of 'embodied subjectivity' across time" (78). The boundaries between trans men, mannish women, and nonbinary people are—and should be—porous, and the theoretical frameworks such categories inspire are malleable. I recall for the reader Gayle Rubin's words, quoted in the introduction, about the permeability of identity categories: "Categories like 'woman,' 'butch,' 'lesbian,' or 'transsexual' are all imperfect, historical, temporary, and arbitrary. . . . Instead of fighting for immaculate classifications and impenetrable boundaries, let us strive to maintain a community that understands diversity as a gift, sees anomalies as precious, and treats all basic principles with a hefty dose of skepticism" (479). Considering *My Ántonia* in light of contemporaneous notions of mannishness is one of many possible readings, one that allows us to conceptualize the possibilities of the pregnant body in new ways.

To wit: it is intriguing that many critics read Ántonia as a fertility goddess despite her clear identification with masculinity.[3] Jim's characterization of Ántonia as "a founder of early races," along with similar phrases sprinkled through the novel, informs most of these readings. Deborah G. Lambert voices a common interpretation when she states that the novel's final image of Ántonia is "a figure of the greatest conventionality: she has become the stereotypical earth mother" (687). This earth mother finale is often seen as a departure from earlier, more radical parts of the novel where Cather depicts Ántonia as enjoying her masculinity. These earlier sections of the novel have resulted in another large body of scholarship reading Ántonia as a queer character. When these two bodies of scholarship overlap, that is, when critics discuss both Ántonia's masculinity and her earth mother finale, her masculinity is almost always explained as temporary or an economic necessity.

Yet numerous traits that Jim describes as masculine in his teenage friend persist when Ántonia takes on the guise of the earth mother who runs an economically successful farm. Readings that explain away Ántonia's masculinity therefore engage in what Halberstam calls a "project of rationalization." As explained in chapter 1, Halberstam argues that authors and critics alike often attempt to neutralize a character's potentially destabilizing gender or sexuality by placing it within a familiar and nonthreatening narrative. Two of the most common methods of rationalization include writing the character into an explanatory framework wherein threatening comportment is an economic necessity or else rationalized as a temporary but understandable transgression, such as that of the tomboy (*Queer Time* 55). Both of these methods occur within *My Ántonia* as well as the critical conversation surrounding it. Terence Martin, for example, explains Ántonia's masculinity as resulting from economic necessity and familial self-sacrifice. He states, "through [the narrator's] eyes we see her as she grows coarse and muscular doing the work of a man on the farm," and later adds, "Ántonia's determination to work for the immediate needs of her family molds her to the land" (306). Economic motive is certainly present, but critics sometimes focus on this motive to the exclusion of Ántonia's enjoyment of the ways farm labor physically "molds her to the land."[4]

Rationalizing Ántonia's masculinity as a phase or economic necessity leaves an important question unasked: is it actually *conventional* to depict a masculine-identified woman as a fertility goddess? Clearly my answer is no. I read *My Ántonia* as a novel that fits Heather Love's definition of "queer": "*queer*, unlike *gay* or *lesbian*, is by definition generalizable . . . *Queer* is the uninvited guest, unexpected but not totally unwelcome, that shows up without visible relations or ties. Its unlocatable quality does not have political effects that can be calculated in advance: queerness can be a force of disruption, but it can also be an unremarkable or merely enlivening presence" (introduction 744). In my reading of the novel, Cather's invocation of a traditional trope, the earth mother, is quietly, unexpectedly disruptive because a mannish woman becomes a symbol of cultural order and harmony. Instead of rationalizing Ántonia's masculinity, this chapter considers the novel's depiction of her mannishness as coextensive with its depiction of her as a fertility goddess. I show that Ántonia retains her masculinity to the end, and that masculinity *facilitates* her status as an excellent mother.

My reading is not meant to overturn or undercut all interpretations of the novel as conservative. Indeed, I agree with ones that read it as an exaltation of the heteronormative family or a nationalistic embrace of American pioneer mythology. Katrina Irving, for instance, argues that *My Ántonia* invokes eugenic fears of immigrants' fertility. Irving's interpretation fits, albeit uncomfortably, with mine. Cather's masculine, immigrant earth mother is by turns radical and traditional, progressive and conservative. Unlike mainstream eugenicists, Cather implies that the fertility of immigrant Others will rejuvenate America. Indeed, to highlight the difference between Cather's novel and more mainstream eugenic-influenced narratives, I briefly compare *My Ántonia* with Charlotte Perkins Gilman's *Herland* (1915). I ultimately demonstrate that, within the eugenic logic of Cather's novel, the community's attempts to help Ántonia assimilate are foolish because the qualities that assimilation would efface are the very same ones that make her an earth mother whose stock will help rejuvenate the anemic American population. The novel gives an untraditional spin to a discourse that nevertheless rests on long-standing notions of a hierarchy of races; similarly, the novel makes a radical declaration for the legitimacy of queer parents and their offspring by placing them in a traditional tableau of domestic harmony. Cather's depiction of mannish pregnancy is queer, then, in a highly qualified way.

This qualified queerness is further complicated by Cather's politics. Despite her aforementioned mannish comportment, Cather "never identified herself with any emergent modern homosexual subcultures," as Love states, adding that Cather was "consistently hostile toward public expressions of same-sex desire" (*Feeling Backward* 74). Given Cather's refusal to identify with queer culture, is it logical to argue, as I do in this chapter, that Cather's writing legitimizes the offspring of queer people? And to furthermore use for this argument a novel like *My Ántonia*, which ends with the titular character ensconced in domestic harmony? My reading builds on Love's argument regarding Cather's stance toward queer culture: "it is her resistance that makes a queer reading of her work unavoidable. Cather's queerness is bound up with her powerful disidentifications, her ambivalence, and her refusal of community" (25). This ambivalence is apparent in the plot of *My Ántonia*, which is itself a prime example of a project of rationalization.

Ántonia's path from a queer teenager in the early chapters of the novel to a mother of ten by the end of it replicates the model Halberstam lays out, wherein "behavior that may seem dangerous and outrageous" is neutralized by returning the offending character "to the comforting and seemingly inevitable matrix of hetero-domesticity" (*Queer Time* 55).[5] Rather than valuing that which is outside the sphere of the legitimate (as does *Nightwood*, the focus of my next chapter), Cather's novel expands the sphere of the legitimate to encapsulate masculine mothers. There is undoubtedly a conservatism to this depiction because legitimacy is still held out as a valuable status and heteronormative kinship relations the route to attaining it. Yet given the fearmongering that swirled around mannish women at the time of the novel's publication, especially the worries that mannish comportment would render these women unsuitable for maternity, Cather's depiction of a masculine woman as earth mother remains remarkable.[6]

Acknowledging the persistence of Ántonia's masculinity has implications extending beyond the critical conversation surrounding the novel. Reading for masculinity and pregnancy in *My Ántonia* allows us to conceptualize differently the relationship between legitimacy and narrative, showing the powerful role of storytelling in the decisions people make about who and what is legitimate. In Cather's novel, these decisions most frequently arise in regard to immigrants and their assimilation to rural midwestern life. The acceptability of Ántonia's masculinity depends on the community's ability to spin a tale about her as an American, which, in the context of Cather's Black Hawk, means a white, heterosexual woman and capable mother. To put it bluntly, the more the community perceives Ántonia as a non-white immigrant, the more they perceive her as masculine and therefore a threat to heteronormativity. The reverse is also true: the more masculine her behaviors are, the more likely the community is to see her as a dark-skinned immigrant. If the project of rationalization is a kind of narrativization that neutralizes forms of gender and sexuality that threaten the social order, then another way to understand this project is the use of narrative to confer or deny legitimacy. By deeming behaviors, activities, or people illegitimate, members of a community render them abject by psychologically pushing threatening forms of gender, sexuality, and race outside the bounds of that community. Narrative is central to the process by which characters in *My Ántonia* determine whether others are legitimate members of a community: someone whose behaviors fit easily into a recognizable, nonthreatening narrative is more likely to be granted legitimacy than if their behaviors fit no recognizable storyline or, worse, a threatening one. *My Ántonia* thereby depicts projects of rationalization in action.

In the pages that follow, I read Jim Burden's narration as a vehicle that moves Ántonia back and forth across the line of legitimacy as his perception of Ántonia changes from a masculine immigrant to a marriageable American woman. In a similar fashion, the events of Ántonia's illegitimate pregnancy (because conceived out of wedlock) are told to Jim by the Widow Steavens. Her story of the pregnancy moves Ántonia's baby from the category of illegitimate to legitimate by describing the "realness" of Ántonia's maternal instincts, as though they can erase the child's status as a bastard. Steavens's voice takes over the narration for several chapters as she tells a tale about Ántonia as a "natural-born mother" (155) despite her masculinity, her pre-marital sexual relations, and her fatherless child. The Widow's story facilitates the novel's conclusion in which Jim once again takes over the narrative, depicting Ántonia as an earth mother who is not only a legitimate American but a mythological hero and harbinger of a better America. Whereas sociology or psychology might tell us that narrative influences people's decisions about who and what is legitimate, literature is better suited for showing how this dynamic plays out in individual lives. A narrative construction itself, *My Ántonia* illuminates narrative as essential to decisions about legitimacy, whether it concerns a child born out of wedlock, an immigrant seeking acceptance in a new country, or the gender of a queer person.[7]

Perceiving Masculinity

Perception is central to any discussion of gender because gender involves a complex interplay of self-identification as well as the interpretations of others. Issues of perception are necessarily at the forefront of any discussion about *My Ántonia*. For starters, almost all events are filtered through a narrator who romanticizes the people and places of his childhood. Irving notes that "the foreign, dark, Catholic Ántonia is presented to us through Jim's white, middle-class, Protestant, male eyes, which to a large extent are those of his community" (91). Jim's story, in turn, is transmitted to us by another, unnamed narrator who presents Jim's text in a lightly edited final version. This mise en abyme encourages readers to confront the constructed-ness of the narrative. *My Ántonia* is not the unvarnished truth of Ántonia's life but Jim's staging of it, a quality emphasized by Jim's deliberate addition of "My" to his initial title "Ántonia."[8] The novel's multiple frame stories and attendant questions of veracity are further complicated by the first narrator's similarity to Cather herself. This first narrator is, in the original 1918 edition, a woman writer who grew up in the rural midwest. Although Cather deleted many of these specificities when she revised the novel for its 1926 reissue, reading Cather as the first narrator remains plausible in the revised version (O'Brien, introduction, xi–xv). Conversely, numerous critics have argued that Jim, rather than the first narrator, is a fictionalized screen for Cather who can safely give voice to her romantic desires for women.[9]

Intriguing as these debates are, I am less concerned here with whether Jim is reliable or a screen for Cather's repressed sexuality, than in his perception of Ántonia as masculine. In this regard, I am strongly influenced by the work of Marilee Lindemann, who argues that power, not credibility, "is what is at stake in *My Ántonia*" (" 'It ain't my prairie' " 487). This is so because the multiple frame stories "foregroun[d] the problem of how women perceive and are perceived in masculinist culture," which means that Cather's novel "broods upon and elucidates profoundly feminist issues, though its author almost certainly did not intend to create a self-consciously 'feminist' work" (486).[10] Like Lindemann, I consider the various ways Jim constructs Ántonia's gender as transgressive, as well as the ways this perception gives rise to gendered forms of policing and legitimizing. Unlike Lindemann, I read Ántonia's masculinity as a stable feature of her identity. Moreover, I broaden the scope to consider female characters' perceptions of Ántonia, too, particularly as her masculinity disrupts and shapes what they think about her pregnancies. Focusing on perceptions of Ántonia's masculinity allows us to see how Jim, the Widow Steavens, and several other neighbors use narrative to withhold and grant legitimacy.

By narrative, I mean weaving Ántonia's behaviors and appearance into a chain of causal events to give them meaning or coherence. This is similar to what Walter Benjamin calls novelistic narrative form. Benjamin compares this to journalism and "storytelling," the latter of which he privileges because it is open-ended. Storytelling, for Benjamin, is a mode in which "the most extraordinary things, marvelous things, are related with the greatest accuracy, but the psychological connection of the events is not forced on the reader. It is left up to him to interpret things the way he understands them" (89). In contrast, novelistic narrative conveys "the overarching 'meaning of life' " and delivers an "implicit analysis that will make sense of it all" (414). Richard H. Millington identifies novelistic narrative throughout Books One, Three, and Four of *My Ántonia*. Like Benjamin, Millington says these narratives are implied rather than overt, "never told but already written into the mind," and that they combine to "construct the overarching, normative narrative of maturity that constitutes middle-class culture in Black Hawk" (701). Although Millington argues that these narratives are "never told," I find them voiced by Jim, Mrs. Burden, the Widow Steavens, and others.[11]

Cather establishes narrative distance by writing into the novel numerous scenes in which characters contradict themselves, change their stories, and espouse short-sighted opinions. As such, readers can see a different side to Ántonia than the one constructed by Jim, Jim's grandparents, and the Widow Steavens. It is in the differences that we can detect these characters building (de)legitimizing narratives around Ántonia. Consider, for instance, the difference between Ántonia's enjoyment and pride in her masculinity and Jim's disparaging narration of it. When she begins working the land at fifteen, after the death of her father, Ántonia glories in her newly developed muscles and tanned skin. She tells Jim: " 'Oh, better I like to work out of doors than in a house!' she used to sing joyfully. 'I not care that your grandmother say it makes me like a man. I like to be like a man.' She would toss her head and ask me to feel the muscles swell in her brown arm" (110). Behaviors like this Jim characterizes as "disagreeable" (67). On another occasion, he has dinner with the Shimerdas at their farm. Ántonia laughs loudly, teases her brother Ambrosch good-naturedly, and eats heartily (67). Jim's reaction is to complain that, "Ántonia ate so noisily now, like a man" (99) and to begin calling her by the nickname "Tony" (100). When Ántonia banters with Ambrosch over who plowed more land, Jim grouses, "Tony could talk of nothing but the prices of things, or how much she could lift and endure. She was too proud of her strength" (69). Her pride is justified, stemming in part from the difference between this summer of plentitude and the months of privation the Shimerdas endured when they first arrived in Nebraska. Whereas they once struggled to grow enough food to feed the family, Ántonia's strength allows her to help support the family. The shape her pride takes suggests that she also enjoys the changes taking place in her body as her muscles become stronger and her skin grows rougher.[12]

The exception to Ántonia's happiness during this summer of farm labor comes when Jim asks on behalf of his grandmother if Ántonia wants to attend school. Her reply indicates the extent to which she now identifies with men: " 'I ain't got time to learn. I can work like mans now. My mother can't say no more how Ambrosch do all and nobody to help him. I can work as much as him. School is alright for little boys. I help make this land one good farm" (66). Thus, she rebuffs Jim's offer by recourse to age and maturity. If she were a young boy she might go to school, but she is now strong and mature enough to work like a man. Yet moments later, Jim catches her crying. She asks, "Sometime you will tell me all those nice things you learn at the school, won't you, Jimmy?" (67). I do not read this scene as suggesting that she regrets having to "work like mans." Evidence of her pride in the work and enjoyment of the changes it makes to her body are too abundant to be consistent with regret of this kind. Rather, I read this scene as evidence of her regret that she cannot work the land and attend school simultaneously. Ántonia identifies both of these occupations with men she admires. She associates manual labor with Ambrosch, consistently comparing her work on the farm to his. She identifies book learning with her father. Immediately after asking Jim to share with her the "nice things" he learns in school, she states, "My father, he went much to school . . . he read so many books that the priests in Bohemie come to talk to him" (67). Because of these associations, I see Ántonia's tears as sadness over the need to decide between two different models of masculinity, both of which she finds appealing. Jim interprets her tears as an indication that she needs saving from this life of toil, but his interpretation rests on the idea that she needs to be more feminine, a judgment Ántonia does not share.

Despite Ántonia's repeated comments about enjoying her embodiment, Jim narrates her masculine behaviors as illegitimate and imitative. The behaviors he likes—politeness, passivity, and helpfulness—he reads as legitimate. In so doing, he makes his own subjective preferences into seemingly objective standards for what constitutes legitimate behavior for women. At one point during this same summer he describes Ántonia as "so gay and responsive that one did not mind her heavy, running step, or her clattery way with pans" (74). This description appears while Ántonia is staying at the Burden household for a week to help Jim's grandmother in the kitchen during harvest time. Jim's word choice, especially "responsive," focuses on her attitude toward others: he likes that she is helpful to his grandmother and open to Jim's suggestions. He is willing to overlook her lack of gracefulness ("clattery ways") as long as her demeanor is docile and she views him as intellectually superior. Passivity, we can thereby understand, is central to Jim's conception of womanliness at this point in the book. The less he perceives Ántonia as docile and suggestible, the more his narrative frames her gender as illegitimate. As if to emphasize this point, shortly thereafter he asks, "why are n't you always nice like this, Tony?"[13] When she asks for clarification, he says, "Why, just like this; like yourself. Why do you all the time try to be like Ambrosch?" His phrasing constructs Ántonia's masculinity as an imitation, something with origins outside her. Ántonia agrees that the reason is external, but points to economic necessity rather than imitation: "If I live here [at Mr. and Mrs. Burden's more comfortable home], like you, that is different. Things will be easy for you. But they will be hard for us" (67). As I have said, Ántonia's masculinization does indeed involve economic necessity, but this necessity conveniently gives cover to her enjoyment by providing an excuse for masculinity.

Attending to scenes such as these allows us to see that what makes Ántonia queer in this community is not her rough ways but her pride in them, her refusal to apologize. Her queering begins at the level of community-defined categories of "masculinity" and "femininity." Jim accepts Ántonia when she rationalizes her gender as an economic necessity. Conversely, Jim's comments are most critical when she resists his advice or shows off her robust physicality. Such demeanor makes it difficult for Jim and others to incorporate Ántonia into a narrative they perceive as acceptable because, as will become clear, they worry that she will not be marriageable, with both homophobia and xenophobia underlying this worry. Narratives that legitimize certain kinds of masculinity in women existed, then as now. In addition to the aforementioned narrative of women doing their duty during wartime, Halberstam observes that a woman whose comportment might seem transgressively masculine in the city is likely to be read in an agricultural context as "simply a hardworking woman who can take care of herself and her farm" (40–41). In the rural Midwest during the interwar years, a certain amount of masculinity in a woman could be squarely within the norm.[14] Jim's own grandmother, whom he describes as an archetype of maternal care and warmth, is "a strong woman, of unusual endurance," who carries around a cane for killing rattlesnakes (15). Similarly, the eldest daughter of the respectable Harling family runs her father's business when he is out of town. Ántonia's masculinity is different, however, because she openly discusses her preference for it. Jim notes that he and his grandmother are not the only ones to find Ántonia's comportment unusual, saying "the farmhands around the country joked in a nasty way about it" (69). The undercurrent to this comment is that she is not behaving like a lady, which relates to the fear that masculinity would render her unmarriageable. Although Cather does not make this point overtly in this section of the novel, we learn later that Jim is romantically attracted to Ántonia. Here, then, is yet another reason for Jim to find Ántonia's masculinity troubling: it makes her unsuitable for Jim's own marriage conquest. Jim's concern for what others think about Ántonia steadily grows, but his concern also makes clear that Cather is interested in issues with broader import than interpersonal disputes between teenagers.

Instead, Cather's novel investigates the ways communities make judgments about legitimacy. And if, as Irving argues, one of Jim's functions is to be a representative of community norms, we see that his tale models on a small scale the ways people use narratives in their determinations about the legitimacy of neighbors. What interests me most are the scenes in which some characters decide that Ántonia's masculinity has become queer and therefore troublesome, while other characters perceive her gender as within the norms of the community. The lack of consensus is valuable from a reader's perspective because these characters justify their determinations to each other through narrative, and their determinations carry an expression of community values. In the farmlands surrounding Black Hawk, masculine behaviors in women are acceptable as long as they are rationalized; preferring them to feminine behaviors is not acceptable. As the following sections demonstrate, the various narratives Jim, his grandparents, and others tell about Ántonia move her back and forth across a hazy line separating illegitimacy from legitimacy. Jim and his grandmother initially react to Ántonia's masculinity by delegitimizing her with homophobic and xenophobic narratives, and later legitimize her by casting her as a damsel in distress who needs rescuing from a hard life. In these sections of the chapter I veer away from discussions of pregnancy, but attending to scenes of community narrativization will help me make an important point about the novel's depiction of a masculine woman as a fertility goddess. Specifically, the very qualities that Jim initially narrates as illegitimate are the same ones he later perceives as a source of rejuvenation for a degenerating American population in his final narrative of Ántonia as earth mother.

Delegitimization through Place, Race, and Time

"Like the land which suffers the attempts of male pioneers to divide it into sections," Helen Wussow argues, "so Cather's central female characters endure efforts to classify them within traditional female roles" (52). In the case of Ántonia, these efforts to classify her gender are yoked to cultural assimilation: immigrants such as Ántonia must be perceived as legitimate women to be considered full-fledged Americans by the inhabitants of Black Hawk and its surrounding farmlands.[15] Ántonia's masculinity makes it hard for Jim to see her as a legitimate member of this American community because he struggles to find a narrative of acceptable womanhood that she fits into. It is his grandmother who eventually locates one. She begins telling a story of Ántonia as a damsel in distress, which Jim latches onto because it is both familiar and lets him think of his friend as someone who needs to be "saved" from her rough life rather than an illegitimate immigrant.

At first, Jim can only understand Ántonia's masculinity as a feature of her foreignness.[16] Mary Paniccia Carden notes that Jim's narration in these chapters "associates [Ántonia] with her brother Ambrosch and her mother, immigrants who behave inappropriately in American spaces" (289). Carden further connects gender and nationality when she argues that Jim "aligns Ántonia with her unacceptable family when she does not conform to his definitions of femininity, thus characterizing gender-role transgression as un-American" (289–90). To Carden's perceptive analysis, I would add that part of what Jim dislikes about Ambrosch and Mrs. Shimerda is that they are not particularly interested in assimilating. For instance, Mrs. Shimerda continues to cook with ingredients and tools that are foreign to Black Hawk, such as dried mushrooms and a "quilt" for keeping food warm (66). Neither she nor Ambrosch is eager to learn English, as Ántonia is, nor to participate in the Burden's cultural activities (such as musical or religious ceremonies), even if Ántonia's father is a keen admirer. The fact that Ambrosch and Mrs. Shimerda are not deferential to the Burdens in these regards facilitates Jim's connection of foreignness to masculinity because, as we know, he considers deference to be a central aspect of femininity. As a result, the narrative he writes of Ántonia at this point in her life is shot through with xenophobia.

In a key passage of this narrative, Jim laments that Ántonia "kept her sleeves rolled up all day and her arms and throat were burned as brown as a sailor's. Her neck came up strongly out of her shoulders, like the bole of a tree out of the turf. One sees that draft-horse neck among the peasant women in all old countries" (96). Jim's similes and metaphors make his disapproval of Ántonia plain. However, the logic behind his disapproval is not obvious and so is worth considering in greater detail. Jim's comparisons suggest that masculine traits are natural and expected among poor, non-American women. American-born Jim thinks that "old," backward countries work their women like they work their horses, which buttresses his focus on ladylike behavior as part of Ántonia's Americanization.

Jean Schwind reads the draft-horse quote as indicating the depth of Jim's distaste for Ántonia's gender: "As Jim sees it, Ántonia's claim to a 'man's' work is more than a violation of Black Hawk's sense of propriety: it is a violation of human nature" (59). I agree with Schwind but would add that Jim's statement also reveals a fear of Ántonia's competence and value. Draft horses are esteemed for their strength, second only to oxen among farm animals. Ántonia's laboring body is essential to her family's survival in this new country, while Jim largely spends his days indoors, engaged in passive or stereotypically feminine behaviors such as studying and helping his grandmother around the house. Jim's language manifests class differences between the Shimerda and Burden families, but it also reveals his perception of Ántonia's masculinity as a threat to his own.[17] To assuage this fear, he casts Ántonia's masculinity as inappropriate and even potentially inhuman. Jim might have been able to accept Ántonia's masculinity if she were in a different place and time (an "old" country), but in the United States, in his childhood friend, Jim cannot abide mannishness. Halberstam argues that queerness has its own timeline, one that is out of sync with heterosexual trajectories such as that which leads from adolescence to marriage to reproduction (*Queer Time* 6). Halberstam finds the possibilities afforded by queer uses of time and space exciting for their potential to create "imaginative life schedules" (1). Here, however, we see a less sanguine approach to the effects of queerness on the perception of time. Ántonia's masculinity causes Jim to perceive her as existing in both the wrong time and the wrong place. That he narrates Ántonia as out of sync with Black Hawk's time and space is one way he marks her queerness.

Jim's queering of Ántonia occurs in tandem with his racialization of her. He describes Ántonia as darker skinned than her sister when he first meets her, and in the middle section of the novel he fixates on skin color in ways that evoke eugenic discourse. Eugenics dominated conversations about immigration and reproduction in the 1910s and 1920s.[18] Linda Lizut Helstern states that eugenicists in the United States "viewed Southern and Eastern Europeans [including Bohemians], who represented the greatest percentage of new immigrants during the first two decades of the twentieth century, as a particular threat to evolutionary progress, ostensibly because they carried less desirable racial traits than Nordics" who comprised the bulk of the prior generation of immigrants (255). This distinction between immigrant communities is clear in *My Ántonia*. Jim depicts the Harlings, a Norwegian family, as hardworking, intelligent, and financially successful. Lena Lingard is also Nordic, a fact Cather emphasizes by including numerous references to her white skin. The beauty of this white skin, combined with her buxom figure, leads to rumors that Lena is promiscuous, but we eventually find out that these rumors have no substance. In the end, Jim shows Lena to be a skillful and sought-after businesswoman. In keeping with the aforementioned racial distinction, Jim's complaints about Ántonia's masculinity often combine with references to her dark skin. We have seen this in several of the passages I have discussed already: when Ántonia says "I like to be like a man," Jim notes that her "muscles swell in her *brown* arm" (emphasis added 74); and in the draft-horse quote, Jim finds fault with her skin because it is "burned as brown as a sailor's" (66). Working the fields would certainly tan her skin, but Jim's repeated union of skin color and masculinity suggests he finds it increasingly difficult to think of Ántonia as a legitimate member of the Black Hawk community because dark skin implies to him a lower or degenerate race.

We must also read Jim's comment for traces of racism against Black Americans.[19] Black women have long been stereotyped as more masculine than their white counterparts and more able to withstand backbreaking work in the fields. Further, the legitimacy of Black women *as* women was a topic of debate at the time of *My Ántonia*'s publication, much as the legitimacy of masculine women was in question. According to Saidiya Hartman, white Americans at the close of the nineteenth century questioned the legitimacy of Black women, asking themselves, "What kind of woman was she, if a woman at all?" (38). With the image of masculine, dark-skinned Ántonia, Cather's novel combines the racism that informed these perceptions of Black women with the bigotry that informed some perceptions of masculine women. The draft-horse quote, then, shows that Jim perceives foreignness as an index for transgressive gender. Combining race and gender amplifies Jim's delegitimization of Ántonia as an American woman.

Coerced Assimilation as "Salvation"

Narrating Ántonia's legitimacy becomes a group effort when Jim's grand-mother begins developing an alternative to Jim's xenophobic narrative. This alternative still condemns Ántonia's masculinity but does so in a way that allows Jim to see his childhood friend as a victim rather than a source of illegitimacy. Jim and his grandmother, as well as his grandfather to an extent, construct narratives around Ántonia in attempts to rationalize her masculinity. They finally land on a damsel in distress story in which Ánto-nia needs saving from a hard life. In practice, however, this "salvation" is coerced assimilation involving Ántonia's labor and gender.

Jim's grandmother rationalizes Ántonia's masculinity by locating its ori-gins in necessity—the demands of farm labor—rather than her preferences. Jim explains that his grandmother said, " 'Heavy field work'll spoil that girl.

She'll lose all her nice ways and get rough ones'" (67). Jim thinks, "She had lost them already" (ibid.). In this instance, "spoil" means *ruin the value of* rather than *indulge* or *pamper*. Because Ántonia is, at the time, responsible, hardworking, and economically successful, Jim's grandmother clearly means field work will ruin Ántonia for marriage and that she needs someone to save her before it's too late. Jim's grandfather disagrees and tries to write Ántonia into a traditional romance plotline, saying, "'she will help some fellow get ahead in the world'" (69). Mr. Burden manifests awareness of an unspoken concern by using the language of heterosexual coupling. Depicting Ántonia tucked away in marriage, her husband's helper rather than his leader, minimizes the threat of her masculinity and possible homosexuality.

Mr. Burden's story, however, does not persuade his wife and grandson. Jim implicitly rejects his grandfather's narrative by embellishing the damsel in distress story his grandmother began. As in folk tales like as Cinderella, a devious family member forces the woman at the center of the story into a life of endless toil from which she cannot extract herself:

> All through the wheat season, Ambrosch hired his sister out like a man, and she went from farm to farm, binding sheaves or working with the thrashers. The farmers liked her and were kind to her; said they would rather have her for a hand than Ambrosch. When fall came she was to husk corn for the neighbors until Christmas, as she had done the year before; but grandmother saved her from this by getting her a place to work with our neighbors, the Harlings. (78–79)

The bare facts of her working conditions tell a different story than that of a damsel in distress. Ántonia is a skilled farmhand bringing in needed income through her labor on farms where the owners treat her well. Combined with the enjoyment she derives from her muscled body while engaged in farmwork, Jim's perception that she needs "saving" is unjustified. However, the damsel in distress story allows him and his grandmother to continue thinking of Ántonia as an upstanding woman rather than a potential threat to the community's gender norms because, in their narrative, Ambrosch forced her into heavy farmwork and masculinity rather than it being her choice.

When Jim and his grandmother put their plan to "save" Ántonia into action, they do so ostensibly for her own good, but also to preserve a certain norm of legitimate behavior for women in the Black Hawk community. We can see this normalizing drive, particularly the emphasis on heterosexuality, most clearly in a conversation between the Burdens and the Harlings. Before hiring Ántonia, Mrs. Harling and her adult daughter, Frances, insist on meeting Ántonia. This meeting, in turn, allows the Harlings to contribute to the story of the damsel in distress who needs help becoming a suitable (read: marriageable) American woman. When the Burdens and the Harlings gather to settle the details of Ántonia's employment, none of them talks much about Ántonia's skills. Rather, they focus on her looks and potential for domesticity. Jim's grandmother says to Mrs. Harling, " 'She'll be awkward and rough at first, like enough . . . but unless she's been spoiled by the hard life she's led, she has it in her to be a real helpful girl' " (81). Note that Mrs. Shimerda does not say that Ántonia is a "helpful girl" now, despite Ántonia's demonstrated abilities on the farm, and even despite the fact that Mrs. Burden herself hired Ántonia to help in the kitchen during harvest time. Mrs. Burden thinks Ántonia has yet to learn some important skills. That these skills are related to domesticity and marriageability is apparent in Mrs. Harling's reply: "I can bring something out of that girl. She's barely seventeen, not too old to learn new ways. She's good-looking, too" (81). That the women's focus is Ántonia's looks and her potential in domestic settings suggests that their primary concern is transforming Ántonia into someone who will make a suitable wife. They assume—incorrectly, it turns out—that men will not find her strength, vitality, and independence attractive and set about to change her ways. This scene displays yet again the importance of narrative in legitimizing Ántonia as an assimilated member of the community. The prelude to the Harlings taking Ántonia into their respected, affluent household is this scene of communal narrativization in which the Harling women contribute to the damsel in distress story. But instead of a male hero, as is usual in folk tales, a matriarch is a more appropriate savior here. Mrs. Harling, once an unassimilated immigrant herself, knows how to make a marriageable American woman out of a rough foreign girl; so much the better that Mrs. Harling is from Norway, where the "better" sort of immigrants come from.

The next phase of Ántonia's life is the part that is easiest, thus far, for Jim to write into a respectable, recognizable narrative. When she first arrives in Black Hawk, Ántonia is "responsive" (to use Jim's term), manifesting a desire for transformation of the kind Jim, Mrs. Burden, and Mrs. Harling have in mind. Ántonia hopes to be "the kind of girl you like better, now I come to town" (82). Some of Ántonia's "rough" ways disappear, but most of the changes concern her external appearance. No longer working in the fields, her body takes on a less muscular shape, and although she wears some items of men's clothing, such as slippers made of Mr. Harling's old coats (82), she also begins to make clothes that Jim describes as "pretty" (92). Yet these changes are superficial compared to the changes effected by her new living arrangement. In Black Hawk, Ántonia becomes more like the kind of girl Jim prefers because she fits more easily into a heterosexual marriage plot. Traits that he reads as masculine in the fields, such as physical strength, are less threatening as potential signs of homosexuality in the context of Black Hawk, where Ántonia works with children in a domestic setting. Her preferences and comportment are unchanged from her time in the fields. She still revels in physical activities, especially if they are outdoors. For instance, she regularly ducks work in favor of playing outside with the Harling children and Jim: "She would race about the orchard with us, or take sides in our hayfights in the barn, or be the old bear that came down from the mountain" (82). Here Jim is not bothered by her robust physicality, as he was when she worked the fields. The difference is that Ántonia's activities occur in the context of childcare. And since Jim suspects that Ántonia has a crush on the oldest Harling boy, Jim can easily continue thinking of Ántonia within the damsel in distress narrative. Having been rescued, Ántonia has begun the happily-ever-after portion of the story where she becomes a bride and a mother. None of this comes to pass in the manner Jim imagines it will—her eventual love interest is a cad and motherhood comes before marriage—but Jim remains invested in a narrative that legitimizes Ántonia as heterosexual and feminine.

Ántonia moreover assimilates to the largest extent she ever will during this phase of her life. Cather's depiction of assimilation is rather ironic, though, because what Jim perceives as Ántonia's "assimilation" consists of imitating peers to obtain social acceptance. One of the clearest examples of this phenomenon occurs when Ántonia begins attending dances in the summertime. Her vigorously healthy body, like that of the other immigrant girls who worked on family farms in their earlier years, makes her attractive in ways that the girls in town cannot hope to match. Jim says of the "country girls" like Ántonia, "out-of-door work had given them a vigor which . . . developed into a positive carriage and freedom of movement, and made them conspicuous among Black Hawk women" (102). Thus, it is Ántonia's vitality that makes her attractive, and this vitality is, as Jim acknowledges, a product of her work outdoors. By contrast, when dancing with the town girls, "their bodies never moved inside their clothes; their muscles seemed to ask but one thing—not to be disturbed" (102). Town boys risk arguments with their town girlfriends just for a chance to dance with a country girl. Ántonia develops scores of admirers, from the iceman who "lingered too long now, when he came to the covered porch to fill the refrigerator," to the "delivery boys" and "young farmers" who turn up to spend time with her (105). Ántonia's "assimilation" is therefore part of the problem. She imitates the behaviors of her peers by attending dances, but the local men are unaccustomed to muscular physicality like hers. Whereas Jim found her physical vigor distasteful in the countryside, it is now irresistible. As with Ántonia's antics among the Harling children, Jim accepts her comportment—even as he is concerned about the romantic competition—because he perceives it within the contours of heteronormative romance.

Legitimacy in the Black Hawk community comes in the form of acceptance from families such as the Burdens and Harlings. Ántonia gains it, but Cather makes plain that their acceptance based on assimilation comes at a cost. Ántonia is happy at times with the Harlings, but she is also "lonesome" and stricken with intermittent "sad spells" (166). In one of the instances that reveals a distance between Cather and her narrator, Jim does not discuss (or seem to notice) her sadness while narrating their lives in Black Hawk. Instead, we hear about it directly from Ántonia in the last section of the novel. A happily married mother of ten by this time, Ántonia tells Jim about her sad spells while reminiscing from the distance of decades. These moments of sadness and loneliness are still present enough in Ántonia's memory that she brings them up almost immediately upon reference to the Black Hawk of their youth, but young Jim failed to include them in his narrative of these years. That they should retain urgency for Ántonia is not surprising, for they precede traumatic events. Shortly after Ántonia begins attending the dances, she leaves the Harling household because of a disagreement over her attendance at them, begins working for a man who attempts to rape her, runs away with her lover, becomes pregnant, and faces single parenthood when her lover abandons her. Thus, assimilation of the kind encouraged by the Harlings and Burdens is hardly something to be sought after. In truth, *My Ántonia* shows assimilation to be a psychologically damaging kind of window-dressing. Ántonia makes external changes to fit more easily into the contours of a life story others see as legitimate. In the process, she sacrifices her happiness and, as we will see in the following pages, experiences events that lead to depression and possible thoughts of suicide.

The Widow Steavens's Narration

Just as Jim's various narratives for Ántonia's early life attempt to adjudicate the legitimacy of her gender, the Widow Steavens's narrative of Ántonia's later years adjudicates her legitimacy as a mother. This adjudication is necessary in part because Ántonia forgoes "assimilation" and returns to masculine comportment while pregnant. The Widow's story successfully legitimizes Ántonia in Jim's eyes, for he is thereafter able to see Ántonia as a real mother and to later spin a tale of her as an archetypal earth mother. Much of the action concerning Ántonia's first pregnancy takes place off-stage, and Jim does not experience it firsthand. Instead, the Widow Steavens takes over the novel's narration for several chapters as she recounts Ántonia's pregnancy and the events leading to it. At the moment when the Widow tells this story, Jim has recently returned to Black Hawk from college and is in town for the summer before moving away again for law school. He has not seen Ántonia since leaving for college and has only heard unflattering rumors of her since. Upon his return, Frances Harling says, "You know, of course, about poor Ántonia" (145). Jim becomes angry at this, thinking: "Poor Ántonia! Every one would be saying that now, I thought bitterly. I replied that grandmother had written me how Ántonia went away to marry Larry Donovan at some place where he was working; that he had deserted her, and that there was now a baby. . . . I was bitterly disappointed in her. I could not forgive her for becoming an object of pity" (145). Jim's disappointment in Ántonia stems from behaviors he perceives as ingratitude: after the Burdens and Harlings worked so hard to position Ántonia within a respectable plotline, she throws it all away on someone Jim considers a "cheap sort of fellow" (148).

Jim is unwilling to associate with Ántonia until he begins to see the outlines of an alternate narrative. Stopping by the local photographer's studio, he sees an image of Ántonia's baby. The image is framed elaborately and displayed publicly, suggesting that Ántonia is proud of the child. He thinks approvingly, "Another girl would have kept her baby out of sight, but Tony, of course, must have its picture on exhibition at the town photographer's, in a great gilt frame" (148). When Ántonia was proud and boastful as a teenage farmhand, Jim was disgusted. When she displays the same behaviors as a mother, Jim is intrigued because the photograph suggests a story of maternal love. Desiring to know more, he seeks out the Widow Steavens. Steavens is the person in Black Hawk best able to tell Jim what happened to his childhood friend because she "helped Ántonia get ready to be married; and she was there when Ántonia came back [after Donovan's abandonment]. She took care of her when the baby was born" (149). The narrative the Widow eventually constructs emphasizes Ántonia's goodness, meekness, and maternal feelings, going so far as to say that "Ántonia is a natural-born mother" (155), despite the persistence of her masculinity through these experiences. The Widow's story helps Jim—and therefore readers, too—see Ántonia as a legitimate mother. As Lindemann states, the Widow's narrative "performs the necessary task of restoring Ántonia's dignity in Jim's eyes (following the birth of her first child out of wedlock) and pronouncing her fit for the symbolic role he will ultimately confer upon her," that of the earth mother (" 'It ain't my prairie' " 496). We can see a project of rationalization in Steavens's narrative: although Ántonia is masculine, unmarried, dark-skinned, and an immigrant, Steavens legitimizes her and the child by creating a narrative around them that defuses perceived threats to the social order. The Widow's narrative repositions Ántonia within the sphere of the socially legitimate.

As several critics have argued, the scenes in which the Widow relays her narrative to Jim are imbued with the trappings of mythology. Before Jim turns the novel's narration over to Widow Steavens, he describes riding a horse to the Widow's home, emphasizing the remoteness of it from Black Hawk (149). Once there, Jim stresses the noble bearing of the Widow (149). Rosowski argues that Cather here revises the tale of the quester (Jim) who seeks information from the oracle (Mrs. Steavens). Jim's long journey to her home, his comparison of Steavens to a Roman Senator, and their ritualistic sharing of food (149) combine to create a mythological atmosphere that represents to Rosowski the "supplication of youth to age, quester to oracle" (447). Particularly interesting for our purposes, Rosowski furthermore likens the Widow to a midwife who assists with both a literal childbirth and a narrative rebirth: "Jim goes to see a midwife for the re-visioning necessary to break the silence surrounding birth" (446–47). Steavens is a midwife because she literally helps Ántonia through pregnancy and metaphorically brings Ántonia back to life in the narrative after an absence of several chapters.

That the Widow's role in the novel is, in part, to adjudicate Ánto-nia's place in the community provides insight into the changeable politics surrounding legitimacy: Who confers and withholds it? Why them? In Ántonia's teenage years, the main questions about her legitimacy concern assimilation and marriageability. Jim, a male, native-born person of approx-imately the same age as Ántonia, is in a position to make determinations about Ántonia's marriageability. His opinions matter a great deal in this particular situation. With regard to Ántonia's legitimacy as a mother, how-ever, he does not have experience or authority to adjudicate convincingly.

Instead, Cather uses the Widow Steavens for that purpose, countering Jim's originally disapproving narrative of Ántonia's motherhood by constructing a more socially acceptable version.

The Widow's authority stems from direct experience with childbirth. The novel does not specify whether Steavens has children of her own, but Steavens describes her postpartum interactions with Ántonia in a matter-of-fact manner that suggests wisdom on the subject. Upon learning that Ántonia gave birth, Steavens immediately heads for the Shimerda household and "went right in and began to do for Ántonia" (155). Her manner is sure and steady, even correcting Ántonia's mother when the latter is about to bathe the baby with an abrasive soap. Steavens's experience would not have been uncommon in rural Nebraska at the time, when doctors were expensive and home birth the norm. A woman in labor usually would have been attended by neighbors and perhaps a trained midwife (Declercq et al. 10). Midwives were most commonly women with children of their own, but in rural communities where travel could be difficult, any woman who was available, rational, and calm under pressure would have been welcomed. Steavens's experience in the birthing room in general and in Ántonia's in particular makes her a far more qualified judge of maternal legitimacy than Jim, who does not have children and who the Widow guesses is "not much interested in babies" (155). Rosowski's description of Steavens as a midwife is thus particularly apt, for it is plausible to read Steavens as a midwife to more of the community's women than only Ántonia.

Nevertheless, the Widow's story does not begin by legitimizing Ántonia as a mother. One of the most striking features of her story is the detail she provides concerning Ántonia's discomfort with pregnancy. Ántonia might enjoy being a mother, but pregnancy is a different matter. She returns to farmwork, performing similar tasks to those she did as a teenager. As before, she wears men's clothing and walks with a heavy step, but has none of the vitality of her earlier days working the fields (153). The Widow describes Ántonia during her pregnancy as "crushed and quiet," and says, "she always looked dead weary" (153). Steavens furthermore notes that Ántonia "was afflicted with toothache; one tooth after another ulcerated, and she went about with her face swollen half the time. She would n't go to Black Hawk to a dentist for fear of meeting people she knew" (153). Ulcerated teeth are common during pregnancy, but here they take on figurative significance as metonyms of her pregnancy. The abscesses continue for the duration and swell up formerly flat planes of her body with painful growths. If Ántonia's body gave her pleasure when field work made it masculine, that body now gives her pain.

Undoubtedly, this pain can be explained in part by the discomfort every person experiences during pregnancy. Furthermore, her malaise can be partly attributed to an emotional cause: shame at being pregnant out of wedlock. As mentioned earlier, Ántonia cares what others think about her and seeks legitimacy in the form of social approval. The Widow Steavens says that people "respected [Ántonia's] industry and tried to treat her as if nothing had happened" (152). Ántonia nevertheless avoids social interactions. Ann Fisher-Wirth notes that "Ántonia is never overtly expelled from the social order [while pregnant]. But she internalizes opprobrium and holds herself apart" (191). Ántonia is ashamed regardless of whether it is self-imposed or otherwise.

Yet the Widow also describes symptoms of depression that are not explained by either social shame or the nature of her work. I surmise that her pregnant body—a form of embodiment often considered the apotheosis of femininity—contributes to Ántonia's emotional state. She tells Steavens:

> It does seem like I ought to make lace, or knit [for the baby] . . . but if I start to work, I look around and forget to go on. It seems such a little while ago when Jim Burden and I was playing all over this country. Up here I can pick out the very places where my father used to stand. Sometimes I feel like I'm not going to live very long, so I'm just enjoying every day of this fall. (153)

This statement tells us that Ántonia feels close to death and is trying to appreciate what time she has left. She does not experience physical complications with pregnancy that would make her death more likely than normal for the time and place. Instead, the statement is suggestive of an emotional malaise. The invocation of her father, who committed suicide in winter, raises the possibility that Ántonia might be contemplating the same. This reference to her father alongside ones to her childhood recall a time when Ántonia was young, a recent immigrant who felt out of place, ill-fitting, and alienated. Her actions while pregnant reenact this rootlessness on a small scale as she wanders far and stays out late while tending the herds. The Widow Steavens explains that Ántonia sometimes brought her cattle "over the west hill" because "it had been dry and the pasture was short, or she would n't have brought them so far," and later, in the winter, Ántonia is caught in a late-day snowstorm because, the Widow says, "she'd been feeling too miserable to get up and drive" the cattle home (153). This wandering, combined with her reminiscences of a lost childhood and pater familias, creates a symmetry between Ántonia's nationality and her pregnancy.

It is plausible, then, to read Ántonia as unhomed in her body while pregnant. Throughout her life, hard, physical work never causes Ántonia's spirits to flag. She is not given to complaining about physical pain, boasting, for instance, of "how much she could lift and endure" (69). She later tells Jim that she does not mind physical labor "if I don't have to put up with sadness" (166). As such, attributing Ántonia's emotional state during pregnancy to the physical discomforts of it seems a misreading; so too is attributing her depression to *only* shame over being pregnant out of wedlock since people generally treat her kindly and she is proud of her baby once born. Instead, I read her depression as also a sign of psychological discomfort with a state of embodiment that traditionally signaled femininity. Whereas Ántonia feels happy with and proud of her body when she perceives it as masculine, she is depressed when her body takes on a shape that most people associate with femininity. Working the fields as a teenager, Ántonia gloried in the increasing masculinity of her body, showing off her muscles and tanned skin. Rather than displaying her pregnant body, Ántonia covers it up with "a man's long overcoat and boots, and a man's felt hat with a wide brim" (153). But even if she covers her swelling belly with men's attire, her swelling teeth are there to remind her of what is beneath the coat.

Despite all of this—the masculinity, the depression, the premarital pregnancy—the Widow is able to spin a tale that legitimizes Ántonia. To begin with, Steavens attributes Ántonia's depression to shame, an interpretation that allows her to position Ántonia as acting within community norms. If shame is the culturally sanctioned response to single motherhood, Ántonia is on the path to redemption if she feels accordingly. The tone of the Widow's story changes after Ántonia gives birth, switching from Ántonia's depression during pregnancy to her pride after giving birth. This latter portion of the narrative brings to fruition the redemption for which Steavens laid the groundwork. She describes Ántonia as proud and content, loving the baby "as dearly as if she'd had a ring on her finger, and was never ashamed of it. It's a year and eight months old now, and no baby was ever better cared-for. Ántonia is a natural-born mother" (155). The conclusion of her narrative thereby grants a kind of retroactive legitimacy to Ántonia and her baby.[20] The claim that Ántonia loved the baby as though it were born in wedlock is a clear example of this kind of narrative legitimizing, but the reference to Ántonia's skillful caregiving also discursively shifts Ántonia into the realm of legitimate mothers. As with Jim, however, the Widow fails to notice how Ántonia's behaviors do not entirely square with the story she is telling and that these behaviors point to a more subversive cause. In both cases, the cause is Ántonia's sense of herself as a masculine person.

Cather is not so single-minded as to imply that narrative is the only factor in community considerations of legitimacy. The Widow Steavens's story does much to legitimize Ántonia and her baby in Jim's eyes, but Jim is the sole listener to the tale. To be sure, the Widow is a respected member of the Black Hawk community, and her acceptance of Ántonia would likely sway others. But it is Ántonia's marriage to Anton Cuzak that cements community acceptance. Anton treats Ántonia's "illegitimate" child as his own, which facilitates the rest of the community's treatment in kind. Moreover, as we will see in the following section, Jim's narrative increasingly focuses on the role of biology in determinations of legitimacy. Nevertheless, the Widow's story precedes Ántonia's marriage and is sufficient to begin changing Jim's perception of Ántonia. Viewed in context with the contemporaneous discourse about mannish women being bad or degenerate mothers, *My Ántonia* is rather remarkable for its affirmation of Ántonia as not just a fertile woman but as an appropriate, skilled mother. The novel is equally noteworthy for the efficacy of Cather's project of rationalization. Jim is an easy target, primed to see his childhood friend in a more positive light. But the Widow's legitimizing narrative worked on critics, too, who largely read Ántonia's earth mother role as her apotheosis, her masculinity as a phase, and the novel's conclusion as a retreat into convention rather than an extension of Cather's engagement with non-normative gender.

Masculine Earth Mother

In the previous two sections of this chapter, I focused on Jim's and then the Widow's narratives to demonstrate their role in moving Ántonia and her baby across the boundary of community legitimacy. In this final section I return to Jim's narration of Ántonia's life. In the earth mother narrative he constructs for her later years, biology—specifically eugenic ideas related to genetic inheritance—rises to the surface as a key factor in Jim's construction of legitimacy. Once Jim settles on narratives of Ántonia as a heterosexual woman and legitimate mother, he rationalizes her remaining masculinity by spinning a tale of her as a mythic earth mother figure. I do not entirely disagree with readings of this section of the novel as a retreat to conventionality. Nevertheless, my reading of the final section also shows Cather at her most radical: Ántonia's masculinity persists to the end and is part of what makes her an excellent mother. At the same time, the novel's endorsement of eugenic principles—albeit an unusual, slightly more open-minded version than that promoted by mainstream American eugenicists—is rooted in deeply racist assumptions of a hierarchy of races.[21]

Cather's brief mythologization of Jim's meeting with the Widow fore-shadows a more extended engagement with myth in Jim's narrativization of Ántonia as earth mother. This territory has been amply covered in Cather criticism (see Carden, Lambert, and Wiesenthal, among others). In sum, the critical consensus holds that the final book of *My Ántonia* invokes earth mother mythology through Jim's use of language that emphasizes the abundant vitality of Ántonia's brood and points to her as the source of it. In one well-known scene, he describes all ten of her children coming up from an underground cellar: "they all came running up the steps together, big and little, tow heads and gold heads and brown, and flashing little naked legs; a veritable explosion of life out of the dark cave into the sunlight. It made me dizzy for a moment" (164). The novel concludes with Jim calling Ántonia "a rich mine of life, like the founders of early races" (171). These scenes and others like it lead Deborah G. Lambert to argue that the final book of the novel, titled "Cuzak's Boys" after Ántonia's married name, shapes Ántonia into a symbol of "nourishment, protection, fertility, growth, and abundance: energy in service to the patriarchy, producing not 'Ántonia's children' but 'Cuzak's boys'" (689). That Cather would draw so overtly on mythology for the novel's conclusion fits with her thematic emphasis on narrative as central to social determinations of legitimacy. Ántonia's life fits the contours of earth mother mythology, which facilitates Jim's narration of her as a legitimate American woman.

Nevertheless, the novel's conclusion is far more radical than Jim real-izes because he overlooks what an unusual earth mother Ántonia makes. Cather depicts Ántonia as a masculine woman in motherhood, with the physical roughening she experiences as a teenage farmhand only accelerating as she has children. When Jim finally reunites with her after twenty years away, he finds "a stalwart, brown woman, flat-chested"; a woman whose hair is "grizzled" and whose skin, "so brown and hardened, had not that look of flabbiness, as if the sap beneath it had been secretly drawn away" that other women have (163). The people of Black Hawk, one imagines, would be more likely to think of a man than a woman if they heard adjectives such as "stalwart," "grizzled," and "hardened" out of context, and Jim uses similar terms to disparage Ántonia's masculinity as a teenage farmhand. Therefore, it is her femininity in Black Hawk that is the aberration because she returns to masculine comportment after a period of assimilation to midwestern standards of womanhood. Indeed, despite Jim's best efforts to the contrary, we can see that if any gender comportment is legitimate or authentic for Ántonia, it is masculinity. With the exception of her first pregnancy—her initial experience of this form of embodiment traditionally thought of as feminine—Ántonia is happier working the land than she was in Black Hawk.

Furthermore, the physical strength Jim found distasteful and threatening now facilitates her success as a mother. Ántonia says, "I belong on a farm. I'm never lonesome here like I used to be in town. You remember what sad spells I used to have, when I did n't know what was the matter with me? I've never had them out here" (166). Immediately thereafter she makes the statement about not minding "a bit of work, if I don't have to put up with sadness" (166). Her claim that the land she and Anton bought needed "a bit of work" is an understatement. Running a successful farm is never easy, and the Cuzak's land requires nearly a decade of toil before it is productive (166). All the while, Ántonia bears nine more children and her body becomes harder, rougher, and flatter (in contrast to the Widow's emphasis on the roundness of Ántonia's pregnant body). Intriguingly, Ántonia chalks up the farm's success to her physical endurance, saying, "We'd never have got through if I had n't been so strong. I've always had good health, thank God, and I was able to help him [Anton] in the fields until right up to the time before my babies came" (166). With these statements, Cather connects Ántonia's success as a mother to her success as a farmer: neither the crops nor the children would be so healthy if not for Ántonia's physical strength. Her farm is at its most fertile when her body is at its most masculine. Moreover, the physical strength and endurance that once disturbed Jim now helps make her a mother capable of providing for her family, and the pride Jim once found distasteful he now finds enchanting.[22] Cather thus subtly implies that Jim was wrong to try to assimilate her because the qualities he would change are the same ones that make her a figure of rejuvenation. Motherhood gives Ántonia cover to be masculine and to work the land as she pleases. She has "proven" her legitimacy as a heterosexual woman through her fecundity. The more children she has, the more masculine her body becomes and the less she needs to apologize for it to maintain the approval of her neighbors.

As should be clear by now, I read Jim's earth mother narrative as springing from the strength of the assumed connection between pregnancy and femininity. This assumption explains why Jim perceives her as a stereotypically feminine figure despite the persistence of her masculinity, and also why he no longer narrates her strength as objectionable as he did before she had children. When Jim first sees Ántonia after the twenty-year absence, he says that her appearance came as "a shock" that takes a moment to reconcile (161). He credits his surprise to the many intervening years between this visit and the last. While this reason is plausible enough, I also read in his reaction a struggle to reconcile Ántonia's masculinity with her maternity, for she is surrounded by children when he first sees her. Critics usually understand the thinness and hardness of her body as an indication that she gave all her vitality to her children and her farm. As I have discussed elsewhere, women sucked dry by multiple pregnancies was a common trope in the interwar years, but these women are usually exhausted and desperate to stop having children (*Conceived*, ch. 1). Ántonia, by contrast, "had not lost the fire of life" and seems as happy and robust as when she was a teenager working the farm (163). Counterintuitively, repeated pregnancy shapes Ántonia's body into a form she prefers by making it harder, thinner, and less feminine. By resisting the impulse to rationalize Ántonia's masculinity as Jim does—holding her gender and her maternity in mind simultaneously—we can see Cather's invocation of the earth mother figure as distinctly radical, not conservative as it is often thought to be.

Cather's narrative positions Ántonia as rooted in the American soil through her farming. This rooting is apparent in an additional way that counters the radical valence of the novel's conclusion. Eugenic-influenced ideas of biology form an important part of Cather's commentary on legitimacy. As discussed earlier, one of the reasons Jim perceives teenaged Ántonia as illegitimate is due to her darkening skin, which he associates with people of "lower" races. Recall, too, Jim's statements about the weakness of the American-born women of Black Hawk, whose bodies ask nothing more than to be left alone. These statements evoke eugenic debates of the day in which America was feared to be degenerating.[23]

The version of eugenics that is ultimately endorsed by the novel is an unusual one in that it affirms the vitality of a poor, uneducated, immigrant woman as having the potential to improve the genetic stock of Americans.

To better gauge the abnormality of the novel's eugenic stance, it is helpful to compare it to another interwar text that deals with reproduction and eugenics, *Herland* by Charlotte Perkins Gilman (originally published in 1915). This utopian novel focuses on three American explorers who "discover" a community of women that has survived on its own, without contact from the outside world, for thousands of years. These women have been able to survive because they developed the capacity for parthenogenesis; and they only give birth to female offspring. The society is defined by reverence for maternity, "unfailing dignity and good taste" (105), "daring social inventiveness," "mechanical and scientific development," "social consciousness," "fair-minded intelligence," "health and vigor" (106). In short, this society manifests qualities that many people in interwar America thought to be contrary to women's nature. According to the novel, Herland was able to develop into a utopian community because of two factors: the *absence* of men and the conscious application of eugenic principles. The women of Herland "devoted their combined intelligence to that problem—how to make the best kind of people" (86). What constitutes the "best" in this society is white, tall, able-bodied; as Beth Sutton-Ramspeck states, the novel depicts Herlanders as "admirably built to bear healthy daughters" (16).[24] The Herlanders who are "found unfit" are not allowed to reproduce (95). Gilman used *Herland* to espouse eugenic beliefs about the perfectibility of the human race. For Gilman, notes Sutton-Ramspeck, "wise marriage could advance human evolution—and prevent degeneration of the human race. . . . For humanity in general to attain Herland's perfection, women must consider reproductive fitness and avoid diseased mates" (15). The women of Herland kept to themselves for two centuries, reproducing parthenogenically and, in the logic of the book, steadily improving their genetic stock through selective reproduction.

Their isolationist tendencies stand in stark contrast to the expansionist version of eugenics that Cather's narrator espouses. Nevertheless, the women of Herland do see a potential benefit in expanding their gene pool and reproductive processes through the addition of men. (According to Herlanders, and to Gilman herself, "bisexual reproduction" is superior to parthenogenesis because it is the method used by the most evolved animals [Sutton-Ramspeck 16].) They are not willing to breed with just any men, however. The narrator refers, with no trace of irony, to the communities nearest Herland as "savages" whose lives are primitive and undeveloped (34). Men from these communities who attempt to infiltrate Herland never return, presumably killed by the athletic Herlanders, who are skilled fighters when pushed to it. Rather, the first men they consider to be viable options for reproductive partners are the three wealthy, white American men who are the protagonists of *Herland*. By contrast, Cather wrote a novel in which a dark-skinned, poor, uneducated immigrant woman is America's best hope for rejuvenation. As I note later, Cather's eugenic vision was racist, classist, and ableist, but it was more expansive that that advocated by contemporaneous authors. Cather's belief in the value of immigrants such as Ántonia had roots in hard work and connection to the land. Indeed, Linda Lizut Helstern argues that the eugenic ideas promoted by anthropologist Franz Boas influenced Cather while writing *My Ántonia*. According to Boas's theory, working the land literally changes one's offspring by changing the "cephalic" or skull shape of the fetus in utero (261). Helstern continues: "Geography and climate, then, the very land that Willa Cather showcases so effectively, makes the infant its own, according to this updated version of eugenic theory. . . . Ántonia had barely reached puberty when she began her physical labor in the fields, and from the ploughing to the threshing, she worked in the fields the entire season she was pregnant with her oldest daughter" (261). Accordingly, Jim's earth mother narrative positions Ántonia and her children as literally and metaphorically part of the American soil. The fruit cave from which Ántonia's children burst forth is a rather obvious metaphor for a womb, with the preserved food it contains nourishing a new, vibrant lineage of Americans. Because Ántonia and her family once lived in an underground dugout similar to this one when they first arrived in the United States, Jim's narrative implicitly, belatedly, legitimizes Ántonia as a product of the American soil, too, through these echoing descriptions (Rosowski 441).

The connection between geography and embodiment occurs elsewhere in Cather's prairie trilogy. The protagonist of *Song of the Lark*, Thea Kronborg, is a singer who finds musical inspiration in Panther Canyon, Arizona. Kronborg "found herself trying to walk as [Native American women] must have walked, with a feeling in her feet and knees and loins which she had never known before—which must have come up to her out of the accustomed dust of that rocky trail" (277).[25] As Kronborg is rejuvenated by her contact with American soil, Jim depicts Ántonia as a potential source of rejuvenation for both the American people and the land, calling her "a rich mine of life, like the founders of early races" (171).

That Jim should portray Ántonia as distinctly American may surprise some readers since Ántonia has, by this point in the novel, dropped many of the traits she learned during her time in Black Hawk. She mostly speaks

Czech at home, mingles with "Bohunk crowd[s]" when away from home, and prepares foods that "Americans don't have," such as spiced plums and kolaches (172, 164). Jim even notes that Ántonia's husband is in the habit of glancing sideways at people "as a work-horse does its yoke-mate" (173), a phrase that echoes his derisive comparison of Ántonia to a draft horse. This time, however, Jim's metaphor expresses approval, for he says that Anton's habit shows "frankness and good-nature" (173). This example shows Cather revising and correcting her narrator's desire for Ántonia's assimilation.

"Americanization," as Cather called it in a 1923 essay, extinguished much of the intelligence, artistry, and skill of Nebraska's immigrant communities, which "spread across our bronze prairies like the daubs of color on a painter's palette. They brought with them something that this neutral new world needed even more than the immigrants needed land. Unfortunately, their American neighbors were seldom open-minded enough to . . . profit by their older traditions" ("Nebraska" 325). Had Ántonia assimilated as Jim once wished, she would have lost the "color" that Black Hawk metaphorically needs, even if her literal color—her skin—was less desired.

Although Cather's narrator does not depict Ántonia's fecundity as threatening, as was common in the interwar years, the novel suggests that only some immigrants make "good stock." In the eugenic logic of the novel, Ántonia's younger brother, Marek, remains part of the "lower" races. Marek is mentally disabled and a poor farmer, consistently overworking the farm animals (71). Jim never describes Marek as part of the land, much less a potential rejuvenator of America. Becoming part of the land through successful farming helps Jim perceive Ántonia as a good immigrant, which in turn allows him to depict her as good stock.[26] The rest of the novel tacitly endorses Jim's position because his own life corroborates the eugenic idea that the American race is degenerating. Jim marries a woman with much more in common with the "town girls" than the "hired girls" from the country, but his marriage is unhappy and childless (7). As Lindemann puts it, "Cather's early fiction . . . sometimes hierarchizes [racial] characteristics in ways that suggest some races are superior to and some more threatening than others. It also demonstrates, however, that normativity is dangerous and destructive, differences can be salubrious, and transgressions can produce beneficial change" (*Willa Cather* 67). In the end, Cather does not correct or alter Jim's consecration of Ántonia as an earth mother. As I have shown, however, this mythological hero is much queerer than he acknowledges. As such, the novel's depiction of gender and pregnancy is a radical counterweight to its depiction of race and nationality.

Masculine Female Characters

Reading *My Ántonia* for its representation of mannish pregnancy helps us appreciate the full range of Cather's engagement with gendered discourse. More broadly, this chapter has shown how a consideration of the rhetoric surrounding masculinity and pregnancy can open up new readings of familiar texts such as *My Ántonia*. As mentioned earlier, Ántonia has much in common with Charlotte Rittenmeyer from Faulkner's *If I Forget Thee, Jerusalem*, which is the focus of chapter 3. Beyond their gender, Ántonia and Charlotte also share an aptitude for art. Several critics have read Ántonia as an oral storyteller. Judith Woolley, for instance, argues that Ántonia's talent is distinctly embodied: "In Jim's description of Ántonia's storytelling, Ántonia's voice—both her physical voice and her artistic style and tone—is unique and striking, with its 'peculiarly engaging quality' and its implied roots in her 'life itself'" (np). Charlotte, you will recall, is a sculptor and painter who runs away from her family to pursue a life suffused with both love and art. Charlotte produces art that Faulkner associates with hardness and masculinity, which therefore makes it "real" or legitimate art in the novel's logic. Conversely, Cather was ambivalent about her protagonist's art form, oral storytelling. Cather valued folk art but knew this opinion diverged from the dominant opinion among the male-centric literary establishment whose respect she coveted; she also knew that folk art is more commonly associated with femininity and that "high" or "real" art was associated with masculinity (Woolley np). Unsurprisingly, then, both Cather and Faulkner shied away from asserting the possibility that legitimate artistic creation and procreation can exist compatibly in a female body. Written art, the "real" kind of art, emanates from a male narrator in Cather's novel (Jim's creation of the manuscript "My Ántonia"), and female biology ultimately gets in the way of artistic creation for Faulkner's female artist.

Comparing these characters reveals less predictable conclusions too. The differences between Charlotte and Ántonia in terms of class, nationality, and race highlight the disparity in opportunities for inverted women in the interwar era. Although Charlotte is not wealthy, she is a middle-class, American-born white woman who moves in artistic communities. As such, she has far more resources available to her than a dark-skinned immigrant woman in rural America. Charlotte is able to arrange an affair with a man who can (at least for a while) make sufficient money to support her; to pursue her art in urban locations, where people have enough interest in her avant-garde creations that she is able to support herself and her lover on the sales; and to feel secure enough to walk away from commercial success when she no longer finds it worthwhile. Ántonia has none of these resources. She works the fields to eat and keep a roof over her head, even if these exigencies do offer cover for the pleasures of masculine embodiment. When Ántonia runs off with a man, he abandons her and she has no option but to return home to work the fields once again. These differences in opportunity will become even more apparent when considered alongside Djuna Barnes's *Nightwood*. The focus of the next chapter, this novel depicts characters for whom no amount of money or privilege would allow them to gain acceptance and social legitimacy. As I will show, Barnes's novel demonstrates the limits of narrative in social determinations of legitimacy.

Chapter 5

"Conceiving herself pregnant before she was"

Parental Impressions and the Limits of Reproductive Legitimacy in *Nightwood*

Similar to *My Ántonia*, the focus of the previous chapter, Djuna Barnes's *Nightwood* (1936) treats masculine procreation sympathetically. And like *My Ántonia*'s positioning of narrative as a powerful force—capable of making a legitimate child from one born out of wedlock—language, stories, and the imagination have the ability to shape kinship in *Nightwood* too. This is where the similarities end. While Cather's novel affirms the value of legitimacy, Barnes's text lampoons it.

In this chapter, I discuss a version of masculine pregnancy that is based on an ancient theory of the gestator-fetal bond called parental impressions. Variations on the theory have circulated widely in folk belief since antiquity, and these beliefs influenced medical and scientific discourse throughout the following centuries, including the twentieth (Mazzoni 6–17). Today, we frequently hear about the effects of the pregnant person's emotions and nutrition on the fetus, but the theory of parental impressions is far more literal than the relationship that medical professionals tend to discuss in the twenty-first century. As Christina Mazzoni explains, in various versions of parental impression theory the pregnant person's "fear of pigs could lead to a cleft palate" and "craving for milk could lead to a white stripe of hair" in the baby (22). Thus, according to parental impression theory, thoughts and desires can literally shape anatomy, which casts the imagination in a role nearly as significant as genetics when it comes to bloodlines and kinship.

Characters in *Nightwood*, I argue, deploy the theory of parental impressions to a specific end: to displace the masculinity of the father onto the body of the gestating mother in an attempt to have sons who embody patriarchal values.[1] The phrasing of my argument may strike some readers as prescriptive and heteronormative, particularly the part about "the masculinity of the father." I use this phrasing advisedly, however, because Barnes was working under the shadow of growing fascist forces and was well aware of the patriarchal foundations of fascist discourse. To reflect this, in *Nightwood* she conflates "the father" with "the ruler." By depicting characters who displace the patriarchal masculinity of this symbolic father onto the mothers in *Nightwood*, the novel queers the figure of the "race mother" and ridicules the grounds on which concepts such as nationalism, legitimacy, and kinship are based.[2] Masculinity writ large is not the object of Barnes's critique—indeed, mannish women are treated sympathetically—but rather patriarchal masculinity.

Barnes's depiction of this different version of masculine pregnancy matters both because it expands our understanding of modernist uses of the trope and because it demonstrates that Barnes scorned the very idea of reproductive legitimacy. Daniella Caselli has persuasively argued that Barnes rejected *literary* legitimacy. Caselli states that in nearly every major text, Barnes's "engagement with genealogy on the thematic level goes hand in hand with a refusal to either acknowledge a literary legacy or to produce lawful [literary] offspring, thus openly waging war against linguistic and literary legitimacy" (4). For Caselli, Barnes's rejection of literary legitimacy manifests in her obfuscation of influences and allusions (3). Barnes heaped intertextual references into her writing and frequently distorted quotations, an approach to source materials that Caselli aptly calls "unreverential and promiscuous" (34). She reads this aesthetic practice as an attempt by Barnes to "unfather" (ibid.) her writing: "The wide variety of intertextual and intratextual references in Barnes produce her text as neither self-sufficient nor belonging to a specific lineage: her texts are bastard offspring, whose similarities and alikeness can be attributed—without much certainty—to a number of progenitors" (86).[3] My argument complements Caselli's by showing that Barnes also rejected reproductive legitimacy and, moreover, it nuances Caselli by demonstrating that Barnes's efforts to 'unfather' offspring (thematically and literarily) were more complex than a straightforward rejection of the heterosexual family. By displacing patriarchal masculinity onto the body of the mother, *Nightwood* undermines the straightness of even the nuclear family, the presumed bastion of state-sanctioned legitimacy. Instead of arguing the legitimacy of queer (pro)creation, as Cather does, Barnes argues the illegitimacy of straight families. This is not to suggest that Barnes advocates a return to genealogical purity, as though modernity had corrupted once-pure family lines. Rather, the point is that reproductive legitimacy—the idea that we can draw lines between bastard and heir, pure and impure, straight and queer—is irredeemably flawed.

The grounds on which Barnes bases this rejection of reproductive legitimacy in *Nightwood* are as complex as they are fascinating, especially for literary scholars. Barnes rejects reproductive legitimacy because, she implies, all kinship is fictional. The idea of fictional kinship, as I am calling it, is an adaptation of the anthropological concept of *fictive* kinship, which denotes "a relationship, based not on blood or marriage but rather on religious rituals or close friendship ties, that replicates many of the rights and obligations usually associated with family ties" (Ebaugh and Curry 189). The term has fallen out of favor, in part because it suggests that fictive bonds are less real or meaningful than blood- or marriage-based kinship (a connotation that was not intended in the term's coinage, as I later explain).[4] *Chosen family* and *chosen kin* are often preferred today, especially in queer communities where these relationships are sometimes stronger than those with families of origin. Barnes depicts kinship as not only *fictive*, in the sense of unreal, but also *fictional*, that is, constituted by narrative and the imagination. Kinship being fictional means that familial ties depend at least as much on narrative and the imagination as on blood- and marriage-based ties. With *Nightwood*, Barnes posits that much of what we think of as fixed regarding kinship (i.e., biology, anatomy, and genealogy) is mutable through the power of parental impressions. As a result, everyone in *Nightwood* is illegitimate because biological ties are no more "real" or stable than any other ones.

The opening scenes of *Nightwood* establish a focus on reproduction and kinship that persists throughout the novel. It begins with the birth of Felix Volkbein under the "Volkbein arms" and the "bifurcated wings of the House of Hapsburg" (4). We soon learn, however, that Felix is not a Volkbein at all. His father, Guido, was an Italian Jew who created an alternate, noble lineage when he needed "an alibi for the blood" in an increasingly fascist Europe (10). Guido fabricates this lineage to save his family from a very real threat, but his choice to claim nobility is also a grab at social status. Felix is aware of the deception and, rather than fleeing from it, becomes obsessed with "Old Europe: aristocracy, nobility, royalty," thinking that "the great past might mend a little if he bowed low enough" (11; 12). He becomes determined to find a wife suited to carry on the fabricated family line. An important aspect of Barnes's commentary on kinship and gender involves Felix's marriage to the woman he chooses for this role, Robin Vote, who is decidedly masculine. After marriage, Robin prepares for motherhood by "conceiving herself pregnant" at Felix's behest (49), which I read as a version of parental impressionism. In the scenes dealing with Robin's pregnancy, thoughts have the power to shape offspring in the womb, both physically and psychologically. Robin's relationships—with Felix and with multiple women after she leaves Felix—form the backbone of the novel's plot. Robin is unfaithful to everyone, and her nighttime escapades in the Paris demimonde cause heartache for Felix and two of her lovers, Nora Flood and Jenny Petherbridge. In their sorrows, they turn to the novel's best-known character, "Doctor Matthew-Mighty-grain-of-salt-Dante-O'Connor" (87). O'Connor is a Tiresian figure who functions as confessor, physician, and psychiatrist for the jilted lovers. Although I do not focus on O'Connor in the present chapter, I discuss this queer character's reproductive longing in the coda.

Barnes bristled at binaries, labels, and categories, particularly those related to gender and sexuality. She famously rejected the label "lesbian," saying "I'm not a lesbian; I just loved Thelma" in reference to Thelma Wood, the woman who inspired the character of Robin Vote (qtd. in Sniader Lanser 165). This statement of Barnes's has vexed generations of lesbian and queer critics who would claim her as their own, but I think Frances M. Doughty is right to reject as irrelevant the question of whether Barnes was a lesbian. Doughty states, "The issue is not whether Barnes was a lesbian or a heterosexual, but that she was neither. . . . Her refusal to take on a lesbian social identity comes not from fear of stigma but from fear of suffocation" (149–50). Labels carry social expectations that Barnes refused to shape her life around. This fact helps us understand the character of Robin Vote, who likewise runs from suffocating identities. Starting with Felix, lovers repeatedly attempt to write Robin's life into their ideas of what her identity should be and how those identities should determine the course of her life. At great psychological cost, she rejects the fictions of kinship others attempt to create for her by becoming a person who is impossible to pin down in any one narrative.

This chapter begins by demonstrating that Barnes displaces the masculinity of the father onto the body of the mother via parental impressions. I then connect this reading to Barnes's rejection of reproductive legitimacy, showing that *Nightwood* positions kinship as fictional and all the characters in the novel as illegitimate, even those who seem to have the greatest claims to legitimacy. Since Robin Vote's rejection of reproductive legitimacy is tied—in ways I will demonstrate—to the notion of travel, this section of the chapter also positions *Nightwood* in a broader constellation of travel narratives featuring pregnant protagonists, particularly Olive Moore's *Spleen*. In the third section of this chapter, I show that Barnes is attentive to both the power of fiction in the realm of kinship as well as the limits of that power. Even though *Nightwood* is a novel concerned with fiction's outsize role in reproductive legitimacy, Barnes nevertheless suggests that not all forms of kinship can or should be legitimized through narrative and the imagination. Indeed, chasing legitimacy—constructing familial fictions in the hopes of gaining it—compounds traumas for many of Barnes's characters.

Before continuing, I want to address my approach to *Nightwood*. It is a beguiling novel for a literary critic. Barnes's writing is so densely allusive and her language so poetic that any direct quote is likely to raise questions and suggest other topics that need following up. Tying up one loose end causes five others to unravel, making criticism a Sisyphean task. Many scholars have noted this quality; it led Caselli to say *Nightwood* "disobeys all the rules it lays down, often at the price of its own inappropriate illegibility" (156). In recognition of the fact that Barnes's language is likely to raise a multitude of questions, I have endeavored to provide rich footnotes that will direct readers to scholarship that addresses the various questions this chapter raises along the way. The footnotes allow me to keep a singular focus on Barnes's engagement with the trope of masculine pregnancy.

Part One: Masculine Mothers and Parental Impressions

The masculinity of pregnant women in *Nightwood* is key to Barnes's rejection of reproductive legitimacy. As with the titular character of Willa Cather's *My Ántonia*, my reading of characters in this book as masculine women is precisely that, *a* reading. The line between mannishness and transness is porous, if it even exists, and I see no benefit in attempting to make the boundary watertight. This is particularly true for texts authored by Barnes, who found labels hateful and wrote characters who defy easy categorization. I have opted for a reading of Hedvig Volkbein and Robin Vote as masculine women because they self-identify as women and also exhibit behaviors and traits that are called masculine in the pages of the book. Mannishness and inversion were the dominant frameworks by which most people in the United States and Europe would have attempted to understand such individuals. Barnes was aware of these frameworks and at times engages them directly in her oeuvre. As such, I find mannishness to be a revealing framework for a consideration of Robin and Hedvig while each is pregnant.

In this section of the chapter, I establish the masculinity of the mothers in *Nightwood* and argue that Barnes was not only familiar with the theory of parental impressions but also that it informed her depictions of masculine pregnancy. I discuss two different versions of masculine pregnancy here. The first will be familiar to readers: masculine women who are physically pregnant. In this category I first consider Robin and then her mother-in-law, Hedvig (Felix's mother). The second version involves men who attempt to impress their thoughts and desires onto the maternal body in a bid to control gestation. Robin and Hedvig are mannish women independent of these impressions, but both of their husbands attempt to displace an additional and very specific kind of masculinity—one with roots in fascism—onto them and thereby their offspring. In my reading of *Nightwood*, Felix and his father, Guido, attempt to shape the physical, emotional, and intellectual composition of their offspring, and they do so primarily through stories and imaginative visions. As one might expect of Barnes, the novel queers the masculinity of "the father" such that it is actually the mother's masculinity that is displaced onto the offspring.

Mannish Pregnancies

The novel's depiction of Robin Vote as masculine is overt. The narrator tells us that strangers who encounter Robin while she is pregnant regard her as "a tall girl with the body of a boy," a person with "broad shoulders" and "feet large and as earthly as the feet of a monk" (50). Pamela Caughie et al. note that Barnes "uses the term 'invert' only once [in *Nightwood*], and that is in relation to Robin Vote" ("Storm Clouds" 235). What is most striking about Barnes's depiction of Robin is that she does not start describing Robin's body as masculine until Robin has conceived. The significance of this shift is largely unrecognized in the critical conversation because of the undertheorized nature of Robin's pregnancy, especially her masculinity during it, despite the novel being the focus of numerous queer readings.[5] In one of these readings, Hannah Roche views Robin "not as a cross-dressing adult but as a childlike gamine figure who, in Freud's terms, has the 'freedom to range equally over male and female objects'" (131). What I want to highlight is the fact that Robin "ranges" over masculine territory while pregnant. The aforementioned description of Robin as having "the body of a boy" occurs just several paragraphs after she conceives. Until this point in the novel, Barnes has described Robin's body largely in terms that connote femininity, as when Robin is introduced to readers as a person with "beautiful" hands and the posture of a dancer (38), or else with adjectives that are gender neutral. In a noteworthy change, Barnes uses overtly male or masculine descriptors while Robin is pregnant. Moreover, these descriptions refer to her body, not just her clothing. Her "broad shoulders" and feet of a monk (50) suggest elements of adult male embodiment. In other words, Robin's masculinity cannot entirely be chalked up to the gamine figure of the New Woman who dresses in masculine clothing. Robin's embodiment while pregnant bears markers of adult masculinity.

Most scholars interested in gender and sexuality focus on Robin's same-sex relationships and sideline her pregnancy. In a way, these readings take a cue from Barnes herself in that they position Robin's marriage and childbirth as diversions from the main point of the novel, namely her relationships with women. Barnes explained that she wrote Robin's marriage and pregnancy into *Nightwood* as a preemptive refutation of the classic Freudian explanation for female inversion, which is one of failure. As Rebecca Jennings explains, female inversion was thought to be a result of " 'arrested development': a girl becoming fixed at an earlier stage of sexual development and failing to reach adult heterosexuality. Much of the literature of the time focused on this issue of maturity, presenting heterosexual—ideally, married—women as mature and inverts as sexually and emotionally immature" (Jennings 886). In the popular imagination, this theory was reduced to the idea that an inverted woman does not know what she is missing ("once she sleeps with a man she won't go back"). Barnes rejected this idea outright. She wrote of the main female characters in *Nightwood*, tongue firmly in cheek, "Well of course those two women would never have been in love with each other if they had been normal, if any man had slept with them, if they had been well f—and had born [*sic*] a child. . . . I married Robin to prove this point, she had married, had had a child yet was still 'incurable' " (qtd. in Plumb xviii). This quote suggests that Barnes wrote Robin's marriage precisely to undermine psychoanalytic theories rather than as a central part of the narrative.

Nevertheless, the intensity of Robin's rejection of motherhood belies an importance not acknowledged in Barnes's flippant comment. Indeed, nothing in Barnes's oeuvre is simple and clear-cut, even if Barnes herself might say otherwise. Although her comment implies that Robin's marriage and pregnancy are no more significant than a rejection of Freudian theories, the marriage plotline dominates the first fifty pages of the novel and engages themes far beyond psychoanalysis, including genealogy, religion, the life cycle, and nationality. To be sure, the refutation of psychoanalysis is there. Pregnancy does the opposite of satisfying Robin; it incites anger. Shortly after giving birth, she confronts Felix "in a fury," shouting, " 'I didn't want him!' " in reference to the child (53).[6] Robin then leaves Felix and the baby for a string of female lovers. She is no more satisfied with these women than she is with Felix, and as Barnes intended, Robin's dissatisfaction cannot be blamed on a lack of heterosexual intimacy and motherhood. Instead, motherhood itself is a catalyst for alienation. As Andrea L. Harris states, "Maternity becomes a means by which Robin understands her distance from femininity" (236). In the sense that femininity is often understood as coextensive with motherhood and pregnancy, this argument holds. That Robin is decidedly not feminine while pregnant does show her distance from societal norms associated with maternity, but Harris's reading also highlights the strength of the ideological connection between pregnancy and femininity, that is, our deep-seated impulse to align the two. After all, Harris elsewhere calls childbirth the "most feminine of acts" (236). Reading *Nightwood* through the lens of masculine pregnancy pushes analysis in a different direction. In my reading of the novel, Barnes challenges us to rethink not only psychoanalytic theories but also the very foundations of our ideas about reproduction by stretching apart the close association between femininity and pregnancy.

Robin's mother-in-law, Hedvig, is a striking refutation of this ideological association. By the end of her life, Hedvig has wholly become an avatar of patriarchal masculinity and dies for its cause. Her husband, Guido, impresses this patriarchal version of masculinity onto her body while she is pregnant with Felix, and she fully embraces this role by the time she passes away. Barnes's depiction of Hedvig directly engages Nazi gender norms, both the expectation of hypermasculinity in men and the insistence on maternal devotion in women. Historian Jill Stephenson characterizes these gender norms as such: "the 'Aryan', 'hereditarily healthy' woman who had not compromised her 'value' by becoming 'asocial' was to marry an equally 'valuable' man and produce several 'valuable' children, to combat Germany's numerical disadvantage compared with its perceived enemies. The Nazi message to women was: be a mother, first, foremost and always, preferably a married mother of several children. . . . All other aspects of a 'valuable Aryan' woman's life had to accommodate that core value; 'worthless' women were to be prevented from reproducing" (14). To be asocial or anti-social, as

I discuss in chapter 1, meant to be shirking one's duties to the nation. In the context of fascist Europe, women who did not reproduce were seen as placing their own comfort over the nation's need for soldiers and workers. The "race mother" is the opposite of the asocial woman. The concept of the race mother, prevalent in fascist Europe, posits that "mothers reproduce bodies not in a social vacuum but for either a dominant or a subordinate group," and that reproduction and childrearing must be controlled so that dominant groups can continue to dominate and grow (Doyle 5).

Unsurprisingly, Barnes's novel refuses easy comparisons: Hedvig is not a simple representative of the race mother, just as her husband, Guido, is not simply Nazi militaristic manhood. Instead, Hedvig is both the race mother and the embodiment of the patriarchy, representing the nation and the military. As mentioned at the outset of this chapter, Hedvig dies giving birth to Felix. Her final act is to "thrust" the infant away "with the gross splendor of a general saluting the flag" (3). The aggressive gesture is a fitting end for someone who went through life with a military bearing, for she had a "goose-step of a stride" and the "slight repercussion of movement common to military men" (6). As Sharon Marcus says, "Hedvig is German militarism" (157).[7] It is this masculinity that Felix later attempts to impress on his offspring and that Robin runs from.

Yet Hedvig's symbolic uprightness is undercut by her queerness as a masculine mother. And because Barnes uses Hedvig as an archetype, she can be read as representing all bloodlines that claim purity. Hedvig's queerness, therefore, raises the specter of inversion and illegitimacy in even the most "valuable" of citizens.[8] Stephenson notes that the value of a woman in fascist Europe was largely tied to her reproduction, stating, "the 'valuable' were of 'Aryan' stock, with no alleged hereditary blemishes through 'Aryan' antecedents marrying and reproducing with people from other races" (12). According to this value system, Hedvig's most obvious offense is that of marrying a "worthless" man in disguise and reproducing with him (recall Guido's fabricated family lineage).[9] Her offense to the Nazi value system goes deeper, however, for her masculinity places her close to the "valueless" women classed as "asocial": lesbians, single mothers, or those women who failed to conform to the rigid gender norms prescribed by the Nazi party (Stephenson 13). If Hedvig is German militarism, her character signals the failures of this system to police divisions between valuable and worthless, legitimate and illegitimate. Hedvig's mannish pregnancy is therefore an important facet of Barnes's depiction of legitimacy as a concept based on dubious distinctions between right and wrong kinds of reproduction.

Further queering the Volkbein line—but also drawing uncritically on antisemitic stereotypes of Jewish men as feminine—Barnes uses reproductive language to describe Felix and Guido.[10] For instance, the elder Guido is described as having a protruding stomach that "brought into prominence the buttons of his waistcoat and trousers, marking the exact centre of his body with the *obstetric* line seen on fruits" (emphasis added 4). Regarding Felix, Barnes frequently uses the term *labor* and its cognates in connection with this character. We read that "Felix labored" with the re-creation of history (46) and that his face is defined by "laborious melancholy" (11). Additionally, Felix is engaged in "making a destiny for himself, through laborious and untiring travail" (46). In the twentieth century, *travail* most frequently referred to "physical or mental work, esp. of a painful or laborious nature," yet at earlier times the term carried a specifically reproductive inflection: "woman's labour, childbirth" ("travail"). (Barnes also engages this older connotation, which I later demonstrate.) As a result of this reproductive language, the Volkbein men can also be read as examples of masculine pregnancies. All members of the Volkbein line, men and women, Jew and Christian, are thereby depicted as illegitimate in the fascist discourse of the day.

The Volkbein marriage and its early demise can be read in part as a satire on the aristocracy's inability to see the inevitable end to their way of life. Guido dies early, passing away from fever six months before his wife dies in childbirth (3). The progenitors of the Volkbein line are dead or dying almost before the novel begins, and the systems of kinship and reproductive legitimacy that defined their lives are shown to be irredeemably flawed. It is important to note that Hedvig is Viennese rather than German (3), and she married an Italian man who falsely claims Austrian aristocratic ancestry. All of these facts implicate Austro-Hungarian aristocracy, Italian fascism, and German militarism in Barnes's critique. The fact that Barnes jumbles all these geographic and political references together implicates the whole rather than any specific tradition and is a manifestation of Barnes's rejection of patriarchal kinship and legitimacy writ large.

Parental Impressions

Archival records suggest that Barnes was aware of parental impression theory and that it informed the masculine pregnancies discussed above. By referring to *parental* impressions as opposed to the more common *maternal* impressions, I am following Wendy Doniger and Gregory Spinner's lead.

They distinguish maternal impressions from paternal ones, and combine the two under the umbrella term *parental impressions*.[11] What they call *paternal* impressions are versions of the theory in which men are believed to have the ability to make impressions on the fetus by dictating what a pregnant person thinks, imagines, and sees during conception or while gestating. This person may or may not be the biological father. Parental impression theory—both maternal and paternal versions—circulated broadly in the interwar years and appear often in modernist literature.

Although the details change across time and place, all versions of parental impression theory posit a strong connection between the developing body of the fetus and the pregnant person's mental and emotional states. This is a much more literal relationship between fetus and gestator than is typically seen today. If modern medicine tells us that the pregnant person's diet and emotional state affect the fetus's well-being, parental impression theory holds that the fetus "saw what the mother saw, heard what she heard and felt what she felt. Any unpleasant sight or unsatisfied desire was echoed, with greater or lesser intensity, in the body of the fetus" (qtd. in Mazzoni 22). For all our claims to scientific rationality in the realm of childbearing, we moderns have not debunked this theory. Christina Mazzoni argues that versions of it persist in contemporary pregnancy manuals that advocate strict management of emotions and diet (22). Maternal impressions are often connected to food, as Mazzoni documents. For instance, some nineteenth-century Europeans believed that a pregnant woman whose craving for strawberries was not satisfied would bear a child with a strawberry-shaped birthmark (11). Although cravings are a commonly referenced source of impressions, they are far from the only one. Some impressions were thought to occur via sight, particularly when pregnant people witness acts of violence or images thought to be unsavory. This fear was so strong in late nineteenth- and early twentieth-century America that it was common to "war[n] pregnant women against entering the sideshow tent" for fear that "the very sight of a freak might be enough to deform the gestating fetus" (Adams 198). It was also believed that physical or psychological trauma experienced by the mother could impact a fetus's physical development. Hence, physical abnormalities of people deemed "freaks' " were "regularly described as the consequence of a trauma experienced by the pregnant mother" (Adams 198). Parental impression theory therefore grants enormous power to the imagination by forging a literal connection between it and the body of the fetus.

Some of the driving forces behind the theory of parental impressions are predictable: rationalization, patriarchal control, and racism. Doniger and

Spinner argue that the theory has likely persisted for so long because it allows men to rationalize away fears about adultery and assert their own paternity despite visual evidence to the contrary: "The theory of parental imprinting was one way of accounting for divergences from the expected norm without admitting the likelihood of actual impregnation by an alienating male" (98–99). Nevertheless, there is evidence to suggest that some women used the theory to their advantage to cover up infidelities. Mazzoni notes that some Italian intellectuals in the nineteenth century argued "that it was women themselves who invented the theory of maternal impressions as a deception against their husbands"; one woman, so the story goes, bore a child who resembled a friend of her husband's but explained away the likeness by claiming that the friend's platonic presence in the household was enough to impress his features on the child (Mazzoni 33). It is plausible, of course, to read this explanation of the theory as an example of misogyny since it makes men into victims of women's supposed duplicity.

The extent to which the body was capable of receiving impressions was shaped by shifting notions of race and evolution. As Kyla Schuller explains, in the nineteenth century, "impressibility was understood to be an acquired quality of the refined nervous system that accrues over evolutionary time through the habits of civilization that transform animal substrate into the cultural grounds of self-constitution" (introduction). The more evolved one was, so the theory goes, the more the body was susceptible to impressions. Where white bodies were thought to be more evolved, they were also thought to be more penetrable by outside forces.

Parental impression theory has roots far earlier than the nineteenth century. It can be found in antiquity and was particularly influential in Europe. Galen, the famous physician of second-century Rome, argued that a child's appearance was affected by what a woman saw and imagined while pregnant (Mazzoni 16). Parental impressions appear in fifteenth-century intellectual theory texts, many of which posited that "the unity between mother and fetus was emblematic of the unity of the world and of the magic relations that governed the universe" (16). The theory persisted throughout the eighteenth and nineteenth centuries in folk wisdom and science. Despite growing skepticism toward the theory in twentieth-century European medical communities, it was still treated seriously as a subject of consideration by leading doctors. For instance, Havelock Ellis devoted a section of *Studies in the Psychology of Sex*, vol. 5 (1906), to maternal impressions, presenting case studies collected "from the best medical periodical literature during the past fifteen years" (218). He admits that it was difficult to understand how impressions might occur given extant medical knowledge but concludes that "our difficulty in conceiving of the process must, however, be put aside if the fact itself can be demonstrated by convincing evidence" (218). What this evidence might be Ellis left unspecified. Sexological texts like Ellis's circulated broadly in intellectual circles in the years between the World Wars. Barnes was familiar with sexology in general and the theories of Ellis in particular (Berni 83–85).

Parental imprinting shows up frequently in interwar literature, including in works by modernists. Doniger and Spinner argue that it was a common theme in European fiction into the twentieth century (113) and cite as an example Joyce's *Portrait of the Artist as a Young Man*.[12] In it, Stephen Dedalus imagines himself "cast[ing] his shadow over the imagination" of the daughters of Ireland's patricians "before their squires begat upon them, that they might breed a race less ignoble than their own" (210). Joyce here uses paternal impressions to demonstrate Stephen Dedalus's hubris—that his imagination would be the one to improve the race—and also to castigate the ruling classes as degenerate. Additional examples of parental impressions in twentieth-century fiction cited by Doniger and Spinner include Goethe's *Elective Affinities* and E. T. A. Hoffman's "The Doubles" (114).[13]

Other modernists followed religious and spiritual movements that promoted variations on parental impression theory, and Barnes was close to several of them. Parental imprinting was "an article of faith" for people who followed the New Thought movement, which was tremendously popular in the United States in the nineteenth and early twentieth centuries (P. Ellis 416). New Thought was an offshoot of Christian Science and was, in the years leading up to *Nightwood*'s publication, best understood as "a religious healing movement" that advocated "mind-cure" principles, claiming that " 'spirit,' 'mind,' or human thought had the power to shape matter, overcome heredity, and mold desire" (Satter 9). As one might expect given this description, parental impressions show up frequently in New Thought treatises. For instance, Alice Bunker Stockham, a physician and New Thought writer, encouraged couples to practice a eugenically tinged form of impression she called "child thoughts" (Satter 148). Stockham urged men to exercise "self-control during sexual intercourse" and women to "guar[d] their thoughts during pregnancy"; doing so would allow the couple to " 'conceive children superior to themselves' " (Satter 148).[14] New Thought grew beyond Christian Science into its own powerful movement and, for a time, boasted more followers. Satter explains that "as early as 1901 William James could report that 'mind-cure principles are beginning to so pervade the air that one catches their spirit at second hand' " (6). Mabel Dodge and Mina Loy read deeply in New Thought texts (Burke, Interview), and Loy converted to Christian Science some time prior to 1914 (Burke, *Becoming* 117). As many critics have noted, Loy and Barnes were friendly during this period; Loy is furthermore the model for the character Patience Scalpel in Barnes's *Ladies Almanack* (Hanscombe and Smyers 112–28). Barnes's own mother converted to Christian Science in the 1930s. Barnes was therefore closely associated with people who would have been familiar with parental impression theory, and she moreover lived in an environment in which one could "catch the spirit of impressionism at second hand," to paraphrase James.

The influence of parental impressionism on *Nightwood* is most apparent in Barnes's depiction of the Volkbein men.[15] Considering first the relatively straightforward example of displaced masculinity in the relationship of the elder Volkbeins, Guido and Hedvig, will make the more complicated dynamic between Robin and Felix easier to understand. Historical records contain many examples of men attempting to shape offspring through thought, the imagination, and desire (Doniger and Spinner 107–12). Guido does the same while Hedvig is pregnant with Felix. The narrator states that he "prepared out of his own heart for his coming child a heart, fashioned on his own preoccupation, the remorseless homage to nobility, the genuflexion the hunted body makes from muscular contraction, going down before the impending and inaccessible, as before a great heat. It had made Guido, as it was to make his son, heavy with impermissible blood" (5). The image Barnes paints here is visceral: the child's heart, muscles, and blood are shaped by Guido's preoccupations. It is moreover literal in the manner of paternal impressions. Downward movement—"going down," kneeling, hiding from hunters—characterizes Guido's shaping efforts. Even the Volkbein name focuses attention to parts of the body that are close to the ground: the name literally translates as "folk" and "leg," which Sharon Marcus reads more figuratively as "foot soldier" (158). These grounding ideas create a child who is heavy with their weight and power. All this shaping happens before Felix is born simply by Guido thinking and genuflecting. By depicting the father as impressing his desires onto the fetus through the mother, Barnes intimates the displacement of an aristocratic version of patriarchal masculinity onto the maternal body.

With Felix, Barnes created a character who stakes his genealogical hopes on a similar ability to impress desired traits onto his child. Felix, the fetus who grows into a man with "impermissible blood," plans to erase his illegitimacy by impressing a stereotypically masculine "destiny" (46) onto

Robin and thereby their child. Rather than the "homage to nobility" that Guido impressed onto him, Felix attempts to impress fascistic patriarchal masculinity onto his child. Immediately upon meeting Robin, Felix decides he will marry her. Robin is ideal for a wife, Felix tells Matthew O'Connor, because she is an American, and "with an American anything can be done" (42). Barnes thereby suggests that Felix likes Robin for a wife because he thinks she is a blank slate onto whom he can write whatever kinship he wants. Robin is furthermore an orphan and seems to have no other relatives (Carlston 52). This means that Robin's genealogy is unfettered by extant connections that could interfere with the fabricated Volkbein line. As Sharon Marcus says, Felix's "restless search for 'pure' racial nobility" serves to "underscore[e] the reality of a Europe in which racial purity has been obscured by mixed marriages and false credentials" (158). To Felix's mind, Americans are removed from this European mixing and falsifying, which ironically makes Robin perfect for his own mixing and falsifying effort because his is the only one in play. Robin's absence of genealogy presents to Felix an opportunity to continue fictionalizing Volkbein kinship from whole cloth.

The novel undermines Felix's efforts, and language is key to this subversion. When the narrator introduces Felix's plans for Robin, language becomes slippery in a way that manifests Barnes's rejection of reproductive legitimacy, suggesting that Felix's fabrications are merely an extreme version of a phenomenon that permeates the very foundations of Western kinship. Caselli argues that a "sliding movement" (159) characterizes Barnes's use of language. Her texts, including but not limited to *Nightwood*, are full of puns and wordplay, so much so that Caselli identifies them as central to Barnes's poetics. Caselli states, "words constantly slide into alternative meanings" in *Nightwood* (159), making this book a " 'place where Contrarieties are equally True' [sic], in which 'Go Down Matthew' cannot be reduced to its 'depraved' meaning without its contrary, and equally true, 'innocent' one" (161).[16] The chapter title "Go Down Matthew" thus refers to Matthew O'Connor's sexual inclinations and to the spiritual "Go Down Moses, let my people go."

Another example—one not discussed by Caselli—is the word *conception*. Barnes makes much of the shifty, slidy qualities of language in her use of this word. Since it can signify the formation of both ideas and embryos, "conception" creates a felicitous connection between mind and body. Barnes exploits this connection, most obviously with the statement that Robin prepared for motherhood by "conceiving herself pregnant" when Felix demands it (49). The central passage concerning Robin's conception reads:

> Coming face to face with her, all that [Felix] could stammer out
> was: "Why is there no child? *Wo ist das Kind? Warum? Warum?*"
> Robin prepared herself for her child with her only power:
> a stubborn cataleptic calm, conceiving herself pregnant before
> she was; and, strangely aware of some lost land in herself, she
> took to going out; wandering the countryside; to train travel,
> to other cities, alone and engrossed. (49)

Felix's use of German here underscores the association in his mind between reproduction and the destiny of "German militarism" he envisions for his off-spring. Because of Barnes's emphasis on wordplay and the power of thoughts to affect reproductive outcomes, I read this passage as the moment Robin's gestation begins. Biological impregnation is not even significant enough to warrant a mention in Barnes's text; it is rendered unnecessary because her wordplay makes one definition of the word "conceive" slide seamlessly into the other definition of it. Felix demands a child, Robin conceives of it mentally, and the pregnancy is achieved.[17] Eight paragraphs later, she is in labor. These paragraphs, plus the one in which Robin conceives, become the nine months of pregnancy.

Barnes further exploits the dual connotation of *conception* through her depictions of parental impressions.[18] In a key passage, part of which I quoted earlier, the narrator states that Felix decides to marry Robin because he sees her as the perfect conduit for a lofty but unspecified destiny: "He had thought of making a destiny for himself, through laborious and untiring travail. Then with Robin it seemed to stand before him without effort. When he asked her to marry him it was with such an unplanned eagerness that he was taken aback to find himself accepted, as if Robin's life held no volition for refusal. He took her first to Vienna" (46). The work Felix thought he would have to undertake—the "laborious and untiring travail"—is rendered unnecessary by linguistic substitution. *Labor*, in the sense of work, slides into the labor of childbirth when Robin accepts his marriage proposal. Barnes achieves this shift through the word *travail*, thanks to the aforementioned dual connotation of work and childbirth. This etymology allows us to see how Barnes uses language to motivate plot (to the extent that *Nightwood* can be said to have a plot). Felix's labors of the mind shift to Robin's labors of the womb. Since the destiny Felix would create is a stereotypically masculine one—written as "a caricature of the masculine in his obsession to identify himself with the line of power" (Lee 209)—language surrounding "labor" is a key indication of Felix's intention to impress patriarchal masculinity onto his wife and future child.

More slippery still, *travail* is the word from which *travel* stems ("travail, n.1."). Correspondingly, talk of labor in the above passage is immediately followed by mention of a trip to Vienna.[19] The purpose of this trip is impressing upon Robin the history and geography of the city that defines his desired (though fictional) genealogical heritage (46–47). Felix takes her to Vienna "in an effort to acquaint her with the destiny for which he had chosen her—that she might bear sons who would recognize and honour the past" (49). Barnes's phrasing implies cause and effect: in order for the sons to recognize the past, the mother must be familiar with this history. Note that the narrator does not say "that she might *raise* sons" who approach history the way Felix desires. Rather, Felix wants Robin to bear sons who are born recognizing and honoring the past. Felix guides Robin around Vienna in order to shape his offspring to his liking. Felix, Barnes implies, would have Robin live out the role of a race mother as his own mother did, and his children embrace the patriarchal destiny he constructed for the family. The death of both of Felix's parents presages the failure of Felix's endeavor.

Exaggeration comes into Barnes's depiction of paternal impressions in the conception of Felix and Robin's child. In this one specific way, Felix's powers outstrip historical examples of impressionism, for he impregnates Robin without sleeping with her. As we saw, he initiates his wife's conception through words rather than deeds. As if impregnation occurred by fiat, by the following sentence Robin has begun "prepar[ing] herself for her child" and "conceiving herself pregnant" (49). These lines further suggest two key ideas that I pick up on in the final section of this chapter: Robin's ability to give birth to a child who will continue the (fictionalized) Volkbein kinship hinges on her intellectual and emotional state, and Robin is alternately passive and active in the reproductive process (preparing, conceiving).

Barnes's depiction of Felix ridicules and exaggerates the idea of parental impressionism even as it takes the cultural power of impressionism seriously. Ridicule appears most obviously in Felix's lack of knowledge of Vienna. His recitation of Austrian history is "confused and hazy" (47), and Robin falls asleep while he recites it (48). His memory is so faulty that his history lesson turns into a combination of "fact and fancy" (48). As a result, any impression that Felix's stories might make on Robin would be imaginative fictions, tales about the way Felix would like history to be rather than the way it occurred. Furthermore, he fails to stir Robin to attention while guiding her around the city—she is never "moved as he is moved" (47)—meaning that the impressions the city might make on the offspring are limited and shallow at best.

TRAVEL NARRATIVES, *NIGHTWOOD*, AND *SPLEEN*

Barnes's use of travel in conjunction with pregnancy—both Felix's attempts to impress history on Robin with a trip to Vienna as well as Robin's wandering of the countryside after "conceiv[ing] herself pregnant"—places *Nightwood* in a constellation of interwar travel narratives that feature pregnant people. This small but distinct body of travel narratives uses pregnancy as a plot device that externalizes their protagonists' self-discovery; their identities grow alongside their bellies. Joyce Kelley analyzes works written by transnational women writers that portray "the inner-mobilization of women through pregnancy. As these women travel externally, their focus shifts inward to contemplate the female body and its creative possibilities" (185). These texts include Katherine Mansfield's *In a German Pension* (1911) and Elizabeth Smart's *By Grand Central Station I Sat Down and Wept* (1945). The pregnant women in these texts bear a family resemblance to the heroes of traditional bildungsromans: the protagonists discover new insights about themselves through a voyage of some sort and end the voyage ready to step into a new role that is purportedly central to the health of the nation. For the traditional bildungsroman, the role is that of a community leader; for the women in Kelley's pregnancy travel narratives, the role is that of a mother.

To an extent, *Nightwood* does mirror this trajectory, yet the purpose is to satirize the genre rather than extend or revise it. The reader will recall that, immediately after conception, Robin becomes "strangely aware of some lost land in herself," which leads her to "wande[r] the countryside; to train travel, to other cities, alone and engrossed" (49). The "lost land within herself" is a rather on-the-nose invocation of self-discovery, marking the gestation section of *Nightwood* as a mock bildungsroman. Since the traditional hero of this form is a young man, and since Robin is described in masculine terms once she conceives, this depiction subtly highlights Robin's masculinity as a pregnant person. Like the classic hero, Robin, too, will return home after her travels in the countryside with greater self-knowledge and a better-defined sense of self.[20] Unlike those young men who return home to take on a role as a leader in the homeland, or the women in pregnancy travel narratives who return home ready to take on motherhood, Robin's return is eventually marked by rejection of Felix's (self-adopted) homeland and of the roles associated with motherhood.

I have much more to say about Robin's rejection of motherhood later in this chapter, but for now I want to draw a comparison between *Nightwood* and another anomalous text in the canon of pregnancy travel narratives. *Spleen* was published in 1930 by Olive Moore, the pen name for the British writer Constance Vaughn (130). Simon Lowe says of the novel, "[*Spleen*] manages to be both experimental and readable, morbid and beautiful. Told through a blurred, jumbled chronology, it is the story of Ruth, a British woman living on a remote Italian island with her severely disabled son. Arriving with her newborn baby Richard, Ruth is perceived by the local residents as 'not a little mad'" because she ignores the existence of her son to the greatest extent possible by turning over his care to servants. Like Robin Vote, the protagonist of *Spleen* rejects maternity and the culture of pro-natalism that forced pregnancy upon her; Ruth's rejection of her son manifests strong ableist and eugenic sentiments that are not dissimilar to many characters' reactions to Robin Vote's son, who is described as "mentally deficient and emotionally excessive" (114). *Spleen* furthermore depicts a direct relationship between mental and physical conceptions.

If anything, *Spleen*'s engagement with ideas surrounding masculine pregnancy discourse, pro-natalism, and mind/body conceptions is more overt than that which appears in *Nightwood*. For instance, when Ruth discovers she is pregnant, she falls into deep distress. Her thoughts regarding her newly discovered pregnancy manifest the extent to which gender norms are tied up with pregnancy: "she did not want her child. . . . She knew it was not possible to her to love a thing she did not know or had not seen. How can one? Yet I am expected to. All women do. I am a woman. Therefore I do. And if I do not?" (20–21). The answer, according to the pro-natalist, binaristic society in which Ruth was raised, is that Ruth's lack of love for her coming child makes her less of a woman. Moore amplifies this supposed lack of womanliness by later associating Ruth with a classic example of male pregnancy: Zeus birthing Pallas-Athene from his forehead. Ruth is only able to accept her pregnancy (a grudging, unbalanced acceptance, but acceptance nonetheless) when she reconceptualizes it as a masculine kind of intellectual creation. "I think," Ruth announces to her husband, "I carry my womb in my forehead" (24). She accepts pregnancy when she makes it into an intellectual endeavor instead of a physical one. The body, in Ruth's perception (and traditionally in Western culture) is inherently gendered: "woman is but the eternal oven in which to bake the eternal bun" (24). These statements suggest that Ruth rejects pregnancy partly because she rejects the cultural construction of maternity that yokes together the body, femininity, and pregnancy. The strength of Ruth's rejection is manifest in her delusional claim about the location of her womb. Because her womb is in her head, she illogically concludes, her offspring will be different and better than that which women have always produced. Ruth claims that she will give birth to "a new form. A being who . . . escaped the worn-out form and order of life" (58). Her eugenic wish for something different is given ironic fulfillment: instead of giving birth to a transcendent being, she gives birth to a son whose deformed feet prevent him from ever walking on the ground.[21]

A useful framework for understanding Moore's depiction of masculine pregnancy in *Spleen* is summed up in a question asked by Margot C. Finn et al. in *Legitimacy and Illegitimacy in Law, Literature, and History*. The authors outline some of the questions raised by the concept of legitimacy. They ask, "How might self-consciously illegitimate behaviour operate as a form of opposition to the dominant codes of legitimate society and what kinds of political agendas does this open up?" (3–4). Ruth's rejection of pregnancy and maternity is precisely this; throughout the book, Ruth is hyperaware of the ways in which her actions buck traditions and norms. She repeatedly questions the purpose of childbearing, refuses advice to rest, and shows little interest in the nursery preparations. Ruth is unbothered by the concern of those around her because she is convinced that she will give birth to "Something new. Something quite different. Something worth having. Something beyond and above it all. Something free that would defy the dreary inevitable round of years" (30). The political agenda that these illegitimate behaviors open up for Ruth is a eugenic one, tied to a desire to create a "better" sort of human.

Building on Kelley's scholarship on travel narratives, Erin Kingsley considers *Spleen* as a key example in a genre she calls "gestational migration." She defines this genre as a category of text that centers on "the physical and psychological movement that occurs when one becomes a mother (a process the field of anthropology terms 'matrescence')" (139). Although Kingsley is mostly interested in psychological movement, she also discusses physical displacement. She notes that Moore's oeuvre is full of protagonists who are living in exile: "each of her extant works explores the figure of a female outlier in a male world. Her characters are fundamentally displaced, unmoored. In *Celestial*, European girls (predominately English and German) attend a convent school far from home; in *Fugue*, the English Lavinia wanders abroad in Germany; and in *Spleen*, the English heroine flees from her husband's estate in England to the tiny island of Foria, Italy after she births a 'monstrous' child" (143). The version of gestational migration that Kingsley finds in Olive Moore's *Spleen* is much closer to that in *Nightwood* than in any of the texts Kelley considers. The protagonists in both Moore's and Barnes's texts reject the role of the mother, and both authors challenge the pro-natalist politics that underpin such roles. Further, both authors use expressly masculine terms to describe their pregnant protagonists, suggesting the possibility of a modernist ideology that links masculinity to a rejection of "the dominant codes of legitimate society" (Finn et al. 3–4) that are related to matrescence.

Part Two: Fictional Kinship

The unwilling conceptions that happen to *Spleen*'s Ruth and *Nightwood*'s Robin resonate with a point made by the anthropologist Kath Weston regarding the extent to which individuals have agency in family structures. She notes that chosen families are significant in part because individuals have a great deal of control over their composition; biological families are generally assumed to be the opposite, entities into which we are born and will forever exist (38). Barnes's depiction of kinship does not exactly upend this dynamic, but it does show pockets of mutability within biological kinship by depicting it as fictional and therefore rewriteable. Weston sees hope in familial mutability. Barnes's text is less than sanguine about the effects of it.

Parental impressions is *how* Barnes displaces the masculinity of the father onto the body of the mother in *Nightwood*. The *why* has to do with the idea of kinship that Barnes depicts. She uses impressions to show that kinship is fictional and everyone illegitimate, thereby undermining the very idea of reproductive legitimacy. Barnes wrote in an era when anthropology had captured the popular imagination, and talk of concepts like kinship was in the air. She had reason to question theories that positioned blood- and marriage-based kinship as the most real, legitimate, or ideal. To say that her own family of origin resisted traditional Western family structures is an understatement. Barnes's father was a polygamist and her grandmother a free love advocate. At age 17, Barnes was coerced into marrying a man three times her senior (Broe 4). She had close relationships with several members of her family, especially her free-loving grandmother Zadel, but the forced marriage among other familial traumas left lasting scars.[22]

We might guess that a writer reared in these conditions would embrace the nuclear family as an alternative to the polygamous one that was the source of harm. Yet *Nightwood* suggests a writer whose thoughts ran in the other direction, away from the notion that the state-sanctioned nuclear family is more legitimate or real than chosen kinship. Neither, however, does *Nightwood* hold up chosen families as an alternative. Instead, the novel rejects the notion of legitimacy entirely. Blood ties exist in *Nightwood*, but the idea of a true, authentic, or pure blood line is something Barnes depicts as a narrative fantasy that nevertheless has tremendous influence and authority. The divide between high and low, insider and outsider, legitimate and illegitimate structures Barnes's novel from the very first page, and the scars these divisions cause are most clearly on display in the traumas that shape the lives of the characters. Barnes's psychosomatic figuration of Robin's masculine pregnancy, and with it Felix's paternal impressions, forms the foundation of Barnes's construction of kinship as fictional. The next section of the chapter explores Barnes's fictional kinship; the third and final section considers the limits of, and the trauma caused by, fictional kinship, arguing that Barnes positions it as a double-edged sword in interwar Europe.

Fictive and Fictional Kinship

Barnes's critique of kinship anticipates debates within the field of anthropology. Lewis Henry Morgan pioneered kinship studies in the 1870s. His methodology set the field's standards and norms for decades to come. Kath Weston, who is best known for her watershed book *Families We Choose: Lesbians, Gays, Kinship* (1991), summarizes the tradition that Morgan established: "Since the time of Lewis Henry Morgan, most scholarly studies of familial relations have enthroned human procreation as kinship's ultimate referent. According to received anthropological wisdom, relations of blood (consanguinity) and marriage (affinity) could be plotted for any culture on a universal genealogical grid" (33–34). For decades after Morgan, anthropologists organized kinship relations based on these principles of biological procreation; they did so, Weston suggests, in their studies of cultures around the globe without wondering whether these principles were appropriate for each particular culture (33–34). Anthropologists began questioning this received wisdom in the mid-twentieth century. Weston's own work on gay and lesbian kinship in the 1980s and 1990s was part of a strand of anthropological work that asked, in effect, "What would happen if observers ceased privileging genealogy as a sacrosanct objective construct, approaching biogenetic ties instead as a characteristically Western way of ordering and granting significance to social relations?" (Weston 33). One result of this epistemological shift was a reframing of the concept of fictive kinship.

As I mentioned at the outset of this chapter, fictive kinship has roots in law as well as anthropology (Schneider 54). Its coinage was not intended to demean or belittle the relationships it describes, despite the implication of unreal or made-up qualities. The term fictive kinship originates in the concept of legal fiction and was originally used as a heuristic for adoption. For instance, the nineteenth-century legal historian Henry Sumner Maine uses the term "legal fiction" to mean "any assumption which conceals, or affects to conceal, the fact that a rule of law has undergone alteration, its letter remaining unchanged, its operation being modified. . . . The fact is . . . that the law has been wholly changed; the fiction is that it remains what it always was" (26). As an example, he cites "the Fiction of Adoption, which permits the family tie to be artificially created" (27). In Maine's view, the fact of what constitutes a family under the law has changed to encompass adopted children; the fiction is that the legal code has always included them. Maine is at pains to explain the usefulness of the concept and rejects the idea that legal fictions deserve "ridicule" as "merely fraudulent" (27). Yet as Weston, David M. Schneider, and other anthropologists have shown, the term does denigrate the kinds of relationships it describes, regardless of intention. Schneider explains: "the reproductive relationship was taken as the central feature of kinship. Kinsmen, then, were those who were related through 'real' biological ties. . . . Even in such instances as ritual kinship, adoption, and the like, the premise is that the social relationship is modeled on the biological; that adoption is only understandable as a way of creating the social fiction that an actual link of kinship exists" (54–55). Dating back to the origins of the anthropological concept, then, consanguineal and affinal kinship were positioned as more "real" or legitimate than fictive kinship since reproductive ties were the default structure against which all others were defined.[23] The connotation of fictive kinship as less real is part of the reason why many anthropologists as well as people outside the field have moved away from its use and opt for *chosen kin* or *chosen family* instead.

Historically, with regard to kinship, queer was to illegitimate as straight was to legitimate. As Weston notes, anthropology long positioned queer people as "outside both law and nature" (4), that is, outside affinal and consanguineal bonds. And it is not just in anthropology that queer people have been considered outside and separate from kinship. Weston explains: "For years, and in an amazing variety of contexts, claiming a lesbian or gay identity has been portrayed as a rejection of 'the family' and a departure from kinship. . . . Two presuppositions lend a dubious credence to such imagery: the belief that gay men and lesbians do not have children or establish last-ing relationships, and the belief that they invariably alienate adoptive and blood kin once their sexual identities become known." (22). In the 1980s, activists in the United States pushed back against these assumptions and argued that chosen families deserve to be recognized as legitimate (Weston 27). In my reading of *Nightwood*, Barnes takes the opposite and more transgressive approach. Instead of positioning queer relations as legitimate, the novel positions straight ones as illegitimate.

The effect is to render the division between illegitimate and legitimate absurd, a binary that is more a measure of political power and storytell-ing ability than anything based in biological "truth" or "realness." Here, too, Barnes anticipates an anthropological critique of kinship by depicting biology as a cultural and linguistic construct.[24] Weston, writing in 1991, argues for approaching "biology as symbol rather than substance" (34). This reframing is an important acknowledgment that not all cultures grant the same importance to biology for structuring relationships; thinking of procre-ation as the inevitable and immutable ground on which kinship relations are built is a Western mindset (34). More intriguing still, at least for scholars of literature, Weston notes that this particular reframing move shifts kinship into the territory of language: "To read biology as a symbol is to approach it as a cultural construct and linguistic category rather than a self-evident matter of 'natural fact.' . . . Neither [chosen nor consanguineal kinship] is inherently more 'real' or valid than the other" (34–35). *Nightwood* operates in a similar framework, wherein biological ties are symbols of power and status. In Barnes's hands, biological ties become fictional constructs that are mutable in the same way that fictive or chosen ties are, thanks to the power of parental impressions.

To be sure, Barnes pushes the notion of biology as a symbol further than Weston. Where Weston makes an argument rooted in cultural atti-tudes toward biology and its relation to kinship, Barnes's critique is rooted in biology itself. As we have seen, her depiction of parental impressions in *Nightwood* makes language and the imagination into forces capable of shaping biology. The novel undercuts the legitimacy of the nuclear family by positioning legitimacy itself as a fiction and all people as queer; every-one from Hedvig to Robin is an illegitimate interloper. I call this thematic approach to family ties "fictional kinship."

The fictionalized kinship of the Volkbeins resonates with an idea that has a long novelistic tradition. The notion that genealogies have roots in fiction was particularly prominent in nineteenth-century British novels, according to Isobel Armstrong. Armstrong argues that the act of creating an elaborate genealogy for characters is "a constructive and a deconstructive project, for to construct not a historical but an imagined family tree is to be sharply aware of the legal, social, and economic rules and protocol, past and present, governing not only primogeniture but class, status, entitlement, and exclusion. To construct may be to collude, but it must always be an act of extreme self-consciousness" (8). In *Nightwood*, Barnes amplifies the constructive and self-aware properties that Armstrong discusses. Barnes created characters who write their own genealogy, and then she constructed the "real" genealogy behind their fictions. For instance, we read about two "life-sized portraits of Guido's claim to father and mother" that bore "a remarkable likeness" to him (9). The narrator then quickly adds, "the likeness was accidental. Had anyone cared to look into the matter they would have discovered these canvases to be reproductions of two intrepid and ancient actors. Guido had found them in some forgotten and dusty corner and had purchased them when he had been sure that he would need an alibi for the blood" (10). The story of Guido's purchase would seem to be the "real" one behind the fictional kinship, yet even this story is quite possibly fictional itself. The portraits "might have been a Mardi Gras whim" on the part of the actors who posed for them (9); as Caselli points out, the "apparently stable truth" of the portraits "is rocked by the use of the subjunctive, which hints at the possibility that nobody actually did care to look into the matter" of Guido's portraits (9). Here as elsewhere, Barnes implies that all kinship is a fiction and no true, real, or pure version exists underneath it all.

By amplifying and complicating the questions that novelists have long asked about genealogy, Barnes suggests that the interwar relationship to kinship is different than it was before, and the difference lies in the degree to which everyone from rulers to commoners were engaged in efforts to fictionalize kinship. The upshot is this: Barnes's depiction of fictional kinship in *Nightwood* is a portrait in miniature of a much broader phenomenon that swept through many countries in the interwar years. This phenomenon is characterized by a drive to exert control over kinship by revising or writing anew cultural narratives about marriage, families, and reproduction.[25] We saw an example of this in the previous chapter. In efforts to curtail the influence of growing immigrant populations, native-born Americans rewrote, in culture and in law, whiteness to exclude immigrant groups including Bohemians like the Shimerdas. In the European context, many examples of such a drive to rewrite kinship stem from the Nazis. For instance, certain individuals were awarded the status of "honorary Aryans," some of whom were "Jews who were defined as possessing Aryan 'spiritual' or mental qualities" (Bartulin 2). In effect, this designation used the thoughts and ideas of these individuals to rewrite their genealogical lineages. The filmmaker Fritz Lang recalled a similar rewriting of his own kinship. When Lang admitted to having Jewish relatives, Joseph Goebbles "laughed and said, 'Mr Lang, we decide who is Aryan'" (Poole 181).[26] Further, just two years after *Nightwood*'s publication, Italy began to issue race laws that stripped Jews of Italian citizenship. Prior to the 1930s, Italy had a reputation as less antisemitic than other European countries, but as R. J. B. Bosworth states, "all was not quite as bright and simple . . . [because] currents of antisemitism did eddy through Italian life" (415; 417). In the 1930s, Italy increasingly emulated Nazi dictates based on scientific racism (Bayor 382). In the mid-1930s, the Italian fascist party began a new project that aimed, as Franklin Hugh Adler states, "to create an entirely new society and transform Italians themselves. Racial policy was an aspect of this development" (286–87). Fascists were advocating nationalism based on "blood and soil" as the most real or legitimate standard around which to construct a nation-state, while at the same time writing fictions about both. This brand of nationalism implicitly comes under fire in my reading of *Nightwood* since the novel points out the always already fictional quality of kinship; blood is the furthest thing from a stable truth.

Nevertheless, Barnes's depiction of Guido suggests that the impulse to fictionalize genealogy cuts both ways. Jews and fascists alike rewrote blood and soil, albeit with widely different power structures available to legitimize their narratives, and, for Jews, under the shadow of the deadly consequences of illegitimacy in interwar Europe. Furthermore, Barnes suggests that even queer communities on the fringes of society are not immune from the drive to fictionalize kinship. Numerous critics have noted that Robin's lovers Nora and Jenny try to mold their relationships with Robin into heteronormative kinship narratives. For example, Carolyn Allen states that "Barnes's text poses Nora Flood and her lover Robin Vote as an intimate couple who alternatively play out (and play on) conventional hegemonic scripts for 'wife and husband' and 'mother and child'" (177). Even the novel's narrator writes Robin into an earth mother narrative similar to the one Jim Burden writes for the protagonist of *My Ántonia* (see chapter 4 for more), although where Cather is earnest about her depiction, Barnes is hyperbolic. Throughout *Nightwood*, Robin is consistently associated with abundant, fecund plant and animal life. Her first appearance in the novel occurs in a hotel room where she is "surrounded by a confusion of potted plants, exotic palms and cut flowers, faintly over-sung by the notes of unseen birds. . . . The perfume that her body exhaled was of the quality of that earth-flesh, fungi. . . . Her flesh was the texture of plant life" (37–38).[27] Miriam Fuchs notes of this scene that "Felix knows instantly that she will one day bear his child and he is overwhelmed by the excessive moisture and fecundity that permeate Robin's bedchamber" (127). All of this fictionalizing—Felix impressing a race mother narrative onto Robin, Jenny and Nora writing her into heteronormative scripts, the narrator constructing an earth mother storyline for her—suggests that narrative and the imagination determine kinship as much if not more than biological ties.

The result is a novel in which the distinction between legitimate and illegitimate breaks down. In *Nightwood*, all kinship is fictional, making consanguineal bonds no more legitimate than fictive ones. (This depiction of Barnes's appears to flatten out differences between kinds of illegitimacy, which is antisemitic in ways I discuss shortly). Everyone, *Nightwood* implies, is illegitimate in one way or another. And if everyone is illegitimate, no one is. Even Hedvig, the novel's avatar of phallic power and representative of eugenic health by virtue of her association with upright Aryanness, also represents illegitimacy through her queerness as a masculine mother. In this way, Barnes implies that drawing clean distinctions between health and illness, eugenic and dysgenic, pure and mongrel, is impossible because all kinship is fictional and rewritable.

Part Three: The Limits of Fictional Kinship

Nightwood is concerned with the immense power of fiction in the realm of kinship. It is also the case, however, that Barnes is attentive to the limits of and harm caused by fictional kinship. Ultimately, fictional kinship is best understood variably: as a tool of the oppressed, as when Guido and Felix attempt to rewrite the script of their own lineage in order to evade deadly antisemitism; and as a tool of oppressors who impress unwanted or inaccurate narratives onto people's lives, such as Felix's attempt to write Robin into a masculine race mother narrative or Nazi efforts to write Jews into bigoted stereotypes. The fact that Felix occupies the role of both oppressor and oppressed shows that Barnes was acutely aware of what we today call the intersectional dynamics of power. This attentiveness to the limits of fictional kinship means that *Nightwood* stakes out quite different territory than Cather's *My Ántonia* with regard to kinship, legitimacy, and masculine pregnancy. Barnes's tale grants tremendous power to narrative as Cather's does, but *Nightwood* implies that some kinds of kinship cannot and should not be legitimized through narrative. I first discuss the ways that Barnes's depiction of Robin's masculine pregnancy suggests that efforts to seek reproductive legitimacy compound trauma. I then move to a discussion of the Volkbein men and the limits to their ability to impress fictional genealogy on their offspring. As Jewish men trying to pass as gentile in fascist Europe, they are unable to completely rewrite the family's biological heritage. Together, these scenes show that the displacement of patriarchal masculinity onto pregnant women in the pursuit of legitimacy reflects multifaceted causes and effects of trauma in interwar Europe.

The Trauma of Robin's Masculine Pregnancy

The trauma of Felix's efforts to impress patriarchal masculinity onto Robin can be seen plainly in *Nightwood's* childbirth scenes. Yet an interesting thing happens during her pregnancy that is far less obvious but undoubtedly consequential to our understanding of this character. The masculinity displaced onto her during pregnancy gives her enough power to reject Felix and the fictional kinship he writes for her. This is not a triumphalist moment in the novel but a trenchant critique of a society that equates silence with femininity. For only once Robin embodies patriarchal masculinity is she able to defy the wishes of her husband. With the trope of masculine pregnancy, Barnes shapes a character who is most often read as a "blank" into one with an identity that is strong enough to resist the narrative Felix wants to force her into. Robin's resistance comes at a steep cost because the means by which she resists Felix is traumatizing, suggesting the hardships attendant upon living a life outside recognizable narrative patterns. As Brian Glavey states, *Nightwood* lodges a "protest against the suffering that results when one's identifications and desires do not match up with the roles one is expected to play in a culture's stories of succession" (758). To be illegitimate is another way to say that one does not match up with roles in stories of succession.

For Robin to escape fictions of kinship, she must become unrecognizable. In the interwar years, queerness did not equal unrecognizability.

Sexology and psychology amplified the recognizability of queers (or at least the assumption that queers could be recognized) by cataloging types—"the invert," "the fetishist," and so forth—and writing them into reductive narratives. Foucault was, of course, one of the first to note the historical linkage between sexual behaviors and storytelling by analyzing the role of confession in the construction of homosexuality. He argues that sexology moved the confessional discourse of sex from the realm of religion to medicine and that the goal of this "machinery of power" was not to suppress deviancy "but rather to give it an analytical, visible, and permanent reality . . . Not the exclusion of these thousand aberrant sexualities, but the specification, the regional solidification of each one" (44). A way to resist "the inhumanity of the madness for order" (Marcus 164) is to be un-label-able, someone difficult to fit within the confines of a single, recognizable narrative, whether it be state-sanctioned narratives of legitimacy or sexology-defined ones of illegitimacy. This unrecognizability is precisely what Barnes depicts Robin attempting, though at great psychological cost.

Saying that Robin attempts or rejects anything cuts against the critical grain because most see her as an empty container for other characters' desires and needs. Charles Baxter voices a common critical assessment of Robin when he calls her "an absent personality: Felix can impress upon her any image he chooses" (1183). Baxter is using impression in the general sense rather than the particularized one of parental impressions. Katherine Fama similarly notes that many characters take Robin's inscrutability as a sign that they can inscribe her into whatever narrative they want: "her silence is a temptation: an apparent blank slate for the projection of desires, a prop for frail narratives. The narrator, Felix, and Nora each over-write Robin" (48). Although Fama suggests that these characters are not entirely successful in their revision efforts, readings such as hers nevertheless echo Felix's sentiments. Recall, for instance, that Felix is "taken aback to find [his marriage proposal] accepted, as if Robin's life held no volition for refusal" (46). To a large extent, these assessments—both Felix's and those of *Nightwood*'s critics—are accurate. For most of her relationship with Felix, Robin passively acquiesces to his plans. *As if* is the key, however, because Robin's life does hold volition for refusal, and my intention here is to show how this volition—this willfulness that hints at an identity—begins to develop at the conception of her child, gestates alongside the fetus, and then is born at the same moment. Displacing masculinity onto the pregnant body is the means by which Barnes brings Robin's identity into being, which is a tragic portrait of the silence and meekness expected of feminine women.

It is my contention that Robin is able to resist Felix's fascist race mother narrative because pregnancy masculinizes her enough to reject the mantle of the race mother.

In stark contrast to Robin's passive acquiescence to Felix's marriage proposal, in childbirth we find Robin "cursing like a sailor" and uttering "loud and frantic cries" of "Oh, for Christ's sake, for Christ's sake!" (52).[28] Robin gives birth to her son and her own identity in the same moment, the latter of which is manifest in a fury and decisiveness that is present nowhere else in the novel. The narrator states, "Robin was delivered" (52), a double-entendre that simultaneously announces the arrival of the child and Robin's identity. Although the birth is a bloody and terrifying one that leaves Robin in a daze, she is nevertheless more lucid than her usual somnambulant state. For a week after, she behaves as if parturition was the first event in her life that "caught her attention" (52). Shortly thereafter she makes two statements that stand out for their decisiveness. I quote the passage in full to capture the strength of Robin's identity in the moment:

> One night, coming home about three, [Felix] found her in the darkness, standing, back against the window, in the pod of the curtain, her child so thrust forward that the muscles in her neck stood out. As he came toward her she said in a fury, "I didn't want him!" Raising her hand she struck him across the face.
>
> He stepped away; he dropped his monocle and caught at it swinging; he took his breath backward. He waited a whole second, trying to appear casual. "You didn't want him," he said. He bent down pretending to disentangle his ribbon. "It seems I could not accomplish that."
>
> "Why not be secret about him?" she said. "Why talk?"
>
> Felix turned his body without moving his feet. "What shall we do?"
>
> She grinned, but it was not a smile. "I'll get out," she said. (53)

This is a portrait of someone suffering from postpartum depression. Hers is not a whole or healthy identity, but there is an identity to be found, a person who has desires and needs and who expresses them verbally, something she had been unable or unwilling to do before. Robin cannot be described here as an "empty center around which [the other characters'] lives and passions spin," as Teresa de Lauretis has asserted (245).

Hints of Robin's developing identity are perceptible before she gives birth. The first indication of her opposition to the role of the race mother appears with the paradoxical "power" we are told she employs when preparing for conception: "a stubborn cataleptic calm" (49). Barnes's combination of adjectives hints at Robin's hamstrung position. Catalepsy implies passivity and immobility, but to be stubborn is to be willful, usually in defiance of others. In stark opposition to the narrator's description of her as cataleptic, Robin prepares for pregnancy by "going out; wandering the countryside; to train travel, to other cities, alone and engrossed" (45). These travels—or more appropriately, travails—contradict the immobility of catalepsy. "Stubborn cataleptic calm" therefore describes a person whose choices are constrained. Resistance through passivity or stillness was an important tenet of New Thought doctrine. In the United States at the turn of the twentieth century, prevailing opinion held that "the role of the middle-class woman was to accommodate her husband's desires, economically (by adjusting their home life to his income) as well as sexually and emotionally" (Satter 124). New Thought activists counseled women to resist this state of affairs through stillness. As Beryl Satter explains, "the 'still' or motionless woman rejected desire, or rather, announced her refusal to mirror man's desire" (124). Robin's stubborn calmness is a similar kind of resistance through passivity.

Robin's will-less acquiescence to marriage has little in common with her furious decisiveness after giving birth. The cause of this dramatic change is, I am suggesting, Felix's impression of patriarchal masculinity onto her gestating body. Barnes further masculinizes Robin's identity because this identity crystalizes in a moment of abandoning a child, a decision that was, at the time, often characterized as masculine since it was thought to be unnatural or even impossible for women to do. This is not to say that abandoning a child actually is a masculine trait but that it was assumed to be so at the time. That Robin should need to embody patriarchal masculinity to resist Felix is a scathing commentary on the restrictions of gender roles, suggesting that femininity is a barrier to a life lived on one's own terms.

Robin manages to slip from Felix's grip because the patriarchal masculinity displaced onto her encourages the expression of anger and exertion of power, which in turn allows Robin to walk away from her husband and the race mother narrative he tried to force her into. This is a pyrrhic victory, however, since escaping this narrative requires what Gilbert and Gubar refer to as "self-obliteration" (*No Man's Land* 360). This tactic makes Robin into a person who is impossible to pigeonhole in any single narrative, which allows her to sidestep the other characters' fictionalizing impulses. Robin

elects self-obliteration over winnowing down her life's story to a recognizable, legitimate narrative. *Nightwood* thereby positions self-obliteration as
a means of resisting totalizing discourses of kinship such as the masculine
race mother. The novel does not endorse either approach—fictionalizing
or self-obliteration—but instead critiques concepts such as legitimacy and
kinship as absurd and attempts to rewrite them as harmful.

ANTISEMITISM AND THE VOLKBEINS

As mentioned earlier, Barnes's novel appears to flatten out differences between
legitimates and illegitimates by rendering the distinction meaningless. Yet
for all *Nightwood*'s championing of illegitimates, the various communities
of outsiders are not, in the end, equal in their disqualification. Barnes's
depiction of queerness as illegitimate is self-aware and critical; her depiction
of Jewish illegitimacy is less so. In other words, Barnes lets some antisemitic tropes stand, where she challenges corollary tropes regarding queer
characters.[29] There is a hierarchy in the way Barnes depicts her outlaws,
as Karen Kaviola argues. Kaviola demonstrates that some types of outsiders—especially queers—are granted more individuality and a fuller human
existence than others. Kaviola's paradigmatic case is that of Robin, who is
complex and unknowable in ways that acknowledge that she is more than
a stereotype of a lesbian. Jewish and Black people are never given the same
acknowledgment and are instead limited to the ambit of stereotyped narratives (174). To Kaviola's points, I add the contrast between Robin's relative
success in taking control over others' attempts to fictionalize her kinship
and the relative failure of the Volkbeins. Although Robin's is a hollow victory—she can only escape kinship narratives through self-obliteration—her
life is nevertheless impossible to reduce to either a masculine race mother
or a character type in sexologists' constructed narratives of inverts.

The same cannot be said of the Volkbeins. Felix's efforts to write his
family's kinship anew fails to secure legitimacy. For although Robin and
Felix's son is legitimate, in the sense of being within the bounds of law
because his parents are married at the time of his birth, the Volkbein line
remains in *Nightwood* a stereotype of "comic and pathetic outsiders" (Kaviola
181). Robin and Felix's son is a poster child for the kind of degeneracy
imagined by critics of masculine women, and his embodiment is suggestive
of the racial degeneracy feared by fascists. As I discuss in the introduction,
Nightwood (1936) was published at a time of intense worry over the effects
of masculinity on women's fertility. Many leading intellectuals argued that

masculinity inhibited women's ability to get pregnant. This led to speculation that if a masculine woman did manage to conceive, she would give birth to degenerate offspring. Michael Davidson says of Robin and Felix's child that his existence is "historically over-determined" by virtue of being disabled, Jewish, and the son of a queer woman who deserts him (*Invalid* 115). And so, although the fictionalized kinship that Guido Volkbein created is powerful enough to secure him wealth and marriage to a woman befitting the sort of background he crafted for himself (befitting to his mind, at least), his efforts to legitimize his family line through fictions of kinship ultimately fail. Guido cannot completely narrativize away his background the way Jim Burden and the Widow Steavens could rewrite the illegitimacy of Ántonia Shimerda's child.

This narrative failure on the part of the Volkbeins is best understood as a manifestation of Barnes's antisemitism. Kaviola argues convincingly that Barnes depicts Jewish blood as particularly durable: "despite the fact that Felix's mother is a Christian, the text insists his most meaningful identity is as a Jew. And although Felix and Robin (who is also a Christian) produce a child, Guido, who is technically one quarter Jewish, the text processes him as a Jew as well. . . . Thus, to be born with any Jewish 'blood' is to remain a Jew forever" (181). Although I generally see more malleability in genealogy than Kaviola does because of the power of parental impressions, I agree with her assessment of the novel's depiction of Jewish blood as durable. The act of fictionalizing kinship is powerful enough to bring about meaningful changes, but there are limits to its power. One obvious limitation is that the Volkbeins were up against fascist forces that were intent on telling stories built on the notion of Jewishness as a pernicious pollutant. But in *Nightwood* a second limitation to the power of fictional kinship comes from Barnes's own antisemitism, which portrays Jewish blood as substantially different from that of other people. The novel's parallel depiction of queers and Jews as illegitimate suggests an intentional pairing that connects Jews and inverts in similar struggles against discourses that try to reduce their kinship possibilities down to fictionalized stereotypes. Barnes ultimately rejects these stereotypes of queers but lets stand the stereotypes of Jews.

This chapter has focused on Barnes's use of masculine pregnancies to portray kinship as a fiction and argued that parental imprinting is the mechanism by which patriarchal masculinity is displaced onto *Nightwood's* mothers. Hedvig's masculinity undermines fascist doctrines of purity and reproductive legitimacy through her queerness, while Robin's masculinity gives rise to a person whose identity is powerful enough to resist the race mother narrative Felix tries to write her into. Through her queer masculine mothers, Barnes suggests that everyone is illegitimate by erasing distinctions between "real" and fictional kinship, bastards and heirs, queer and straight. Reading *Nightwood* for its depictions of masculine pregnancy, therefore, demonstrates Barnes's rejection of the very concept of reproductive legitimacy, while it also expands our understanding of the ways modernists engaged with masculine pregnancies by revealing a deployment of the trope—parental impressions—that is distinct from the others discussed in this book.

Through parental impressions, *Nightwood* suggests that kinship is malleable or open to a wider degree of revision than is usually acknowledged. In this regard, Barnes's novel is similar to *My Ántonia*. The two books together paint a nuanced picture of masculine pregnancy. As we saw in the previous chapter, Cather writes an earth mother narrative for Ántonia Shimerda, and this character finds satisfaction in being inscribed into this well-known narrative. The narrative gives Ántonia's neighbors a way to understand her masculinity. The community grants her and her family social legitimacy as Americans, as members of the Black Hawk community, and, in the case of Antonia, as a "real" woman. Antonia deeply desires this kind of acceptance and therefore finds fulfillment in being seen as an earth mother. Barnes depicts a character for whom this kind of legibility within a familiar narrative is suffocating.

Despite the significant differences between *Nightwood* and *My Ántonia*, these two texts nevertheless take masculine pregnancy seriously, contending with the discourse surrounding it and the effects of that discourse on queer people. Conversely, Ezra Pound, and to an extent William Faulkner, viewed masculine women (pro)creators as a threat to their status as authors. Their depictions of masculine pregnancy, which generally took the shape of metaphorical rather than literal pregnancy, attempted to position queer creation as illegitimate and debased. By considering this spectrum of depictions, this book has provided glimpses of "the conditions of exclusion and inequality" that shaped queer lives in the interwar years, as well as "alternative trajectories" for masculine pregnancy, to use Heather Love's terms (29). As I explained in the introduction, Love's theory of criticism informed the two-part structure of this book, in which both aspects of criticism—the critical and the imaginative—are considered in tandem. In so doing, we keep the past and the future, the politics of oppression and of hope, in view. Yet even this robust framework cannot possibly capture the full picture of literary depictions of masculine pregnancy. It is to these additional avenues for critical consideration that I turn in the coda.

Coda

Masculine Pregnancies beyond Modernism

Throughout this book, I have endeavored to pry apart the assumed connection between femininity and pregnancy that informs many conversations about reproduction. I began from a premise that is relatively uncontroversial, at least in academic circles: gender is not a binary. From this premise, it follows quite obviously and logically that some people with the capacity to bear children are not feminine, and some are not women. If we grant, as we should, that trans men are men, we must also grant the reality of pregnant men here and now. Furthermore, this book has operated on the assumption that pregnancy does not increase femininity. To be sure, some people lean into their femininity during pregnancy, but this change is neither inevitable nor necessary. Many resent social customs that channel them into femininity, as with a clothing industry that piles ruffles onto clothes for pregnant people. *Pregnant Butch*'s Teek—to return to a character I discuss in the introduction—leans in the opposite direction, hoping pregnancy will offer opportunities to wear more masculine clothing. For Teek, who notes that pregnancy counterintuitively *increases* the extent to which people perceive her as male (her pregnancy reading as a beer belly), the practical need to find pregnancy clothes that are not feminine presents an exciting opportunity. Teek declares, "Oboy! I get to wear suspenders! Hooray for pregnancy! I love dramatic masculine costume, but it usually comes off as **drag**. Having a legitimate **structural** excuse to wear it is a **chance of a lifetime**" (emphasis original, 3). That Teek uses a pregnant body to legitimize suspender-wearing suggests some of the complex ideological linkages among reproduction, gender, and authenticity that I have been exploring throughout this book: that she thinks she needs an excuse to wear suspenders; that she refers to a "legitimate" excuse as though desire is not sufficient;

that reproductive legitimacy is a social good, conferred and denied on the fly with others, as much as a formalized legal concept concerning bastardy; that a pregnant belly becomes a "structural excuse" for overtly masculine clothing. Each of these linkages raises questions that resonate with the ones explored in the preceding chapters. They also suggest the persistence of literary depictions of masculine pregnancy across time and space; as in the early twentieth century, so in the early twenty-first. And although Teek identifies as a woman, her pregnancy is in a constellation with other forms of queer embodiment that include pregnant men.

As this book has demonstrated, stories of masculine pregnancy are prevalent in early twentieth-century texts if we look for them. This is even true for depictions of mannish pregnant women, although this figure has been all but invisible in critical conversations about literature published before the twenty-first century. The problem as I see it is not that authors failed to include mannish pregnant women in their works but rather that critics have not been reading for this figure. Instead, the conversation has tended to engage in projects of rationalization, to refer again to Halberstam's phrase, by ignoring, downplaying, or rationalizing a pregnant character's masculinity, or else by emphasizing traits perceived as feminine when a mannish character becomes pregnant. If, however, we widen our critical aperture to include mannish women, we begin to see the relationship between masculinity, pregnancy, and legitimacy in a dramatically different light.

I have focused on two facets of this newly illuminated relationship in modernism: the oppressive as well as emancipatory ends to which masculine pregnancies were deployed; and the modernist fascination with the concept of legitimacy that goes beyond the bio-legal status of the offspring (whether the child is a bastard or an heir) to include the pregnant person's body (whether masculinity renders the gestator unfit for [pro]creation). As such, the keywords around which I structured this book—masculinity, pregnancy, creativity, and legitimacy—provide insight into the ways modernist writers adapted reproductive tropes for the twentieth century. These keywords led me to analyze modernist writers who queered reproduction—Willa Cather and Djuna Barnes—as well as those who reaffirmed heteronormative structures of kinship and reproduction, including Ezra Pound and, to an extent, William Faulkner. Different as they are, these authors have in common a firm belief in the power of narrative to shape how people think about reproductive legitimacy. The texts studied here pit biology against the imagination in an ideological struggle over the determinants of reproductive legitimacy. They implicitly pose a question: which is more important when a community determines what kinds of (pro)creation are legitimate, the material body or the stories we tell about it? Taken together, these texts test the limits of what narrative can do with regard to kinship and legitimacy, the extent to which narrative shapes, revises, and is even constitutive of legitimacy. Although some of these authors suggest that biology—genes and heredity as well as anatomical sex—is the salient factor, none deny that the stories we tell about reproduction undergird kinship systems.

The relationship between narrative and reproduction is key to one of the most important revelations found in this book: modernist authors sometimes combined masculinity and pregnancy in ways that attempt to loosen the cultural shackles around women and queer people. To state it another way, these texts do the opposite of what critics usually assume, which is that women and queers are always on the losing side when masculinity and reproduction combine. The chapters in this book show that modernist authors sometimes combined these discourses to emancipatory ends. Often, the difference between winners and losers, legitimate and illegitimate, oppressors and the oppressed, hinges on the story that a community tells about the reproducing body.

It would be impossible for a single book to fully map literary explorations of legitimacy, pregnancy, creativity, and masculinity. After all, in this book I have opted for depth over breadth, focusing on four authors, all writing in English, all hailing from the United States, and all writing in the interwar years. Yet the framework I developed for analyzing depictions of masculine pregnancy is portable to other time periods, literary movements, and fields of study. Indeed, the ideological linkages mentioned above regarding Teek's response to pregnancy clothing suggests some of the possibilities afforded by an analysis of contemporary literature through the lens of masculine pregnancy. In the remaining pages of this coda, I elaborate on this point after discussing two additional areas where further research should prove fruitful.

First, there is much work left to be done within modernist studies, Anglophone and not. Texts depicting metaphorical and literal depictions of masculine pregnancy include F. T. Marinetti's *Mafarka the Futurist* (1909) and Guillaume Apollinaire's *The Breasts of Tiresias* (1903). Additionally, *Nightwood*'s Matthew O'Connor is an obvious choice for consideration through the lens of masculine pregnancy. The novel provides no indication that he is ever pregnant, yet reproduction is closely tied to his identity.[1] Reading this character through the lens of masculine pregnancy turns the tale of Matthew O'Connor into one of a man who spouts stories in a failed attempt to find among them a narrative that legitimizes his life and dreams of procreation. His deepest wish in life is to "boil some good man's potatoes and toss up a child for him every nine months by the calendar" (98), but he lacks access to biomedical technology that would make this wish possible. This technology still does not exist today, although doctors in Europe were beginning to attempt womb transplants in the early twentieth century.[2] Suggestively, O'Connor also lacks a cultural context in which this kind of gendered embodiment is socially acceptable for men, as agricultural work provides context for masculine women in *My Ántonia*. Therefore *Nightwood*—even though I demonstrate in chapter 4 that the novel is a testament to the immense power of storytelling—implies that some kinds of kinship cannot be legitimized through narrative. Then as now, pregnancy for trans men and nonbinary people is far from socially legitimate. Instead, it is often conceptually invisible in social discourse, as I discuss in the introduction (and when it is visible, it is often met with derision or hostility). In most contexts, reproductive legitimacy rests on the gestator being legible as feminine. Pessimistic though it may be about the value of state-sanctioned legitimacy and blood-based kinship, *Nightwood* does make queer pregnancy more imaginable by depicting a male character whose subjectivity forms around the kernel of a desire to be pregnant. In this regard, I see a similarity—albeit a slant rhyme rather than an exact one—between O'Connor and several other well-known characters in twentieth-century literature, such as *Ulysses*'s Leopold Bloom (1922) and Biff Brannon from *The Heart Is a Lonely Hunter* (1940).

Second, depictions of masculine pregnancy offer new angles on key debates in queer theory. The texts under consideration in *Masculine Pregnancies* engage the relationship between the individual and society; that is, between pregnancy as a condition affecting an individual person and the social import of reproduction. In this regard, these depictions can be understood as forerunners to debates about the antisocial thesis, a controversial lodestar for the field of queer theory over the last two decades. The reader will recall from the introduction that the antisocial thesis holds that social life is organized around the Child (an archetypal image of a child more so than flesh-and-blood children); this ideology also positions queers as non-reproductive, which effectively excludes queer people from social life and simultaneously others them as threats to a social order structured around the nuclear family. One major strand of queer theory advocates leaning into this exclusion—embracing the antisocial epithet to unravel a social fabric that is deeply homophobic—by living for the present rather than the future. A second major strand rejects the premise of the antisocial thesis and suggests a focus on futurity instead of presentism.

I am suggesting here that I see in the figure of the mannish pregnant woman a pathway for reframing the debate. If, as the antisocial thesis claims, social life excludes queerness, this is not to suggest that proponents of the thesis are unaware of the fact that some queer people can and do have children. The antisocial thesis focuses instead on queerness and kinship in symbolic terms: not individual queer people but Queerness as it is constituted in the West. This particular construction of queerness—non-reproductive and a challenge to the social order—goes some way toward explaining the unimaginability of mannish pregnancy that I explore in the introduction and that subtends Teek's ability to pass as male in *Pregnant Butch*. As I have discussed throughout this book, mannish pregnancy challenges dominant social constructions of pregnancy, gender, and legitimacy. By extending this discussion to the antisocial thesis, it is possible to see that mannish pregnancy presents a challenge to various social constructions of queerness, too, by virtue of representing a person who is both queer and enmeshed in systems of reproductive futurism. Rather than erasing this challenge by feminizing mannish characters when they become pregnant, reading for mannish pregnancy has the potential to shift ideas about queerness, kinship, and pregnancy. The presence of queer reproductive desire in interwar literature suggests that the questions raised by the antisocial thesis are perennial rather than newly sprung in the late twentieth century.

Third, investigations into depictions of mannish pregnancy in literary traditions other than the modernist are likely to be fruitful. Although a locus of scholarship on queer pregnancy in Early Modern literature is taking shape, very little literary scholarship exists on queer pregnancy in general and mannish pregnancy in particular.[3] One of the most obvious places to start addressing this dearth is with the works of female-identified and nonbinary writers of the twenty-first century, to which I have already alluded. The contemporary publishing landscape has seen an explosion of pregnancy narratives with queer themes that build on the previous century's developments in sex and gender theory. In addition to *Pregnant Butch*, works such as Rachel Cusk's *A Life's Work* (2001), Meiko Kawakami's *Breasts and Eggs* (2008), Lidia Yuknavitch's *The Chronology of Water* (2010), Maggie Nelson's *The Argonauts* (2015), and Rivka Galchen's *Little Labors* (2016) are just a few of the recently published books that merit consideration for the ways their authors combine discourses of masculinity and pregnancy to emancipatory as well as oppressive ends. In general, I see these texts as pushing further than modernists did toward the emancipatory end of the spectrum, depicting versions of masculine pregnancy that allow for a wider range of self-expression than most modernists could even imagine.

Final Thoughts

Despite the widely accepted premise on which *Masculine Pregnancies* is founded (gender is not a binary), acknowledgment of a logical extension of that premise (not all pregnant people are feminine) is surprisingly rare. Even among people who study gender and sexuality, it is still common to assume that femininity "goes with" pregnancy, to imply that masculinity is incompatible with pregnancy, or to discuss "pregnant women" instead of "pregnant people." This fact gives us a sense of the depth and pervasiveness of the femininity-pregnancy assumption. The people who study gender and work daily to undermine heteronormativity fall prey to this faulty assumption.

Therefore, my grandest hope for *Masculine Pregnancies* is also the note on which I conclude because last words have staying power: this book encourages us to resist easy associations between pregnancy and femininity and to broaden our ideas of reproductive legitimacy to include forms of reproductive embodiment beyond that of the feminine woman when we talk, write, and think about reproduction. We do a disservice to authors and the characters they create by rationalizing away female masculinity during pregnancy. This book is a call to reread depictions of reproduction with an expanded awareness of the various forms that masculine pregnancy takes, as well as a greater willingness to see mannish pregnant women as legitimate (pro)creators.

Notes

Introduction

1. Teek, like Summers, identifies as a butch woman.

2. Breasts do not necessarily indicate someone assigned female at birth, of course; augmentation and reconstruction are among the most common plastic surgeries.

3. Philosopher Koert van Mensvoort's transphobic reaction is characteristic: "At first I thought this first pregnant man was a hoax, but after I saw it on *Oprah* I realized it must be 'real'. Well, the pregnant man is actually a former woman who had a sex change but kept ~~her~~ his reproductive organs. Welcome to the 21st century!" (word crossed out in original text).

4. The perceived newness of queer pregnancy is further fostered by the perception of reproductive biomedical technology as perpetually futuristic. There is a limited truth to this perception. In vitro fertilization and other reproductive technologies have opened possibilities for people of all genders in the last few decades, which leads to an ideological linkage between queer pregnancy and reproductive technology. Yet reproductive technologies are hardly new phenomena (the condom is one, after all). These technologies tend to retain the sheen of newness in the popular imagination even when they are decades old, due in part to the way they are depicted in novels, TV shows, and movies.

5. Robin Silbergleid, for instance, identifies the genre of queer motherhood narratives as one that begins in the 1990s. Silbergleid includes in this category the following texts: "Cherríe Moraga's *Waiting in the Wings* (1997), Anne Lamott's *Operating Instructions* (1993), Carole Maso's *The Room Lit by Roses* (2000), Harlyn Aizley's *Buying Dad* (2003), A. K. Summers's *Pregnant Butch* (2014), and Jennifer Finney Boylan's *Stuck in the Middle with You* (2013)," as well as Maggie Nelson's *The Argonauts* (2015).

6. I discuss race, femininity, and pregnancy discourse further in subsequent chapters. See especially chapters 1 and 5. See also Hazel Carby's *Reconstructing Womanhood*.

7. Although trans male pregnancy is not the same as pregnancy in butch or mannish women, their intellectual and literary histories overlap in ways I detail in chapter 1. Further, distinguishing between mannish women and trans men is an endeavor that is complex and often fruitless. I discuss the scholarly debates surrounding such distinctions in chapter 4. See also Jack Halberstam's "Butch/FTM Border Wars and the Masculine Continuum" and Jen Manion's *Female Husbands*. For scholarship on transmasculinity, see Jay Prosser's *Second Skins*. For trans studies work in modernism, see Heaney's *The New Woman* (2017), Pamela Caughie's work on Lili Elbe, and Jaime E. Hovey's work on Joan of Arc. Outside modernist studies, trans studies scholarship is particularly robust on the early modern period. See especially the 2019 special issue of the *Journal for Early Modern Cultural Studies* on trans studies (Chess, Simone, et al., vol. 19, no. 4).

8. In chapter 1, I detail this ignorance of the history of reproduction.

9. Laura L. Behling, writing in 2001, summed up the state of the field on mannish women in the interwar years: "Critical analysis of the female sexual invert in early-twentieth-century American literature is scant and is founded on two major studies, Jeannette H. Foster's *Sex Variant Women in Literature* (1954) and Lillian Faderman's *Surpassing the Love of Men* (1981). Other critics, including Marilyn Farwell, Judith Butler, Terry Castle, Bonnie Zimmerman, Martha Vicinus, Diana Fuss, and Carroll Smith-Rosenberg, have approached the components of this large field, but none has attempted the comprehensiveness of Foster and Faderman" (26). The field has expanded somewhat since publication of Behling's book in 2001, but the texts she lists remain touchstones. Among the most important recent work on mannish women in Britain is Deborah Cohler's *Citizen, Invert, Queer* (2010) and much of Laura L. Doan's oeuvre, including "Topsy-Turvydom: Gender Inversion, Sapphism, and the Great War."

10. Harris 236. Scores of literary critics have subtly suggested that pregnancy is incompatible with masculinity by implying that the state is inevitably, unquestionably, feminine. Paradigmatic examples of pregnancy-as-feminine discourse in the critical conversation include Elizabeth Sacks's claim that use of the childbirth metaphor (comparing the writing of a book to pregnancy) manifests "unconscious or repressed feminine elements in the masculine psyche" (5); Foster's statement that a mannish female character is "feminized by early pregnancy" (231); and Susan Stanford Friedman's argument that pregnancy leads Anaïs Nin to use the childbirth metaphor to "advocate a feminine form of writing" ("Creativity and the Childbirth Metaphor" 72).

11. Among texts that center male characters and authors, Michael Davidson's "Pregnant Men: Modernism, Disability, and Biofuturity in Djuna Barnes" is perhaps the most sustained examination of male pregnancy in modernism in recent years (the article was later revised into a chapter in *Invalid Modernism*). *Modernism and Masculinity* (2012), edited by Natalya Lusty and Julian Murphet, is an excellent collection containing essays by thirteen scholars on widely varying topics. Yet in all

these essays, only seven combined pages mention pregnancy, childbirth, or conception. Most of these mentions are brief, perhaps a paragraph in passing, and none mentions mannish women. Foster's *Sex Variant Women in Literature*, which was published in 1956 and is still an important work of scholarship on mannishness, makes occasional reference to pregnancy in the narratives she studies, but these are generally limited to a recital of plot points rather than analyses of the phenomenon. See, for instance, Foster's discussion of *Méphistophéla* (1890) by the French author Catulle Mendès, or her reading of Luz Frauman's *Weiberbeutel* (1901), a book that centers on a woman who is such a skilled hypnotist she is able to induce pregnancy in a man (Foster 100–4 and 221–23, respectively).

12. The most influential of these works include Susan Stanford Friedman's "Creativity and the Childbirth Metaphor: Gender Difference in Literary Discourse" (1987), Terry J. Castle's "Lab'ring Bards: Birth 'Topoi' and English Poetics 1660–1820" (1979), Susan Gubar's " 'The Blank Page' and the Issues of Female Creativity" (1985), and vol. 2 of Sandra Gilbert and Susan Gubar's *No Man's Land: The Place of the Woman Writer in the Twentieth Century* (1989), especially pp. 374–376.

13. Edelman's book rekindled debates over the antisocial thesis. This thesis, as Benjamin Kahan summarizes it, "argues that all social life and sociality—encompassing the good life, happiness, and citizenship—is organized by heterosexuality and reproductive futurism (emblematized by the figure of the child) and constitutively excludes queerness" (811). Reproductive futurism is an ideology that sees the future as "requiring not only reproduction but also protection and that therefore represents futurity in the image of the innocent child"; it excludes queerness because this same ideology understands homosexual people as failing to "reproduce the family in a recognizable form" and therefore also failing to "reproduce the social" (Dean 827; 826). The best-known articulations of the antisocial thesis were developed by Leo Bersani in *Homos* (1995), followed by Lee Edelman in *No Future* (2004), both of whom argue that queer people should embrace rather than critique right-wing ideas about homosexuality as undermining the social fabric (Dean 826). By rejecting the futurity represented by the Child, Edelman argues, homosexuals can disrupt a social fabric that has visited so much violence on queer people. A panel at the 2005 MLA conference (later published as a cluster in *PMLA*) attempted to reframe the debate by expanding the archive of antisociality (Halberstam) and directing attention to understudied aspects of Bersani's work, including "trac[ing] new forms of sociability, new ways of being together" (Dean, 827). José Esteban Muñoz's contribution to the cluster refuses the premise of the antisocial thesis entirely. He rejects the presentism that defines Edelman's work, which is emblematized in the title of Edelman's aforementioned book. Muñoz, in his essay for the cluster as well as in his later *Cruising Utopia* (2009), argues against "the assertion that there is no future for the queer by arguing that queerness is primarily about futurity. Queerness is always on the horizon" ("Thinking Beyond" 825). Taken together, the cluster demonstrates the limitations of the totalizing negativity that characterizes Bersani's and Edelman's work.

14. The oldest definition for *legitimate* in the *OED* is "conforming to the law or to rules; sanctioned or authorized by law or right principles; lawful; proper." The first recorded use was in 1460 ("legitimate").

15. Thanks to Rebecca Colesworthy for this idea.

16. Regarding the childbirth metaphor, Friedman similarly argues that "male paternity of texts has not precluded their paternity of children. But for both material and ideological reasons, maternity and creativity have appeared to be mutually exclusive to women writers" ("Creativity" 52).

17. For instance, a panel at the 2020 MLA conference on "Queer Pregnancies in Early Modern Literature" featured work by Andrzejewski, Simone Chess, and Christine Varnado.

18. A paradigmatic example of childbirth metaphors in writing by Black American men appears in Jean Toomer's *Cane* (1923), which concludes with a "birth-song" to celebrate the arrival of a book that the narrator describes as a "gold-glowing child" (117). I discuss *Cane* further in chapter 2.

19. Raymond Stephanson defines this line of inquiry as one concerned with the "literal and figurative connections between creative male mind and reproductive systems" (1). The correlation between male physical fertility and creative output exists, in part, because "the phallus, or erect penis, has represented to numerous civilizations the root of inspiration and creative power, and, as such, the source of natural fertility" (Johnson 23). Scholarship on physical and metaphorical male pregnancy includes Raymond Stephanson's *The Yard of Wit: Male Creativity and Sexuality, 1650–1750* (2003), Sherry Velasco's *Male Delivery: Reproduction, Effeminacy, and Pregnant Men in Early Modern Spain* (2006), and Michael Davidson's chapter "Pregnant Men: Biofuturity in Djuna Barnes and Virginia Woolf" in *Invalid Modernism* (2019; more on this chapter later). See also Matt Franks's article "Breeding Aliens, Breeding AIDS: Male Pregnancy, Disability, and Viral Materialism in 'Bloodchild'" (2019), which discusses a 1984 short story by Octavia Butler, and Alicia Andrzejewski's "'For her sake': Queer Pregnancy in *A Midsummer Night's Dream*" (2019).

20. Emma Heaney reads *Nightwood*'s Matthew O'Connor as trans but not pregnant. Michael Davidson reads O'Connor as pregnant but not trans. I discuss *Nightwood* in detail in chapter 5; I discuss Matthew O'Connor in the coda. For memoirs of a trans woman in the interwar era, see Pamela Caughie's essay "The Temporality of Modernist Life Writing in the Era of Transsexualism," which discusses the life of Lili Elbe. Elbe was an early recipient of gender affirmation surgery. Her fourth surgery was a uterus transplant; Elbe died in 1931 of complications from this surgery.

21. People who identify as women are not the only ones who gestate physical offspring, but the assumption that they are undergirds much of the literature and scholarship discussed in this book. Furthermore, historical discourse surrounding pregnancy in particular and women in general rests on this assumption. When discussing such discourse, I occasionally refer to "pregnant women" (or similar locutions) in recognition of the fact that queer reproduction was not part of the

historical discussion. I have also quoted from sources that assume pregnant people are exclusively women. These sources are indispensable, and quoting from them allows me to build on previous generations of scholarship that might not have recognized variability in reproductive embodiment. When not referring to this scholarship or historical understandings of pregnancy, I use gender-neutral terms such as "pregnant people" or "gestators."

Chapter 1

1. Foster argues that World War I may have increased the rate of same-sex encounters: "the war opened a number of men's jobs to women, increased their financial and personal independence, and encouraged tendencies toward masculine simplicity in dress. It also brought about that relaxation of sexual standards in general for which the 1920s have become notorious. Taken together, these alterations in women's status are held by some social historians to have increased female variance" (153–54). Foster defines "female variance" as female "persons having emotional experiences with others of their own sex" and considers variance as similar to inversion (11). Foster also notes that wars tend to increase the incidences of sex variance since wartime experiences often segregate the sexes (men at the front; women on the home front) and place young people in situations of heightened emotional intensity at an age when sex is particularly interesting (242).

2. The roots of *legitimacy* in law, rules, and principles differentiate it from related concepts such as *normativity*. For more, see Cryle and Stephens's *Normality: A Critical Genealogy* and Wiegman and Wilson's "Introduction: Antinormativity's Queer Conventions."

3. See Zunshine's *Bastards and Foundlings: Illegitimacy in Eighteenth-Century England* (2005)

4. Scholarship on the New Woman includes Sally Ledger's *The New Woman*, Elaine Showalter's *A Literature of Their Own*, Lyn Pykett's *The "Improper" Feminine*, Patricia Murphy's *Time Is of the Essence*, Ann Heilmann's *New Woman Fiction*, and Ann Ardis's *New Women, New Novels*.

5. Other terms for mannishness included "masculo-femininity" and "viraginity" (Behling 46). Sexological and psychoanalytical debates about viragos and masculo-feminine women were widespread in the United States and England during the interwar years, as D'Emilio and Friedman (241) and Laura Behling (3) demonstrate.

6. This debate is ongoing. Scholars still discuss the ethical implications of labeling, particularly when chosen by someone other than the labeled individual. See, for instance, Halberstam's "Transgender Butch: Butch/FTM Border Wars and the Masculine Continuum."

7. My phrasing owes much to Susan Stryker's definition of the subject matter of trans studies. Stryker states, "Most broadly conceived, the field of transgender

studies is concerned with anything that disrupts, denaturalizes, rearticulates, and makes visible the normative linkages we generally assume to exist between the biological specificity of the sexually differentiated human body, the social roles and statuses that a particular form of body is expected to occupy, the subjectively experienced relationship between a gendered sense of self and social expectations of gender-role performance, and the cultural mechanisms that work to sustain or thwart specific configurations of gendered personhood" (Stryker, "(De)subjugated Knowledges," 3). I am not arguing that the characters I study are trans—mostly because they do not attempt nor desire to live as men—but trans critical frameworks are helpful for thinking through depictions of mannish pregnancy. Furthermore, the ability and even desirability of categorizing historical figures using modern terminology is complicated. Where does a researcher draw the line between a butch woman and a trans man? What makes the researcher the best arbiter? I discuss these complications further in chapter 4.

8. Characters in, respectively, *The Well of Loneliness* (1928) and *The Heart Is a Lonely Hunter* (1940).

9. See also Cohler, who notes, "In late nineteenth-century England, gender inversion was primarily a sign of cultural, rather than sexual, transgression. It was not until after the Great War that masculine or mannish women were consistently labeled 'homosexual' in British culture. This signification of gender deviance becomes clear when read through public discourses of geopolitics and racial citizenship: at the turn of the twentieth century, masculine women signified a national or eugenic threat more often than a homosexual symptom" (x). For more on the racial associations with mannishness, see chapter 3.

10. While outside the scope of this book, mannish women appear throughout literary history, not just the twentieth century. As Vicinus states, "for centuries Eurocentric cultures have recognized and imagined the masculine woman" (xxiii).

11. Foster noted in 1956 that early twentieth-century sexologists attempted to locate the source of inversion, which Foster refers to as variance, in the body: "Following the lead of the biological sciences, students of the problem attempted to classify homosexuals. The subjects were variously divided into 'true' or born and "pseudo" or elective; 'masculine' and 'feminine' in general appearance; active and passive in the sexual role; homosexual and bisexual. But the determining data were less objective than is desirable for close classification. . . . The resulting confusion seems now to argue against, rather than for, the claim of somatic causation of variance" (149).

12. Authors were justified in this fear; witness the censorship trial of *The Well of Loneliness* in 1928.

13. See also the introduction, where I discuss the absence of Black mannish pregnancy in interwar literature.

14. See, for example, Lisa Tickner, who writes that masculinity was "in crisis in the years after 1900 or, to put it more locally, that a combination of factors made

the assertion of a virile and creative masculinity both imperative and problematic. Some of these originated in the art world itself and other [sic] pressed upon it from outside" (48). See also Natalya Lusty's introduction to *Modernism and Masculinity*.

15. To be sure, female modernists were apt to compare writing to pregnancy. For example, Virginia Woolf likens bad writing to "horrid little abortion[s]" in *A Room of One's Own* (102). Nevertheless, most of the critical discussion surrounding childbirth metaphors centers on their use by male authors (Friedman's "Creativity and Childbirth Metaphors" essay is an exception). The opposite is true with regard to scholarship on modernism and reproduction more generally, where the focus is on women writers. Works in this area include Allison Berg's *Mothering the Race*, Beth Widmaier Capo's *Textual Contraception*, Layne Craig's *When Sex Changed*, Laura Doyle's *Bordering on the Body*, Daylanne K. English's *Unnatural Selections*, my own *Conceived in Modernism*, and Christina Hauck's multiple articles on birth control and early twentieth-century literature, including "Why Do the Ramsays Have So Many Children?: Birth Control and *To the Lighthouse*." Erin Kingsley has written extensively on pregnancy in modernism; see especially "Birth Giving, the Body, and the Racialized Other in Jean Rhys's *Voyage in the Dark* and *Good Morning, Midnight*" and "'In the centre of a circle': Olive Moore's *Spleen* and Gestational Immigration." Jane Garrity writes about disability politics and reproduction in "Olive Moore's Headless Woman."

16. See Lusty and Kingsley for more on the masculinization of pregnancy.

17. See, for instance, Friedman's "Creativity and Childbirth Metaphors," Sandra M. Gilbert and Susan Gubar's "Cross-Dressing and Re-Dressing," in *No Man's Land*, vol. 2, Gilbert's "Potent Griselda: D. H. Lawrence's *Ladybird* and Literary Maternity," Gubar's "'The Blank Page' and the Issues of Female Creativity," and Yeager's "The Poetics of Birth."

18. Davidson admits his reading of male pregnancy as disability is "hyperbolic" and could strike readers as "a stretch" (120).

19. While Cox's summary of the debate is useful, it is limited by the exclusion of pregnant men and nonbinary people from its purview.

20. According to the US Equal Employment Opportunity Commission, "impairments resulting from pregnancy (for example, gestational diabetes or pre-eclampsia, a condition characterized by pregnancy-induced hypertension and protein in the urine) may be disabilities under the Americans with Disabilities Act (ADA)" ("Pregnancy Discrimination").

21. The phrasing of Cox's argument suggests the lack of uniformity among feminist scholars: is pregnancy a "limitation" or "heightened biological functioning"? (Cox 448–49).

22. For instance, in 2019 a pregnant prisoner in New York was forced to endure childbirth while handcuffed. As Ashley Southall writes, "New York State law prohibits shackling pregnant prisoners during labor and delivery, but the police accompanying the woman left her in chains anyway" ("She Was Forced").

In 2013, *The New York Times* reported that lawmakers in California "called for an investigation into a new report that nearly 150 women behind bars were coerced into being sterilized over the last decade" (Medina).

23. Davidson notes that the title of his book, *Invalid Modernism* (the book in which the chapter on male pregnancy appears), works two ways: "my title contains something of a *double entendre* depending on whether one places the accent on the first or second syllable of 'invalid,' whether one refers to a 'sick' or 'ill' modernism—one in a state of convalescence—or a modernism invalidated by elements that challenge artisanal autonomy" (8). The framework of in*valid* modernism is less problematic from a feminist perspective, but I nevertheless find illegitimacy a more illuminating conceptualization because it reveals important continuities in the cultural imagination surrounding pregnancy and bastardy.

Chapter 2

1. Jaffe notes briefly that Pound depicts himself as a surgeon rather than a midwife (127) but does not contextualize this note within medical history.

2. For more on childbirth metaphors, see Castle and chapter 1 of this book.

3. As many feminist critics have discussed, Eliot's poem has much in common with Hope Mirrlees's *Paris* (1919), first published by Virginia and Leonard Woolf's Hogarth Press. Julia Briggs refers to *Paris* as "modernism's lost masterpiece" (261), while Bruce Bailey, Melissa Boyde, and others have noted that Eliot likely read *Paris* prior to composing *The Waste Land*. See also Suzanne Henig's "Hope Mirrlees: Queen of Lud."

4. See Sorensen Emery-Peck for a detailed analysis of Vivien Eliot's editorial influence on *The Waste Land*. Vivien's emendations are printed in *The Waste Land: A Facsimile and Transcript of the Original Drafts Including the Annotations of Ezra Pound*, edited by Valerie Eliot, Tom's second wife. Valerie's efforts to recover and edit the drafts of the poem, which were long believed lost, contributed substantially to critical understanding of *The Waste Land*'s composition history. Pound states in the preface to the facsimile: " 'The mystery of the missing manuscript' is now solved. Valerie Eliot has done a scholarly job which would have delighted her husband" (*The Waste Land: A Facsimile* ii).

5. After publication, Eliot responded to Conrad Aiken's praise of *The Waste Land* by sending him a clipping about menstruation from *The Nursing Mirror and Midwives' Journal* [often quoted as *The Midwives Gazette* following Aiken's mistaken memory], with various words underlined: "blood," "mucus," "shreds of mucus," "purulent offensive discharge" (*Letters of T.S. Eliot* 43). That Eliot would choose an article in *The Nursing Mirror and Midwives' Journal* as representative of *The Waste Land* is not as significant as it first seems, for he did not have to seek out the journal. As Valerie Eliot and John Haffenden explain, "TSE did not have to

look far for his cutting: F&G [Faber & Gwyer, his employer] had just taken over publication of that periodical, so recent issues were to be found at their new offices" (*Letters of T.S. Eliot* 43). It is therefore likely that Eliot saw the publication lying around at work, not that he sought it out. Nevertheless, the clipping reinforces the idea that Eliot conceptualized poetry in reproductive terms, thinking of his poetic output in terms of the childbirth metaphor, and of *The Waste Land*, in particular, as unsuccessful because his contribution was feminized.

6. Beginning in the 1990s, Susan Merrill Squier and Christina Hauck produced, independently, some of the most insightful scholarship on modernism and the social history of reproduction. Hauck's "Through a Glass Darkly" and "Abortion and the Individual Talent" are particularly relevant here as they address reproductive discourse in *The Waste Land*. Beth Widmaier Capo's *Textual Contraception* and Layne Parish Craig's *When Sex Changed* focus on depictions of birth control in twentieth-century literature, as does my own *Conceived in Modernism*. Paul Peppis discusses birth control and sexology in "Rewriting Sex: Mina Loy, Marie Stopes, and Sexology." For compelling recent essays on pregnancy in modernist literature, see "Olive Moore's Headless Woman" by Jane Garrity, " 'In the centre of a circle': Olive Moore's *Spleen* and Gestational Immigration," by Erin Kingsley, and "Birth Giving, the Body, and the Racialized Other in Jean Rhys's *Voyage in the Dark* and *Good Morning, Midnight*," also by Kingsley. Joyce E. Kelley discusses pregnancy as a travel trope in the chapter " 'I am going on and on to the end of myself where something else begins': Travel, Pregnancy, and Modernism." On abortion in American literature, see Karen Weingarten's *Abortion in the American Imagination: Before Life and Choice, 1880–1940*. Daylanne K. English's *Unnatural Selections: Eugenics in American Modernism and the Harlem Renaissance* is an important study of reproduction and race.

7. See, for instance, the comparison between idea development and childbirth in Plato's *Symposium*, 36–42.

8. The dispute between midwives and medical men has a long and complex history dating back to at least the thirteenth century. For more, see Donnison, Cahill, and Stacey.

9. Similar attitudes existed among physicians in the United States. See Barker-Benfield, especially chapter 7.

10. Although attendance by midwives in the first half of the twentieth century rose to as much as 60% at times, this increase is attributable to WWI, when large numbers of medical men were sent to the front, and to changes to insurance policies, particularly relating to the establishment of the Ministry of Health in 1919 (Donnison 192).

11. Susan Stanford Friedman suggests that these visits reignited their romantic relationship (*Psyche Reborn* 300n16).

12. Despite much interest in the *Cantos*, relatively little scholarship exists on this particular poem, and the composition history has many gaps in it. An early,

undated draft does not contain the parenthetical phrase "lightning was midwife," suggesting it was a late addition that could have been inspired by Pound's visit to H. D. in the maternity ward (Pound, Canto V: Typescript). It is even plausible that Pound began work on Canto V in response to H. D.'s first pregnancy. He started drafting it just a few months after the stillbirth.

13. Carole R. McCann succinctly describes the Comstock Act: "Named for its author, Anthony Comstock, this 1873 amendment to the U.S. Postal Code prohibited the shipping of obscene materials on both public and private freight carriers. All information and devices that could 'be used or applied for preventing conception' were included among the obscene materials proscribed under the law" (23).

14. Pound was not alone in thinking surgically about metaphors at this time. Issues of *The New Age* contain numerous pieces in which authors compare writing and writing-adjacent roles to surgery. Consider, for instance, T. W. Pateman's "Conversation with a Realist" from the March 12, 1914 issue. In this article, Pateman argues that writers should be as selective in their choice of topics as surgeons with scalpels. He states, "your surgeon has a better ideal. He doesn't tackle malformities just because he likes them, because they exist, he only deals with them to restore health. How do you think that principle would do for the writer?" (589). In a similar line, Pateman later argues, "the writer should use his tools—they can cut like the surgeon's—but only to further health of character" (589). It is hard to imagine Pound agreeing with the idea that writing should improve moral health. Yet the idea that surgeons are paragons of skill, judgment, and intelligence—an idea I read in "SAGE HOMME"—is nevertheless apparent in both Pound and Pateman. So too is the idea that artists and professionals connected to the arts would be wise to emulate surgeons. These ideas echo throughout *The New Age* in the years between 1914 and 1921. The rhetoric surrounding surgeons in these references differs dramatically from the rhetoric then common with regard to midwives, the latter of which tended toward the sloppy, ignorant, and unhygienic.

15. Koestenbaum discusses the gendered implications of Eliot suffering from hysteria, a condition closely associated with women.

16. See, for instance, Sterne, *Tristram Shandy*, 78. Pound also published "The Dialogues of Fontanelle," in *The Egoist*, vol. 3 no. 9 (1916), which includes the following: "Ah, Socrates, I knew . . . that you called yourself the midwife of their thoughts conducting accouchement" (133).

17. See, for instance, Moody (53) for pan pipe translation, and Ricks and McCue (551) for ulcer translation.

18. As Morantz-Sanchez notes, Sims's medical legacy needs to be considered in its historical context, which includes Sims's operations on enslaved women, without anesthesia, and in situations that negated their ability to give informed consent. Moreover, the rest of Sims's career was undistinguished, which raises questions about his ability to make such a discovery in the absence of "the racial and class system that made these women available to him as human guinea pigs"

(93–94). The growing attention to this historical context led recently to a statue of Sims being relocated from Central Park to Brooklyn's Green-Wood Cemetery, near Sims's grave, where it will be placed on a lower pedestal that will include reference to this history (Zhang par. 14).

19. J. Marion Sims's grandson, John Allan Wyeth, was a poet who occupied some of the same circles as Pound. In 1926, Wyeth took up residence in Rapallo, Italy, where he almost certainly met Pound. Dana Gioia explains: "Although there is no documentary evidence that Wyeth knew Pound (who moved from Paris to Rapallo in 1924), the English-speaking community was so small that it would have been unlikely for them to have missed one another" (256). Gioia also states that "Wyeth family members have confirmed the friendship" with Pound (257). The timeline makes it impossible for Wyeth and his family connections to have exerted influence on Pound's thinking in 1922, but it is possible they had an influence on Pound's later reproductive rhetoric.

20. C-sections are today an important preventative measure for people likely to develop obstetric fistulae (Wall 11). I have not been able to determine if this recommendation was common in 1922.

21. See, for instance, Rachel Blau DuPlesssis, "Propounding."

22. Rachel Blau DuPlessis reads this line as signifying a metaphorical pregnancy wherein the poet gestates phallic materials because of the shape of the mandrake root and the plant's long association with fertility ("Propounding" 393).

23. Nevertheless, the feminine women do not have much more success. Jessica Hays Baldanzi notes that "Instances of failed reproduction in *Cane* far outweigh the book's successful births, which are not only scarce but wholly metaphorical and atmospheric" (np).

24. See, for instance, MacKethan and Bone.

25. I am not suggesting that childbirth is easy; see chapter 1 for more.

Chapter 3

1. Of *Jerusalem*, for instance, Cynthia Dobbs argues that the pregnant female body in this novel symbolizes "monstrous fluidity" and "malevolent nature" (821). Of *Mosquitoes*, Ted Atkinson echoes other critics' assessment of it as a poorly executed novel of ideas: "Typical of this genre, *Mosquitoes* contains repeated digressions that seem to serve no further purpose than allowing a budding novelist to work through thoughts on various topics of interest" (3). See also Claus Daufenbach, who states that *Mosquitoes* has "obvious flaws" (547), and John Earl Bassett, who argues that it is "his most imitative work" (50). Even still, all these critics conclude that *Mosquitoes* reveals much about Faulkner's developing aesthetic.

2. On Faulkner's familiarity with sexology, see Rado 14, Duvall 155–56, and Michel 8.

3. See Bauer (99) and Heilmann (117–54)

4. On the more capacious definition of inversion, see also Bauer 87–89 and Funke, "The Case," 134–35.

5. For more on the racial underpinnings of the gender binary, see Kyla Schuller's *The Biopolitics of Feeling.*

6. Yet culture and the economy did undeniably contribute to the ideology of masculinity in the 1920s. Chris Forth argues that the American labor movement in the early years of the twentieth century "insisted upon the working man's right to a certain standard of living that would allow him to meet 'civilized needs,' thus initiating a reorientation of proletarian male identity away from production towards consumerism" (157). In the 1920s, men's participation in the consumer marketplace, long associated with femininity, became acceptable to an extent.

7. On Faulkner's gendered attitudes toward the literary marketplace, see also Michel, 7–8.

8. On hermaphroditism, John C. Avise states, "approximately 99% of all [vertebrate] species consist of separate-sex individuals, meaning that each individual is either male or female. Most of the other 1% of vertebrate species are hermaphroditic, and essentially all of these are fishes" (xi). Among hermaphroditic fish, only a small proportion is "selfing," that is, reproducing by self-fertilization (xii).

9. The "ladder of nature" had a stronghold on scientific thinking for hundreds of years; this stronghold was barely beginning to loosen in the early years of the twentieth century as Darwin's ideas took root (Gopnik 40).

10. Minrose Gwin argues that the deletion of this scene, along with several others like it, is most likely attributable to the publisher and not Faulkner (130–32).

11. Faulkner's belief that sex fosters artistic creation is well-documented. See, for example, Golden, 737.

12. The novel interweaves two distinct narratives, "Old Man" and "The Wild Palms." "The Wild Palms" is the story of Charlotte and Harry. "Old Man" takes place during the Mississippi River flood of 1927. While it also deals with reproduction, the specific reproductive topics that "Old Man" engages are outside the scope of this book.

13. The most obvious example of incest as a threat to identity is that of Quentin's attraction to Caddy in *The Sound and the Fury,* but other examples abound. See also Rado, 20, 26.

14. Many critics, such as Janet Carey Eldred, read the abortion as the event that puts an end to Charlotte's art rather than pregnancy. As my timeline shows, however, months pass between the conception and the abortion, during which time she does not create art of any kind. Pregnancy is therefore the more likely precipitating event.

15. In this stance, the novel is not entirely at odds with prevailing attitudes toward reproductive control in the 1930s. The difficulties associated with supporting

a family during the depression brought about broader acceptance of abortion and birth control. For more, see Henninger, Weingarten, Craig, and Capo.

16. The full quote is "What was it you told me nigger women say? Ride me down, Harry" (186). Charlotte thereby connects transgressive sexuality with race, a combination familiar to readers of Faulkner's novels. The relationship between race and sex in this scene is complex and part of a broader pattern in Faulkner's oeuvre. For more on Faulkner's association of transgressive sex with race, see Guttman.

17. The characterization of excessive, uncontrollable liquid as feminine is echoed in "The Old Man" plotline of *Jerusalem*. Cynthia Dobbs explores this characterization at length.

Chapter 4

1. Laura L. Doan discusses perceptions of mannish women during wartime in "Topsy-Turvydom: Gender Inversion, Sapphism, and the Great War." For more on queer lives and virtuous narratives, see Jaime E. Hovey, "Gallantry and Its Discontents: Joan of Arc and Virtuous Transmasculinity in Radclyffe Hall and Vita Sackville-West."

2. Critics long suspected that Cather was romantically attracted to women. Sharon O'Brien's *Willa Cather: The Emerging Voice* (1987) provides ample evidence to substantiate these suspicions. While it is certainly possible to read *My Ántonia* through the lens of same-sex attraction and Ántonia as a cipher for Cather—as many critics have done—I resist reading female masculinity as *necessarily* a screen for a "truer" identity (as though Ántonia/Cather would be a feminine-identified lesbian if only she lived in a time and place where it were socially possible).

3. Rosowski captures the frequency of Earth mother readings when she argues that Cather concludes the novel with Ántonia's fulfillment of her "destiny as a natural born mother—undeniably, an Earth Mother. Ántonia as Earth Mother? The description has become so standard that it is easy to pass over how revolutionary is Cather's revisioning of Western myths that depict women" (441). Rosowski's argument is that the Earth mother myth is usually a threatening one, in that man is thought to be delivered from Eden into a chaotic world; the earth to which the character is mother is dangerous and unpredictable. Thus, Cather's representation of Ántonia as a nurturing figure is a dramatic revision of the myth. Like Rosowski, I too see the depiction of Ántonia as Earth mother as subtly revolutionary; but where Rosowski sees revolution in Cather's removal of threat, I see it in the depiction of a masculine woman as a fertile, maternal figure.

4. Blanche H. Gelfant's rationalization takes a different form. In her reading of *My Ántonia*, "thoroughgoing masculinization" is a "punishment" leveled on Ántonia for "sexual involvement—and for the breezy pleasures of courtship" (378).

This reading removes the perceived social threat of Ántonia's masculinity by erasing her pleasure in it. For additional readings that rationalize Ántonia's masculinity, see Clasen and Gilbert and Gubar ("Lighting Out"). Another method by which critics position Ántonia's masculinity as inauthentic is by reading it as a symptom of burgeoning same-sex attraction. While this line of criticism is not a rationalization of the kind Halberstam discusses, because it embraces rather than explains away an alleged social threat, it does nevertheless position female masculinity as temporary or a mask for other desires. Readings in this vein are generally biographical, arguing that Ántonia (or sometimes Jim) is an avatar for Cather, and often conflating gender and sexuality by assuming that Ántonia's masculinity is a manifestation of same-sex attraction because Cather was masculine and attracted to women (Worden 82).

5. Halberstam is referring specifically to trans people in this context. While I would not argue that Ántonia is trans in an identitarian sense, determinations of this kind are ultimately impossible to make for reasons I discuss in the introduction. Nevertheless, reading Cather's novel through the lens of trans theory would undoubtedly be productive. For more on considerations "of superficially 'non-trans' topics through a trans critical lens," see Carter, Getsy, and Salah's Introduction to the TSQ special issue on trans cultural production.

6. See the introduction for more on mannish women and maternity in the popular imagination.

7. Laura L. Behling's perceptive reading of fiction published in the years surrounding the 1920 ratification of the Nineteenth Amendment in the United States considers masculine women and narrative attempts to "return them to femininity and heterosexuality" as a backlash against the successes of woman suffrage movement (82–83). Behling argues that within many popular narratives of the time, "women who failed to achieve traditional femininity and, more specifically, those women who clearly showed signs of masculine womanhood and sexual inversion were subjected to a fate that removed the stigma of their gender and sexuality anomalies by first demasculinizing them and then seducing them with heterosexuality" (83). Unlike the narratives Behling considers, however, Cather does not end the novel with Antonia's seduction into heterosexuality. Cather's narrative continues after the seduction to include some of the dangers of heterosexuality (reproduction out of wedlock and its accompanying social stigma), as well Antonia's re-masculinization when she moves back to the country and resumes farming.

8. Jim tells the first narrator: 'Here is the thing about Ántonia . . . I suppose it hasn't any form. It hasn't any title, either.' He went into the next room, sat down at my desk and wrote across the face of the portfolio the word 'Ántonia.' He frowned at this a moment, then prefixed another word, making it 'My Ántonia.' That seemed to satisfy him" (8). Appending "My" to the title emphasizes the subjective quality of the narrative.

9. See, for instance, O'Brien (Emerging Voice 127–41).

10. Cather did not identify as a feminist, but she also did not ascribe to notions of gender as static and biological. Angus Fletcher explains that Cather "saw

masculinity as dynamic and context dependent, a view that aligned her with early twentieth-century feminists like Charlotte Perkins Gilman and with contemporary queer culture more broadly" (117).

11. For more on *My Ántonia* and storytelling, see Woolley.

12. Mary Paniccia Carden identifies a similar dynamic at work in *O Pioneers!* Carden notes that this novel's masculine protagonist, Alexandra Bergson, claims that "the demands of circumstance compel her deviant femininity and attributes agency not to her desire and skill but to 'conditions' produced by frontier life" (281). Yet Paniccia Carden argues that Bergson's masculinity cannot be boiled down to the exigencies of farm life because "Cather insists that Alexandra's relation to the land is rooted deeper" (281).

13. References are to the 2015 Norton critical edition of *My Ántonia*, which retains the typographical preferences of the novel's original publishing house, including contractions such as "are n't." O'Brien explains in a footnote to the text that "this unusual spacing for contractions, which occurs throughout *My Ántonia*, was a typographical oddity favored by Houghton Mifflin for all its writers" (10).

14. As Halberstam argues, rural queer life takes on a different form than in metropolitan areas, and the former is poorly understood (35). A corrective underway in queer studies addresses this geographical imbalance. Rural queer lives are the focus of studies such as *Queering the Countryside* (2016), edited by Gray, Johnson, and Gilley, and Carol Mason's *Oklahomo* (2015). These studies demonstrate that non-urban queer lives are far richer and more varied than urban-focused scholarship might imply.

15. The town's name, Black Hawk, speaks to a time when the area was populated by Indigenous peoples. While outside the scope of this chapter, issues of legitimacy, nationality, and belonging also inhere in the conflicts between white settlers and Native Americans in ways that inform Cather's novel. For more, see Fischer, "Pastoralism and Its Discontents: Willa Cather and the Burden of Imperialism."

16. Discourse connecting masculine women and foreignness was common in the years preceding *My Ántonia*'s publication. See, for example, the following claim from Edward Allsworth Roth's *Changing America: Studies in Contemporary Society* from 1912: "Society can have the kind of woman it wants. Take the women of eastern Prussia, for instance. These peasant women bear a child in the morning; in the afternoon they are out in the field. . . . I have seen them, and what a type they are, squat, splay-footed, wide-backed, flat-breasted, broad-faced, short-necked—a type that lacks every grace that we associate with woman" (qtd. in Behling 40).

17. For more on the intersection of class and gender in Cather, see Margaret Marquis.

18. As discussed in chapter 1, Southern and Eastern European immigrants were also denigrated on political grounds. Matthew Frye Jacobson documents changes to American perceptions of immigrant race, noting that the period from the 1850s to the 1920s saw the rise of a "regime of racial understanding" for immigrants that was defined by "cataloguing the newcomers as racial types, pronouncing upon their

innate, biological distance from the nation's "original stock," and speculating as to their fitness for citizenship" (14).

19. My thanks to Korey Garibaldi, whose questions at the 2019 Space Between conference pushed my thinking in this direction. For more on racialization of immigrants, see Noel Ignatiev's *How the Irish Became White* and Janis P. Stout's *Willa Cather: The Writer and Her World*, especially the chapter "Coming to America/ Escaping to Europe."

20. Isobel Armstrong discusses "retrospective legitimization," explaining that "European and Scottish civil law . . . after 1601, allowed children to be retrospectively legitimized by their parents' marriage, a practice not recognized by English common law" (38–39).

21. For this point I am indebted to Linda Lizut Helstern, who states, "Never in *My Ántonia* does [Cather] deny outright the racial hierarchy posited by the eugenics movement. Rather, she uses it to point out the logical fallacy of linking negative inherited traits exclusively with the lower races" (262).

22. Ántonia does manifest stereotypically feminine traits after becoming a mother, such as distaste for violence and a desire to comfort. These traits exist alongside ones Jim identifies as masculine. Considered in context with the debates of the day surrounding masculine women, I read the novel as implying that masculine comportment does not erase maternal tendencies but rather complements them.

23. See chapters 1 and 5 for more on eugenic discourse in the interwar years.

24. The male characters frequently discuss the gendered attributes of Herland- ers, with one character in referring to them as "boys" (111) and "neuters" (121), and the other two men arguing for their femininity. As such, a consideration of *Herland* through the lens of masculine pregnancy would prove quite productive.

25. For more on embodiment in *Song*, see Nealon 69–74.

26. Nevertheless, as noted before, the strength of the pregnancy-femininity association causes Jim to think Ántonia has assimilated—that is, feminized—more than she has.

Chapter 5

1. My phrasing is an adaptation of Michael Davidson's. He argues that *Nightwood* challenges readers to consider "what happens when reproduction is removed from female biology and shifted discursively onto other bodies" (120).

2. Barnes's rejection of legitimacy prefigures the contemporary rejection of respectability politics, especially gay marriage, among many in gay communities. Scott Herring explains that Barnes's rejection is made manifest in her ridicule of Radclyffe Hall and Hall's partner, Una Troubridge, whom Barnes called "'Tilly Tweed-in-Blood' and 'Lady Buck-and-Balk'" (Herring, *Queering* 18). Herring argues that Barnes's ridicule "now seems quite prescient" because she satirized them "for

their commitment to gay marriage and desire for a normalizing, state-sanctioned existence" (166).

3. Caselli briefly situates Barnes's bastard aesthetic within interwar literature. She states, "Rather than adopting, like H. D.'s late poetry, a language of parturition and generation in opposition to widely circulating masculine modernist metaphors of forging (adopted by Joyce, Pound, and Eliot), Barnes's oeuvre counterfeits, so that one is never sure if the coin is based, clipped, blanched, or true. Pen Performer, Dobrujda, the Lady of Fashion, Dan Corbeau, Dan Pasquin [Barnes's pen names and avatars] are promiscuously 'loose' characters (also figured in Wendell Ryder's hilariously phallic nicknames) who produce bastard offspring and ruthlessly expose the workings of the Law of the Father by refusing the modernist purity of original creation, even when conceived as the impossibility of originality" (88). Readers interested in bastardy in Barnes's oeuvre are encouraged to consult the scholarship on *Ryder*. Although I do not consider *Ryder* in this chapter because it does not depict masculine pregnancies, there is a possible instance of maternal impression in the birth of Amelia's last child.

4. With regard to the "realness" of biological kinship, anthropologist Kath Weston states, "biogenetic attributes are supposed to demarcate kinship as a cultural domain, offering a yardstick for determining who counts as a 'real' relative," and yet this "realness" is a Western cultural construct because "not all cultures grant biology this significance for describing and evaluating relationships" (34).

5. Davidson discusses masculinity and pregnancy in *Nightwood* but focuses on Matthew O'Connor. For more on Davidson's analysis, see chapter 1.

6. Scholars who discuss this scene as one of postpartum depression include Ery Shin and Courtney Musselman.

7. In a watershed argument, Marcus argued against early readings of *Nightwood* as an apolitical text, demonstrating that it must be read in light of European fascism. See also Carlston, who argues that Hedvig's parturition scene "inverts Mussolini's famous dictum that war is to men what childbirth is to women by parodically metaphorizing childbirth as a scene of military spectacle and then letting Hedvig disappear from the (hi)story. War is not a substitute for childbirth, it is implied; giving birth, rather, is war, a war in which there is little glory and the victims leave nothing to posterity" (80). Furthermore, Barnes's depiction of Hedvig and Guido is informed by her relationship with Ernst "Putzi" Hanfstaengl, a German man who attended Harvard and remained in New York to run his father's art gallery there. Barnes and Putzi were engaged between 1914 and 1916 (Herring 68). He broke off the engagement because Barnes was American. As Scott Herring states, "Putzi Hanfstaengl told her that he must have a German wife for his children" (72). Putzi then returned to Germany, where he became a supporter and then confidant of Hitler's. He held the position of chief minister of the foreign press for the Nazi party from 1932 to 1937 (69).

8. There is a long tradition of scholarship on the relationship between fascism and homosexuality, perhaps most famously summed up in Adorno's adage "totality

and homosexuality belong together" (*Minima Moralia* 46). John Champagne notes that Italian fascism was undergirded by worry that Italian men lacked the virility and masculinity of their European counterparts (9). The demasculinization of the Volkbein men engages stereotypes of two peoples, that of effeminacy in Jewish and Italian men. For more on fascism and homosexuality, see Andrew Hewitt's *Political Inversions: Homosexuality, Fascism, and the Modernist Imaginary* and Barbara Spackman's *Fascist Virilities*.

9. Hedvig is skeptical of Guido's claims to aristocracy, believing Guido's assurances of his barony "as a soldier 'believes' a command. Something in her sensory predicament—upon which she herself would have placed no value—had told her much better" (7). Hedvig's skepticism suggests that she had a better grasp than her husband on the historical forces that were voiding the aristocracy's legitimacy.

10. For more on Barnes's antisemitism and uncritical engagement with stereotypes of Jewish men as feminine, see Lee 209–11 and Goody 188–92. I incline to Catherine Setz's argument that although Barnes intended "to show a sympathy for the plight of the Jews (as stated in Barnes's 1930 application for a Guggenheim Memorial Foundation Fellowship) . . . the novel instead simply negates Jewish history by expressing Felix Volkbein as a Christianized form of aesthetic pain" (Setz 374).

11. The term *parental impressions* has the benefit of encompassing, in theory at least, pregnant men and nonbinary people. In practice, however, examples of impression theory have historically been strictly heteronormative. Therefore, Doniger and Spinner's overview of parental impressions does not encompass the gestational influence of trans men on the fetuses they carry or other kinds of queer pregnancy.

12. See also Persephone Emily Harbin 179–81.

13. Livia Arndal Woods provides literary historical context on maternal impressions, noting that they appear frequently in pre-nineteenth century literature, "only to recede from view for much of the mid- and late nineteenth century along with frank representations of sexuality and pregnancy more generally" (119). References begin to show up again shortly before the interwar years. Woods explains that "at the *fin-de-siecle* when pregnancy re-appears as something more than just the narrative moral lesson it has been for most of the century prior, impression theories seem to re-appear alongside it . . . the deployment of outdated theory in *fin-de-siecle* fiction suggests that notions of impression are doing something in late-Victorian fiction, specifically acting as a way of sketching the unarticulated spaces of women's bodies and minds in order to express rising unease with the disruptive social and physical potential of the unconscious mind" (119). Jeanette H. Foster's discussion of Philip Cuisin's *Clémentine, Orpheline et Androgyne* (1819) provides evidence of parental impressions in nineteenth-century France, which remained quite frank about sexuality while British literature became less explicit. Foster notes that Cuisin locates the origins of his protagonist's "passionate intensity" in prenatal influence: "Her mother, we are told, had during pregnancy been very friendly with a Persian

ambassador to the French court, and had been 'saturated' with his oriental tales. Thus, the daughter was predestined to love "avec l'exaltation d'une Persane" (61).

14. At its highest point in 1936, the year of *Nightwood*'s publication, Christian Science had 296,000 followers, a meteoric increase from its beginnings in 1879 as a congregation of 26 people. Christian Science membership began to taper off in the 1930s, while New Thought continued to grow. New Thought was less doctrinal than Christian Science, which largely explains its broader popularity. Where Christian Science is a discrete religion closely associated with its founder, Mary Baker Eddy, New Thought was less rule-bound and could therefore encompass a broader variety of people's existing spiritual and moral beliefs. The New Thought movement was closely associated with women's groups, especially those agitating for suffrage, and attracted a mostly female following (Satter 5–6).

15. Maternal impressions are a present though less potent force during Robin's pregnancy. At one point while pregnant, Robin attempts "to think of the consequence to which her son was to be born and dedicated. She thought of the Emperor Francis Joseph" (50), a key figure in the "destiny" Felix desires for his son. Even in this moment of acquiescence to Felix's impressions, her thoughts drift away from the Emperor and toward "women in history" who challenged patriarchal control such as "Louise de la Vallière, Catherine of Russia, Madame de Maintenon, Catherine de' Medici, and two women out of literature, Anna Karenina and Catherine Heathcliff" (51). Robin's outright rejection of Felix's plans comes later, after she gives birth.

16. Caselli here draws on William Blake and his influence on Barnes's style.

17. Readers interested in self-conceptions ("conceiving herself pregnant") are encouraged to refer to my discussion of parthenogenesis and "selfing" in chapter 2. See also Brian Glavey, who discusses the passage in which Jenny Petherbridge is described as giving off an odor "of a woman about to be accouche" (758).

18. In *The Masculine Woman in America*, Laura L. Behling analyzes Barnes's exploitation of the dual connotation of *conception* in *Ladies Almanack*, particularly with regard to the sterility of same-sex couples. See chapter 5, "Marketing Mockery," especially 141–56.

19. Felix's birth year (1880) is significant because it is "the beginning of one of the decades that would see a rise of anti-Semitism," and the place of his birth, Vienna, holds special importance as "the city to which many Eastern European Jews fled to escape persecution" (Kaviola 179).

20. Travel of the kind associated with the bildungsroman was still largely a male privilege in the interwar years. Through the mid-twentieth century, Western women were discouraged from traveling unless they went to a "safe, civilized territory" with a chaperone (Netzley ix). Further, long-standing gendered associations around travel persisted into the interwar years. Sidonie Smith explains that "travel has generally been associated with men and masculine prerogatives" (x) because "travelers affirm their masculinity" through "behaviors, dispositions, perspectives, and

bodily movements displayed on the road, and through the narratives of travel that they return home to the sending culture. Thus, travel functions as a defining arena of agency" (ix). The bildungsroman, with travel as a central feature, is therefore an apt genre for depicting Robin's developing identity during pregnancy.

21. Richard's disability is a frequent topic of discussion in the scholarship on *Spleen*. Erin Kingsley summarizes the discussion as such: "In the extant criticisms surrounding Moore, all take a stab at the meaning of Richard. [Renée] Dickinson claims that Ruth's attempt to create 'something new' in Richard corresponds to the modernist dictum to 'Make it New,' and that Richard's deformity means Moore is 'insistently skeptical of modernism's emphasis on the new, where the 'it' of 'make it new' is also vague and leaves open the option for monstrosity.' [Jane] Garrity argues that Richard is a 'physical manifestation of the argument that maternity is incompatible with intellectual and artistic activity.' [Maren Tova] Linett reads Richard as representative of 'the woman writer's monstrous text' and symbolic of Moore's problematic belief that women cannot create as men can, they can only dumbly reproduce" (" 'In the centre of a circle' " 145–46).

22. Letters between Zadel and Djuna have led some to speculate that their relationship was incestuous. See Caselli, 129–34, on the critical debate surrounding their relationship. Of Barnes's marriage, Mary Lynn Broe states, "Barnes was married in a home ceremony to Percy Faulkner, the brother of her father's second wife and a man three times her age. She left immediately for Bridgeport, Connecticut, surfacing again in 1912, enrolled as an art student at Pratt Institute. (The years 1909–1912 are among the curious gaps or omissions in the Barnes chronology)" (4).

23. See also Janet Carsten's *After Kinship*. Note that *fictive kin* is not identical to *chosen kin*.

24. See also James Joyce's explorations of kinship, particularly in *Ulysses* and *Portrait of the Artist as a Young Man*. For example, Persephone Emily Harbin says, "In *Portrait*, heredity is discussed almost entirely through the mother. In *Ulysses*, Stephen makes explicit his reasoning, arguing 'Paternity may be a legal fiction' " (185).

25. This drive to fictionalize kinship is not a phenomenon unique to interwar Europe. Kinship has been negotiated in sundry other places and times. Weston, for instance, discusses waves of social agitation in the United States, noting that the 1980s saw a surge of activism with regard to gay families. Where movements before the '80s focused on the rights of gay people to continue associating with families of origin, "what set this new discourse apart was its emphasis on the kinship character of the ties gay people had forged to close friends and lovers, its demand that those ties receive social and legal recognition" (21–22). As in interwar Europe, these negotiations had weighty implications. Weston explains: "The material and emotional consequences that hinge upon which interpretation of kinship prevails are truly far-reaching. Who will be authorized to make life-and-death decisions when lovers and other members of gay families are hospitalized or otherwise incapacitated?

Will court rulings continue to force some parents to choose between living with their children and living with a lesbian or gay partner? Should a biological grandfather who has never spoken to his grandchild because he disapproved of his daughter's lesbianism retain more legal rights vis-a-vis that child than a nonbiological coparent who has raised the child for ten years?," and so forth (5).

26. See also Wette 81.

27. With reference to the scene introducing Robin to readers, Harker states that Barnes's descriptions of Robin "move from sky (birds) to earth (earth-flesh fungi), to touch (the plant-like texture of her flesh), and to sight (luminous phosphorus glowing)" (258). Harker notes that this depiction of a queer woman as fecund and "the most natural creature in the world" is a direct rejection of interwar scientific discourse that saw queerness as sterile and unnatural ("Genderqueer" 258). This depiction furthermore stands in stark contrast to a scene in Faulkner's *Mosquitoes* in which ecological fecundity is depicted as threatening. Faulkner likens tree roots to "sluggish umbilical cords" that emerge "from out the old miasmic womb of a nothingness latent and dreadful" (169). I consider this passage in depth in chapter 3.

28. Barnes often forges a connection between sex and death in childbirth scenes. Alex Goody argues that a central image of Barnes's is "the marriage bed, the site of pleasure and the pain and blood of parturition" (167). I would add to this point Robin's reading selection immediately before parturition: the memoirs of Marquis de Sade (51).

29. As Kaviola states, the narrative perspective of *Nightwood* is antisemitic: "Again and again, the narrative insists that a Jew is not one of 'us.' . . . the opening passage questions the 'advisability of perpetuating that race which has the sanction of the Lord and the disapproval of the people' (1). Not only is Felix's birth questionable simply because he is a Jew, the suspicions one might have about another Jewish birth are called 'well-founded'" (179).

Coda

1. "Doctor" O'Connor is a loquacious, incessant storyteller whose medical specialty is obstetrics, though as Andrea L. Harris says, he is "an unlicensed quack" (233). Barnes describes the detritus that clutters O'Connor's home as a mixture of medical supplies and women's toiletries: "medical books . . . covered with dust," "a rusty pair of forceps, a broken scalpel . . . some twenty perfume bottles, almost empty, pomades, creams, rouges, powder boxes and puffs" (85). His rusty, unused forceps and lack of official sanction make him ideologically closer to the midwives of interwar Europe (in the popular imagination, that is) than to the scrupulous medical men that Ezra Pound emulated. O'Connor's alignment with women goes deeper than his profession, for he frequently wears lipstick and occasionally women's

clothing. The novel makes clear that O'Connor is a father but has not given birth to biological offspring. Michael Davidson reads O'Connor as a man who is metaphorically pregnant.

2. Caughie, "The Temporality of Modernist Life Writing in the Era of Transsexualism: Virginia Woolf's *Orlando* and Einar Wegener's *Man Into Woman*." See also my discussion of inversion in chapter 3.

3. See chapter 1 for more on Early Modern scholarship on queer pregnancy.

Bibliography

A. E. R. "Views and Reviews: The Terrified Twins." *The New Age*, vol. 25, no. 14, 1919, pp. 233–34.

Adam, Ruth. *A Woman's Place, 1910–1975*. 1975. Persephone Books, 2000.

Adams, Rachel. *Sideshow U.S.A: Freaks and the American Cultural Imagination*. U of Chicago P, 2001.

Adler, Franklin Hugh. "Why Mussolini Turned on the Jews." *Patterns of Prejudice*, vol. 39, no. 3, Routledge, Sept. 2005, pp. 285–300.

Adorno, Theodor W. *Minima Moralia: Reflections from Damaged Life*. Translated by E. F. N. Jephcott, Verso, 1978.

Allen, Carolyn. "The Erotics of Nora's Narrative in Djuna Barnes's *Nightwood*." *Signs: Journal of Women in Culture and Society*, vol. 19, no. 1, U of Chicago P, Oct. 1993, pp. 177–200.

Andrzejewski, Alicia. "'For Her Sake': Queer Pregnancy in *A Midsummer Night's Dream*." *Shakespeare Studies*, vol. 47, 2019, pp. 105–11.

Apollinaire, Guillaume. *The Breasts of Tiresias: Opera Buffa in Two Acts with Prologue*. 1917. Edited by Francis Poulenc, Heugel: Représentation exclusive pour le monde entier, A. Leduc, 1970.

Ardis, Ann L. *New Women, New Novels: Feminism and Early Modernism*. Rutgers UP, 1990.

Armstrong, Isobel. *Novel Politics: Democratic Imaginations in Nineteenth-Century Fiction*. Oxford UP, 2016.

Armstrong, Martin. "Wanted—A Musical Censorship." *The New Age*, vol. 15, no. 13, 1914, pp. 305–6.

Armstrong, Tim. *Modernism, Technology, and the Body: A Cultural Study*. Cambridge UP, 1998.

Atkinson, Ted. "Aesthetic Ideology in Faulkner's *Mosquitoes*: A Cultural History." *Faulkner Journal*, vol. 17, no. 1, Fall 2001, pp. 3–18.

Auerbach, Nina. "Review of *The Madwoman in the Attic: The Woman Writer and the Nineteenth-Century Literary Imagination*." *Victorian Studies*, vol. 23, no. 4, Indiana UP, 1980, pp. 505–7.

Avise, John C. *Hermaphroditism: A Primer on the Biology, Ecology, and Evolution of Dual Sexuality*. Columbia UP, 2011.

Bacigalupo, Massimo. " 'Safe with My Lynxes': Pound's Figure in the Carpet?" *Ezra Pound's* Cantos: *A Casebook*, edited by Peter Makin, Oxford UP, 2006.

Bailey, Bruce. "A Note on *The Waste Land* and Hope Mirrlees' *Paris*." *T. S. Eliot Newsletter*, vol. 1, no. 2, 1974, pp. 3–4.

Baker, Jean H. "Women's History." *American Heritage*, vol. 55, no. 6, 2004, pp. 66–68.

Baldanzi, Jessica Hays. "Stillborns, Orphans, and Self-Proclaimed Virgins: Packaging and Policing the Rural Women of *Cane*." *Genders*, 42, U of Colorado Boulder, 2005.

Barker-Benfield, G. J. *The Horrors of the Half-Known Life: Male Attitudes Toward Women and Sexuality in 19th-Century America*. Routledge, 1976.

Barnes, Djuna. *Nightwood*. 1936. New Directions, 2006.

Barnes, Djuna. *Nightwood: The Original Version and Related Drafts*. 1936. Edited by Cheryl J. Plumb, Dalkey Archive Press, 1995.

Barnes, Djuna. *Ryder*. 1928. Edited by Paul West, Dalkey Archive Press, 1990.

Barnes, Robert. "The Registration Of Midwives." *The Times*, 1 Aug. 1895. The Times Digital Archive. http://tinyurl.galegroup.com/tinyurl/9aPWZ2.

Bartulin, N. *Honorary Aryans: National-Racial Identity and Protected Jews in the Independent State of Croatia*. Springer, 2013.

Bassett, John Earl. "Faulkner's *Mosquitoes*: Toward a Self-Image of the Artist." *The Southern Literary Journal*, vol. 12, no. 2, 1980, pp. 49–64.

Bauer, Heike. "Theorizing Female Inversion: Sexology, Discipline, and Gender at the Fin de Siècle." *Journal of the History of Sexuality*, vol. 18, no. 1, 2008, pp. 84–102.

Baxter, Charles. "A Self-Consuming Light: *Nightwood* and the Crisis of Modernism." *Journal of Modern Literature*, vol. 3, no. 5, Indiana UP, 1974, pp. 1175–87.

Bayor, Ronald H. "Italians, Jews and Ethnic Conflict." *The International Migration Review*, vol. 6, no. 4, 1972, pp. 377–91.

Behling, Laura L. *The Masculine Woman in America, 1890–1935*. U of Illinois P, 2001.

Ben-Merre, David. *Figures of Time: Disjunctions in Modernist Poetry*. State U of New York P, 2018.

Benjamin, Walter. "The Storyteller: Reflections on the Works of Nikolai Leskov." *Illuminations*, edited by Hannah Arendt, Schocken Books, 1986, pp. 83–109.

Berg, Allison. *Mothering the Race: Women's Narratives of Reproduction, 1890–1930*. U of Illinois P, 2001.

Berni, Christine. " 'A Nose-Length into the Matter': Sexology and Lesbian Desire in Djuna Barnes's *Ladies Almanack*." *Frontiers*; Lincoln, vol. 20, no. 3, 1999, pp. 83–107.

Bersani, Leo. *Homos*. Harvard UP, 1996.

Bland, Lucy, and Laura Doan, editors. *Sexology Uncensored: The Documents of Sexual Science*. U of Chicago P, 1999.

Blotner, Joseph. *Faulkner: A Biography*. Vintage Books, 1991.

Bone, Robert. "Jean Toomer's *Cane*." *Cane*, by Jean Toomer. Edited by Rudolph P. Byrd and Henry Louis Gates Jr., Liveright, 2011, pp. 180–85.

Bosworth, R. J. B. *Mussolini's Italy: Life under the Dictatorship 1915–1945*. Penguin, 2005.

Bourke, Joanna. *Dismembering the Male: Men's Bodies, Britain, and the Great War*. U of Chicago P, 1996.

Boyde, Melissa. "The Poet and the Ghosts Are Walking the Streets: Hope Mirrlees-Life and Poetry." *Hecate: A Women's Interdisciplinary Journal*, vol. 35, no. 1–2, 2009, pp. 29–41.

Briggs, Julia. "Hope Mirrlees and Continental Modernism." *Gender in Modernism: New Geographies, Complex Intersections*, edited by Bonnie Kime Scott, U of Illinois P, 2007, pp. 261–70.

Broe, Mary Lynn, editor. *Silence and Power: A Reevaluation of Djuna Barnes*. Southern Illinois UP, 1991.

Brown, George. "The Registration Of Midwives." *The Times*, 12 Apr. 1899. The Times Digital Archive. http://tinyurl.galegroup.com/tinyurl/9aPVs7.

Burke, Carolyn. *Becoming Modern: The Life of Mina Loy*. U of California P, 1997.

Burke, Carolyn. *Interview with Carolyn Burke about Her Mina Loy Biography*. Interview by Pam Brown, Oct. 1998, http://jacketmagazine.com/05/mina-iv.html.

Burnett, L.D. "A Material World of Ideas." *Society for US Intellectual History*. https://s-usih.org/2018/10/a-material-world-of-ideas/. Accessed 14 Oct. 2018.

Bush, Ronald. *The Genesis of Ezra Pound's* Cantos. Princeton UP, 1976.

Butler, Judith. *Gender Trouble: Feminism and the Subversion of Identity*. 1990. Routledge, 2006.

Cahill, Heather A. "Male Appropriation and Medicalization of Childbirth: An Historical Analysis." *Journal of Advanced Nursing*, vol. 33, no. 3, 2001, pp. 334–42.

Caloyeras, Aliki Sophia. "H. D.: The Politics and Poetics of the Maternal Body." PhD diss., U of Pennsylvania P, 2012.

Capo, Beth Widmaier. *Textual Contraception: Birth Control and Modern American Fiction*. Ohio State UP, 2007.

Carby, Hazel V. *Reconstructing Womanhood: The Emergence of the Afro-American Woman Novelist*. Oxford UP, 1989.

Carden, Mary Paniccia. "Creative Fertility and the National Romance in Willa Cather's *O Pioneers!* And *My Ántonia*." *Modern Fiction Studies*, vol. 45, no. 2, 1999, pp. 275–302.

Carlston, Erin G. *Thinking Fascism: Sapphic Modernism and Fascist Modernity*. Stanford UP, 1998.

Carsten, Janet. *After Kinship*. Cambridge UP, 2010.

Carter, J. B., et al. "Introduction." *TSQ: Transgender Studies Quarterly*, vol. 1, no. 4, Jan. 2014, pp. 469–81.

Caselli, Daniela. *Improper Modernism: Djuna Barnes's Bewildering Corpus*. Ashgate, 2009.

Caserio, Robert L., et al. "The Antisocial Thesis in Queer Theory." *PMLA*, vol. 121, no. 3, Modern Language Association, 2006, pp. 819–28.

Castle, Terry J. "Lab'ring Bards: Birth 'Topoi' and English Poetics 1660–1820." *The Journal of English and Germanic Philology*, vol. 78, no. 2, 1979, pp. 193–208.

Cather, Willa. "Nebraska: The End of the First Cycle." *My Ántonia.* edited by Sharon O'Brien, Norton, 2015, pp. 312–28. First published in *The Nation,* 5 Sept. 1923.

Cather, Willa. *My Ántonia.* 1918. Edited by Sharon O'Brien, Norton, 2015.

Cather, Willa. *O Pioneers!* 1913. Edited by Sharon O'Brien, Norton, 2008.

Cather, Willa. *The Song of the Lark.* 1915. Vintage, 1999.

Caughie, Pamela L. "The Temporality of Modernist Life Writing in the Era of Transsexualism: Virginia Woolf's *Orlando* and Einar Wegener's *Man Into Woman.*" *MFS Modern Fiction Studies*, vol. 59, no. 3, Sept. 2013, pp. 501–25.

Caughie, Pamela L., et al. "Storm Clouds on the Horizon: Feminist Ontologies and the Problem of Gender." *Feminist Modernist Studies*, vol. 1, no. 3, Sept. 2018, pp. 230–42.

Champagne, John. *Aesthetic Modernism and Masculinity in Fascist Italy.* Routledge, 2013.

Chauncey, George. "From Sexual Inversion to Homosexuality: Medicine and the Changing Conceptualization of Female Deviance." *Salmagundi*, no. 58/59, 1982, pp. 114–46.

Christian, Barbara. *Black Women Novelists: The Development of a Tradition, 1892–1976.* Greenwood Press, 1980.

Chess, Simone, et al. "Introduction: Early Modern Trans Studies." *Journal for Early Modern Cultural Studies*, vol. 19, no. 4, 2019, pp. 1–25.

Clasen, Kelly. "Feminists of the Middle Border: Willa Cather, Hamlin Garland, and the Female Land Ethic." *CEA Critic: An Official Journal of the College English Association*, vol. 75, no. 2, 2013, pp. 93–108.

Coffman, Chris. *Gertrude Stein's Transmasculinity.* Edinburgh UP, 2018.

Cohler, Deborah. *Citizen, Invert, Queer: Lesbianism and War in Early Twentieth-Century Britain.* U of Minnesota P, 2010.

Cox, Jeannette. "Pregnancy as 'Disability' and the Amended Americans with Disabilities Act." *Boston College Law Review*, vol. 53, no. 2, 2012, p. 443.

Craig, Layne Parish. *When Sex Changed: Birth Control Politics and Literature between the World Wars.* Rutgers UP, 2013.

Cryle, P. M., and Elizabeth Stephens. *Normality: A Critical Genealogy.* U of Chicago P, 2017.

Cusk, Rachel. *A Life's Work: On Becoming a Mother.* Picador, 2003.

D'Emilio, John, and Estelle B. Freedman. *Intimate Matters: A History of Sexuality in America.* 3rd ed., U of Chicago P, 2012.

Daufenbach, Claus. "A Portrait of the Modernist as a Young Aesthete: Faulkner's *Mosquitoes.*" *Amerikastudien/American Studies*, vol. 42, no. 4, 1997, pp. 547–58.

Davidson, Michael. "Pregnant Men: Modernism, Disability, and Biofuturity in Djuna Barnes." *Novel: A Forum on Fiction*, vol. 43, no. 2, June 2010, pp. 207–26.

Davidson, Michael. *Invalid Modernism: Disability and the Missing Body of the Aesthetic*. Oxford UP, 2019.

de Lauretis, T. "Queer Texts, Bad Habits, and the Issue of a Future." *GLQ: A Journal of Lesbian and Gay Studies*, vol. 17, no. 2–3, Jan. 2011, pp. 243–63.

Dean, Tim. "The Antisocial Homosexual." In 'The Antisocial Thesis in Queer Theory' Special Issue of PMLA." *PMLA*, vol. 121, no. 3, Modern Language Association, 2006, pp. 826–28.

Declercq, Eugene, et al. "Where to Give Birth? Politics and the Place of Birth." *Birth by Design: Pregnancy, Maternity Care and Midwifery in North America and Europe*, edited by Raymond de Vries et al., Routledge, 2001.

Dieffenbach, John. "On the Cure of Vesico-Vaginal Fistula, and Laceration of the Bladder and Vagina." *The Lancet*, vol. 2, no. 1835–36, 1836, pp. 754–58.

Diethe, Carol. "Introduction to *Mafarka the Futurist*." *Mafarka the Futurist: An African Novel*, by F. T. Marinetti, Middlesex UP, 1998.

Doan, Laura L. "Topsy-Turvydom: Gender Inversion, Sapphism, and the Great War." *GLQ: A Journal of Lesbian and Gay Studies*, vol. 12, no. 4, Sept. 2006, pp. 517–42.

Doan, Laura, and Chris Waters. "Introduction: Homosexualities." *Sexology Uncensored: The Documents of Sexual Science*, edited by Lucy Bland and Laura Doan, U of Chicago P, 1999, pp. 41–45.

Dobbs, Cynthia. "Flooded: The Excesses of Geography, Gender, and Capitalism in Faulkner's *If I Forget Thee, Jerusalem*." *American Literature*, vol. 73, no. 4, Dec. 2001, pp. 811–35.

Doniger, Wendy, and Gregory Spinner. "Misconceptions: Female Imaginations and Male Fantasies in Parental Imprinting." *Daedalus*, vol. 127, no. 1, MIT P, 1998, pp. 97–129.

Donnison, Jean. *Midwives and Medical Men*. Heinemann, 1977.

Doughty, Frances M. "Gilt on Cardboard: Djuna Barnes as Illustrator of Her Life and Work." *Silence and Power: A Reevaluation of Djuna Barnes*, edited by Mary Lynn Broe, Southern Illinois UP, 1991, pp. 137–54.

Doyle, Laura. *Bordering on the Body: The Racial Matrix of Modern Fiction and Culture*. Oxford UP, 1994.

Dukes, Ashley. "Drama." *New Age*, vol. 6, no. 12, Jan. 1910, pp. 282–83.

DuPlessis, Rachel Blau. " 'Virile Thought': Modernist Maleness, Poetic Forms and Practices." *Modernism and Masculinity*, edited by Natalya Lusty and Julian Murphet, Cambridge UP, 2014, pp. 19–37.

DuPlessis, Rachel Blau. "Propounding Modernist Maleness: How Pound Managed a Muse." *Modernism/modernity*, vol. 9, no. 3, 2002, pp. 389–405.

Duvall, John N. "Faulkner's Crying Game: Male Homosexual Panic." *Faulkner and Gender*, edited by Donald M. Kartiganer and Ann J. Abadie, UP of Mississippi, 1996, pp. 48–72.

Ebaugh, Helen Rose, and Mary Curry. "Fictive Kin as Social Capital in New Immigrant Communities." *Sociological Perspectives*, vol. 43, no. 2, Sage Publications, Inc., 2000, pp. 189–209.

Edelman, Lee. *No Future: Queer Theory and the Death Drive*. Duke UP, 2004.

Eldred, Janet Carey. "Faulkner's Still Life: Art and Abortion in *The Wild Palms*." *The Faulkner Journal*, vol. 4, no. 1–2, 1988, pp. 139–58.

Eliot, T. S. *The Letters of T. S. Eliot: Volume 4: 1928–1929*. Edited by Valerie Eliot and John Haffenden. Yale UP, 2013.

Eliot, T. S. *The Waste Land: A Facsimile and Transcript of the Original Drafts Including the Annotations of Ezra Pound*. Edited by Valerie Eliot. Harcourt Brace Jovanovich, 1974.

Ellis, Havelock. *Erotic Symbolism: The Mechanism of Detumescence; the Psychic State in Pregnancy*. F. A. Davis Company, 1906.

Ellis, Havelock. "Sexual Inversion in Women." *Alienist and Neurologist*, vol. 16, no. 2, 1895, pp. 141–58.

Ellis, Patrick. "A Cinema for the Unborn: Moving Pictures, Mental Pictures and Electra Sparks's New Thought Film Theory." *British Journal for the History of Science*; Norwich, vol. 50, no. 3, Sept. 2017, pp. 411–28.

Faderman, Lillian. *Surpassing the Love of Men: Romantic Friendship and Love between Women from the Renaissance to the Present*. Morrow, 1981.

English, Daylanne K. *Unnatural Selections: Eugenics in American Modernism and the Harlem Renaissance*. U of North Carolina P, 2004.

Fama, Katherine A. "Melancholic Remedies: Djuna Barnes's *Nightwood* as Narrative Theory." *Journal of Modern Literature*, vol. 37, no. 2, 2014, p. 39.

Farwell, Marilyn R. "Toward a Definition of the Lesbian Literary Imagination." *Signs*, vol. 14, no. 1, U of Chicago P, 1988, pp. 100–18.

Faulkner, William. *As I Lay Dying: The Corrected Text*. 1930. Vintage Books, 1990.

Faulkner, William. *If I Forget Thee, Jerusalem* [*The Wild Palms*]. 1939. Vintage, 1995.

Faulkner, William. Introduction to *Sanctuary*, Modern Library, 1932, pp. v–viii.

Faulkner, William. *Mosquitoes*. 1927. Liveright, 1955.

Faulkner, William. *Selected Letters of William Faulkner*. 1929. Edited by Joseph Blotner, Random House, 1977.

Faulkner, William. *The Sound and the Fury: An Authoritative Text, Backgrounds and Contexts, Criticism*. Edited by Michael Edward Gorra, 3rd ed., Norton, 2014.

Finn, Margot C., et al., editors. *Legitimacy and Illegitimacy in Law, Literature, and History*. Palgrave Macmillan, 2010.

Fischer, Mike. "Pastoralism and Its Discontents: Willa Cather and the Burden of Imperialism." *Mosaic: A Journal for the Interdisciplinary Study of Literature*, vol. 23, no. 1, 1990, pp. 31–44.

Fisher-Wirth, Ann. "Out of the Mother: Loss in *My Ántonia.*" *Cather Studies,* vol. 2, 1993, pp. 41–71.

Fletcher, Angus. "Willa Cather and the Upside-Down Politics of Feminist Darwinism." *Frontiers: A Journal of Women Studies,* vol. 34, no. 2, 2013, pp. 114–33.

Forbes, T. R. "The Social History of the Caul." *The Yale Journal of Biology and Medicine,* vol. 25, no. 6, 1953, pp. 495–508.

Ford, Mark. "Ezra Pound and the Drafts of *The Waste Land.*" *The British Library,* 13 Dec. 2016. https://www.bl.uk/20th-century-literature/articles/ezra-pound-and-the-drafts-of-the-waste-land.

Forth, Christopher E. *Masculinity in the Modern West: Gender, Civilization and the Body.* Palgrave Macmillan, 2009.

Foster, Jeannette Howard. *Sex Variant Women in Literature.* Naiad Press, 1985.

Foucault, Michel. *The History of Sexuality: An Introduction.* 1976. Vintage, 1990.

Franks, Matt. "Breeding Aliens, Breeding AIDS: Male Pregnancy, Disability, and Viral Materialism in 'Bloodchild.' " *The Matter of Disability: Materiality, Biopolitics, Crip Affect,* edited by David Mitchell et al., U of Michigan P, 2019, pp. 182–203.

Fremantle, Francis. "The Midwives Bill." *The Times,* 8 Apr. 1910. The Times Digital Archive. http://tinyurl.galegroup.com/tinyurl/9aPVK8.

Friedman, Susan Stanford. "Creativity and the Childbirth Metaphor: Gender Difference in Literary Discourse." *Feminist Studies,* vol. 13, no. 1, 1987, pp. 49–82.

Friedman, Susan Stanford. *Psyche Reborn: The Emergence of H. D.* Indiana UP, 1987.

Frye Jacobson, Matthew. *Whiteness of a Different Color: European Immigrants and the Alchemy of Race.* Harvard UP, 1998.

Fuchs, Miriam. "Dr. Matthew O'Connor: The Unhealthy Healer of Djuna Barnes's *Nightwood.*" *Literature and Medicine,* vol. 2, no. 1, 1983, pp. 125–34.

Funke, Jana. "Radclyffe Hall." *Bad Gays* podcast. Huw Lemmey and Ben Miller, hosts. 27 July 2020.

Funke, Jana. "The Case of Karl M.[artha] Baer: Narrating 'Uncertain' Sex." *Sex, Gender and Time in Fiction and Culture,* edited by Ben Davies and Jana Funke, Palgrave Macmillan, 2011, pp. 132–53.

Fuss, Diana. *Essentially Speaking: Feminism, Nature and Difference.* Routledge, 1989.

Gabe, Jonathan, and Michael Calnan. "The Limits of Medicine: Women's Perception of Medical Technology." *Social Science & Medicine,* vol. 28, no. 3, pp. 223–31.

Galchen, Rivka. *Little Labors.* New Directions, 2016.

Garrity, Jane. "Olive Moore's Headless Woman." *MFS Modern Fiction Studies,* vol. 59, no. 2, 2013, pp. 288–316.

Garrity, Jane. *Step-Daughters of England: British Women Modernists and the National Imaginary.* Manchester UP, 2003.

Gelfant, Blanche H. "The Forgotten Reaping-Hook: Sex in *My Ántonia.*" *American Literature,* vol. 43, no. 1, Mar. 1971, pp. 60–82.

Gilbert, Sandra M. "Potent Griselda: 'The Ladybird' and the Great Mother." *D. H. Lawrence: A Centenary Consideration*, edited by Peter Balbert and Phillip L. Marcus, Cornell UP, 1985, pp. 130–61.

Gilbert, Sandra M., and Susan Gubar. "Lighting Out for the Territories: Willa Cather's Lost Horizons." *No Man's Land: The Place of the Woman Writer in the Twentieth Century, Volume 2: Sexchanges.* Yale UP, 1991, pp. 169–212.

Gilbert, Sandra M., and Susan Gubar. *No Man's Land: The Place of the Woman Writer in the Twentieth Century.* Vol. 2. Yale UP, 1989.

Gioia, Dana. "The Unknown Soldier: The Poetry of John Allan Wyeth." *The Hudson Review*, vol. 61, no. 2, 2008, pp. 253–68.

Gioia, Ted. "The First Postmodern Novel." Fractious Fiction, 15 July 2013. http://www.fractiousfiction.com/tristram_shandy.html.

Glavey, Brian. "Dazzling Estrangement: Modernism, Queer Ekphrasis, and the Spatial Form of *Nightwood*." *PMLA*, vol. 124, no. 3, Modern Language Association, 2009, pp. 749–63.

Glover, Susan. *Engendering Legitimacy: Law, Property, and Early Eighteenth-Century Fiction.* Bucknell UP, 2006.

Gold, Matthew K. "The Expert Hand and the Obedient Heart: Dr. Vittoz, T. S. Eliot, and the Therapeutic Possibilities of *The Waste Land*." *Journal of Modern Literature*, vol. 23, no. 3, 2000, pp. 519–33.

Golden, Mason. " 'Fluid Currency': Money and Art in Faulkner's *If I Forget Thee, Jerusalem*." *Modernism/Modernity*, vol. 20, no. 4, 2013, pp. 729–46.

Goody, Alex. *Modernist Articulations: A Cultural Study of Djuna Barnes, Mina Loy and Gertrude Stein.* Palgrave Macmillan, 2007.

Gopnik, Alison. "How Animals Think." *The Atlantic*, May 2019, pp. 40–42.

Gorham Doss, Crystal. "Brett Ashley and the Flapper Tradition." *Teaching Hemingway and Gender*, edited by Verna Kale, Kent State UP, 2016, pp. 104–13.

Gray, Mary L., et al., editors. *Queering the Countryside: New Frontiers in Rural Queer Studies.* NYU P, 2016.

Greenwood, Major. "Midwives Registration Bill." *The Times.* June 24, 1895. The Times Digital Archive. http://tinyurl.galegroup.com/tinyurl/9aPTT2.

Gubar, Susan. " 'The Blank Page' and the Issues of Female Creativity." *The New Feminist Criticism: Essays on Women, Literature, and Theory*, edited by Elaine Showalter, Pantheon, 1985, pp. 292–313.

Guttman, Sondra. "Who's Afraid of the Corncob Man? Masculinity, Race, and Labor in the Preface to *Sanctuary*." *Faulkner Journal*, vol. 15, no. 1–2, 2000 1999, p. 15.

Gwin, Minrose. *The Feminine and Faulkner: Reading (Beyond) Sexual Difference.* U of Tennessee P, 1990.

H. D. *End to Torment* Notebooks, book 1. Box 38, Folder 1016. YCAL MSS 24 Series II H. D. Papers. American Literature Collection, Beinecke Rare Book and Manuscript Library, Yale U, New Haven, CT. 11 Sept. 2019.

Halberstam, Jack. *In a Queer Time and Place: Transgender Bodies, Subcultural Lives.* NYU P, 2005.

Halberstam, Jack. *Female Masculinity.* Duke UP Books, 1998.

Halberstam, Jack. "The Politics of Negativity in Recent Queer Theory." *PMLA*, edited by Robert L. Caserio, vol. 121, no. 3, Modern Language Association, 2006, pp. 823–24.

Hall, Radclyffe. *The Well of Loneliness.* 1928. Wordsworth Editions, 2014.

Hammer, K. Allison. "Epic Stone Butch." *TSQ: Transgender Studies Quarterly*, vol. 7, no. 1, Feb. 2020, pp. 77–98.

Hanscombe, Gillian E., and Virginia L. Smyers. *Writing for Their Lives: The Modernist Women, 1900–1940.* Women's Press, 1987.

Harbin, Persephone Emily. *Transforming the Race-Mother: Motherhood and Eugenics in British Modernism.* 2008. Vanderbilt U, PhD dissertation.

Harker, Jaime. "Genderqueer: Literary and Gender Experimentation in Twentieth-Century American Literature." *Gender in American Literature and Culture*, edited by Jean Lutes and Jennifer Travis, Cambridge UP, 2021, pp. 255–70.

Harker, Jaime. "Queer Faulkner: Whores, Queers, and the Transgressive South." *The New Cambridge Companion to William Faulkner*, edited by John T. Matthews, Cambridge UP, 2015, pp. 107–18.

Harris, Andrea L. "The Third Sex: Figures of Inversion in Djuna Barnes's *Nightwood*." *Genders*, no. 19, 1994.

Hartman, Saidiya V. *Wayward Lives, Beautiful Experiments: Intimate Histories of Social Upheaval.* Norton, 2019.

Hauck, Christina. "Abortion and the Individual Talent." *ELH*, vol. 70, no. 1, 2003, pp. 223–66.

Hauck, Christina. "Through a Glass Darkly: 'A Game of Chess' and Two Plays by Marie Stopes." *Journal of Modern Literature*, vol. 21, no. 1, 1997, pp. 109–19.

Hauck, Christina. "Why Do the Ramsays Have So Many Children?: Birth Control and *To the Lighthouse*." *Virginia Woolf: Emerging Perspectives*, edited by Mark Hussey and Vara Neverow, Pace UP, 1994, pp. 115–20.

Hawthorne, Nathaniel. *The Scarlet Letter and Other Writings: Authoritative Texts, Contexts, Criticism.* 1850. W.W. Norton, 2004.

Heaney, Emma. *The New Woman: Literary Modernism, Queer Theory, and the Trans Feminine Allegory.* Northwestern UP, 2017.

Heilmann, Ann. *New Woman Fiction: Women Writing First-Wave Feminism.* Macmillan/St. Martin's Press, 2000.

Helstern, Linda Lizut. "*My Ántonia* and the Making of the Great Race." *Western American Literature*, vol. 42, no. 3, Fall 2007, pp. 254–74.

Hemingway, Ernest. *The Sun Also Rises.* Scribner Paperback Fiction, 1926.

Henig, Suzanne. "Hope Mirrlees: Queen of Lud." *Virginia Woolf Quarterly*, vol. 1, no. 1, 1972, pp. 8–22.

Henninger, Katherine. "'It's a Outrage': Pregnancy and Abortion in Faulkner's Fiction of the Thirties." *The Faulkner Journal*, vol. 12, no. 1, 1996, pp. 23–41.

Herring, Scott. *Queering the Underworld: Slumming, Literature, and the Undoing of Lesbian and Gay History*. U of Chicago P, 2007.

Hewitt, Andrew. *Political Inversions: Homosexuality, Fascism, & the Modernist Imaginary*. Stanford, 1996.

Hovey, Jaime E. "Gallantry and Its Discontents: Joan of Arc and Virtuous Transmasculinity in Radclyffe Hall and Vita Sackville-West." *Feminist Modernist Studies*, vol. 1, no. 1–2, May 2018, pp. 113–37.

Huxley, Aldous. *Brave New World*. 1932. Harper Perennial, 2006.

Ignatiev, Noel. *How the Irish Became White*. Routledge, 1995.

"inversion, n." *OED Online*, Oxford UP. www.oed.com/view/Entry/99005. Accessed 23 July 2018.

Irving, Katrina. "Displacing Homosexuality: The Use of Ethnicity in Willa Cather's *My Ántonia*." *MFS Modern Fiction Studies*, vol. 36, no. 1, 1990, pp. 91–102.

Izenberg, Gerald N. *Modernism and Masculinity: Mann, Wedekind, Kandinsky Through World War I*. U of Chicago P, 2000.

Jaffe, Aaron. *Modernism and the Culture of Celebrity*. Cambridge UP, 2005.

Jennings, Rebecca. "'The Most Uninhibited Party They'd Ever Been to': The Postwar Encounter between Psychiatry and the British Lesbian, 1945–1971." *Journal of British Studies*, vol. 47, no. 4, 2008, pp. 883–904.

Johnson, Allan. *Masculine Identity in Modernist Literature: Castration, Narration, and a Sense of the Beginning, 1919–1945*. Palgrave Macmillan, 2018.

Johnson, Barbara. "Apostrophe, Animation, and Abortion." *Diacritics*, vol. 16, no. 1, 1986, p. 28.

Joyce, James. *A Portrait of the Artist as a Young Man: Authoritative Text, Backgrounds and Contexts, Criticism*. 1916. Edited by John Paul Riquelme, Norton, 2007.

Joyce, James. *Ulysses*. 1922. Edited by Hans Walter Gabler, Vintage Books, 1993.

Joyce, James. *Ulysses*: Episode III. *The Little Review*, vol. 5, no. 1, 1918, pp. 31–45. The Modernist Journals Project (searchable database). Brown and Tulsa Universities, ongoing. www.modjourn.org.

Joyce, James. *Ulysses*: Episode IX. *The Little Review*, vol. 6, no. 1, 1919, pp. 17–35. The Modernist Journals Project (searchable database). Brown and Tulsa Universities, ongoing. www.modjourn.org.

Joyce, James. *Ulysses*: Episode X. *The Little Review*, vol. 6, no. 3, 1919, 28–47. The Modernist Journals Project (searchable database). Brown and Tulsa Universities, ongoing. www.modjourn.org.

Kahan, Benjamin. "Queer Sociality After the Antisocial Thesis." *American Literary History*, vol. 30, no. 4, Oxford Academic, Nov. 2018, pp. 811–19.

Kaivola, Karen. "The 'beast turning human'; Constructions of the 'Primitive' in *Nightwood*." *Review of Contemporary Fiction*, vol. 13, no. 3, Dalkey Archive Press, Fall 1993, p. 172.

Kawakami, Mieko. *Breasts and Eggs*. Translated by Sam Bett and David Boyd, 2020.

Keay, J. H. "Doctors and Midwives." *British Medical Journal,* vol. 2, no. 2133, 1901, p. 1506.

Kelley, Joyce. *Excursions into Modernism: Women Writers, Travel, and the Body*. Routledge, 2019.

Kenner, Hugh. "The Waste Land." *T. S. Eliot's* The Waste Land, edited by Harold Bloom, pp. 7–34. Bloom's Modern Critical Interpretations. New York: Chelsea House, 2006.

Kingsley, Erin M. "Birth Giving, the Body, and the Racialized Other in Jean Rhys's *Voyage in the Dark* and *Good Morning, Midnight*." *Philological Quarterly*, vol. 94, no. 3, 2015, pp. 291–312.

Kingsley, Erin M. " 'In the centre of a circle': Olive Moore's *Spleen* and Gestational Immigration." *Feminist Modernist Studies*, vol. 1, no. 1–2, May 2018, pp. 138–56.

Koestenbaum, Wayne. *Double Talk: The Erotics of Male Literary Collaboration*. Routledge, 1989.

Lakoff, George, and Mark Johnson. *Metaphors We Live By*. U of Chicago P, 2003.

Lambert, Deborah G. "The Defeat of a Hero: Autonomy and Sexuality in *My Ántonia*." *American Literature*, vol. 53, no. 4, 1982, pp. 676–90.

Larsen, Nella. *Quicksand*. 1928. *An Intimation of Things Distant: The Collected Fiction of Nella Larsen*, Anchor Books, 1992, pp. 29–162.

Ledger, Sally. *The New Woman: Fiction and Feminism at the Fin de Siècle*. Manchester UP, 1997.

Lee, Judith. "*Nightwood*: 'The Sweetest Lie.' " *Silence and Power: A Reevaluation of Djuna Barnes*, edited by Mary Lynn Broe, Southern Illinois UP, 1991, pp. 207–18.

Leitao, David D. *The Pregnant Male as Myth and Metaphor in Classical Greek Literature*. Cambridge UP, 2012.

" 'legitimate, Adj., Adv., and n.' " *Oxford English Dictionary*, OED Online, June 2020. www.oed.com/view/Entry/107112.

Lindemann, Marilee. " 'It Ain't My Prairie': Gender, Power, and Narrative in *My Ántonia*." *My Ántonia*. 1918, edited by Sharon O'Brien, Norton, 2015, pp. 479–97.

Lindemann, Marilee. *Willa Cather: Queering America*. Columbia UP, 1999.

Love, Heather. "Introduction: Modernism at Night." *PMLA*, vol. 124, no. 3, 2009, pp. 744–48.

Love, Heather. *Feeling Backward: Loss and the Politics of Queer History*. Harvard UP, 2007.

Lowe, Simon. "To Be the Outsider: On Olive Moore's *Spleen*." *Cleveland Review of Books*, 28 Oct. 2021. https://www.clereviewofbooks.com/home/olive-moore-spleen-review.

Lusty, Natalya, and Julian Murphet, editors. *Modernism and Masculinity*. Cambridge UP, 2014.

Maclean, Marie. *The Name of the Mother: Writing Illegitimacy*. Routledge, 1994.

Maine, Henry Sumner. *Ancient Law: Its Connection with the Early History of Society and Its Relation to Modern Ideas*. London, John Murray, 1861. *Internet Archive*. http://archive.org/details/ancientlawitsco18maingoog.

Manne, Kate. *Down Girl: The Logic of Misogyny*. Oxford UP, 2019.

Marcus, Jane. "Laughing at Leviticus: *Nightwood* as Woman's Circus Epic." *Cultural Critique*, no. 13, 1989, p. 143.

Marinetti, Filippo Tommaso. *Mafarka the Futurist: An African Novel*. 1909. Translated by Steve Cox and Carol Diethe. Edited by Carol Diethe, Middlesex UP, 1997.

Marquis, Margaret. "The Female Body, Work, and Reproduction in Deland, Cather, and Dreiser." *Women's Studies*, vol. 32, no. 8, Dec. 2003, p. 979–1000.

Martin, Terence. "The Drama of Memory in *My Ántonia*." *PMLA*, vol. 84, no. 2, 1969, pp. 304–11.

Mason, Carol. *Oklahomo: Lessons in Unqueering America*. State U of New York P, 2015.

Mazzoni, Cristina. *Maternal Impressions: Pregnancy and Childbirth in Literature and Theory*. Cornell UP, 2002.

McCann, Carole R. *Birth Control Politics in the United States, 1916–1945*. Cornell UP, 1994.

McCullers, Carson. *The Heart Is a Lonely Hunter*. 1940. Houghton Mifflin, 2004.

McHaney, Thomas L. *Introduction to Mosquitoes: A Facsimile and Transcription of the University of Virginia Holograph Manuscript*. Edited by Thomas L. McHaney, Bibliographical Society of the University of Virginia and the University of Virginia Library, 1997.

McIntosh, T. "Profession, Skill, or Domestic Duty? Midwifery in Sheffield, 1881– 1936." *Social History of Medicine: The Journal of the Society for the Social History of Medicine*, vol. 11, no. 3, 1998, pp. 403–20.

McIntosh, T. *A Social History of Maternity and Childbirth: Key Themes in Maternity Care*. Routledge, 2013.

Medina, Jennifer. "California Is Facing More Woes in Prisons." *The New York Times*, 15 July 2013. *NYTimes.com*.

Michel, Frann. "Faulkner as a Lesbian Author." *The Faulkner Journal*, vol. 4, no. 1–2, Fall 1988/ Spring 1989, pp. 5–20.

Miller, James E., Jr. "T. S. Eliot's 'Uranian Muse': The Verdenal Letters." *ANQ*, vol. 11, no. 4, 1998, pp. 4–20.

Millington, Richard H. "Willa Cather and 'The Storyteller': Hostility to the Novel in *My Ántonia*." *American Literature*, vol. 66, no. 4, 1994, pp. 689–717.

Moody, A. David. *Ezra Pound: Poet: Volume I: The Young Genius 1885–1920*. Oxford UP, 2009.

Moore, Olive. *Spleen*. 1930. Dalkey Archive Press, 1996.

Morantz-Sanchez, Regina. *Conduct Unbecoming a Woman: Medicine on Trial in Turn-of-the-Century Brooklyn*. Oxford UP, 1999.

Muñoz, José Esteban. *Cruising Utopia: The Then and There of Queer Futurity*. NYU P, 2009.

Muñoz, José Esteban. "Thinking Beyond Antirelationality and Antiutopianism in Queer Critique." *PMLA*, edited by Robert L. Caserio, vol. 121, no. 3, Modern Language Association, 2006, pp. 825–26.

Murphet, Julian. "Towards a Gendered Media Ecology." *Modernism and Masculinity*, edited by Natalya Lusty and Julian Murphet, Cambridge UP, 2014, pp. 53–67.

Murphy, Patricia. *Time Is of the Essence: Temporality, Gender, and the New Woman*. State U of NY P, 2001.

Musselman, Courtney. "Autobiographical Representations: Family in Djuna Barnes's *Nightwood*." *The Explicator*, vol. 74, no. 2, Routledge, 2016, pp. 107–9.

Nealon, Christopher S. *Foundlings: Lesbian and Gay Historical Emotion Before Stonewall*. Duke UP, 2001.

Nelson, Maggie. *The Argonauts*. Graywolf Press, 2016.

"Notes of the Week." *New Age*, vol. 7, no. 14, 1910, pp. 313–14.

O'Brien, Sharon. "Introduction." *My Ántonia*, by Willa Cather. 1918, Norton, 2015, pp. vii–xxiii.

O'Brien, Sharon. *Willa Cather: The Emerging Voice*. Harvard UP, 1997.

Orwell, George. *1984*. 1949. Edited by Erich Fromm, Signet Classic, 1961.

Ostriker, Alicia. "Body Language: Imagery of the Body in Women's Poetry." *The State of the Language*, edited by Leonard Michaels and Christopher Ricks, U of California P, 1980, pp. 247–63.

Parker, Andrew. "Ezra Pound and the 'Economy' of Anti-Semitism." *Boundary 2*, vol. 11, no. 1/2, 1982, pp. 103–28.

Pateman, T. W. "Conversation with a Realist." *The New Age*, vol. 14, no. 19, 1914, pp. 588–89. *The New Age ser. 2 v. 14 (Nov 1913–April 1914)*. HathiTrust. org. 11 Nov. 2019.

Pender, Elizabeth, and Cathryn Setz, editors. *Shattered Objects: Djuna Barnes's Modernism*. Pennsylvania State UP, 2019.

Peppis, Paul. "Rewriting Sex: Mina Loy, Marie Stopes, and Sexology." *Modernism/modernity*, vol. 9, no. 4, 2002, pp. 561–79.

Plato. *Plato's Symposium*. c. 385–370 BCE. Reprint translated by Seth Benardete, U of Chicago P, 2001.

Poole, W. Scott. *Wasteland: The Great War and the Origins of Modern Horror*. Counterpoint, 2018.

Pound, Ezra, and William Carlos Williams. *Pound/Williams: Selected Letters of Ezra Pound and William Carlos Williams*. Edited by Hugh Witemeyer, New Directions, 1996.

Pound, Ezra. " 'The Dialogues of Fontanelle.' " *The Egoist*, vol. 3, no. 9, 1916, pp. 133–34.

Pound, Ezra. "Doggerel Section of Letter to Marianne Moore." *The Gender of Modernism: A Critical Anthology*, edited by Bonnie Kime Scott, Indiana UP, 1990.

Pound, Ezra. "Paris Letter." Box 157, Folder 6808. YCAL MSS 43 Ezra Pound Papers. American Literature Collection, Beinecke Rare Book and Manuscript Library, Yale U, New Haven, CT. 10 Sept. 2019.

Pound, Ezra. "Paris Letter: Ulysses." Box 157, Folder 6803. YCAL MSS 43 Ezra Pound Papers. American Literature Collection, Beinecke Rare Book and Manuscript Library, Yale U, New Haven, CT. 10 Sept. 2019.

Pound, Ezra, et al. "Portrait d'une Femme." New Selected Poems and Translations. New Directions Pub. Corp., 2010.

Pound, Ezra. "SAGE HOMME. Letter to T. S. Eliot, 24 Jan. 1922." *The Poems of T. S. Eliot: Collected and Uncollected Poems*, edited by Christopher Ricks and Jim McCue, Johns Hopkins UP, 2015.

Pound, Ezra. "Translator's Postscript." *The Natural Philosophy of Love*, by Remy de Gourmont. Translated by Ezra Pound, Boni and Liveright, 1922, pp. 206–19.

Pound, Ezra. Canto V: Typescript. Box 70, Folder 3127. YCAL MSS 43 Ezra Pound Papers. American Literature Collection, Beinecke Rare Book and Manuscript Library, Yale U, New Haven, CT. 10 Sept. 2019.

Pound, Ezra. *The Letters of Ezra Pound, 1907–1941*. Edited by D. D. Paige, Faber and Faber, 1951.

Preda, Roxana. "Cantos Project: Canto V," 17 Sept. 2018.

"Pregnancy Discrimination." *U.S. Equal Employment Opportunity Commission*, https://www.eeoc.gov/pregnancy-discrimination. Accessed 1 Dec. 2021.

Prosser, Jay. *Second Skins*. Columbia UP, 1998.

Pykett, Lyn. *The "Improper" Feminine: The Women's Sensation Novel and the New Woman Writing*. 1992. Routledge, 2006.

Quayson, Ato. *Calibrations: Reading for the Social*. U of Minnesota P, 2003.

Rabaté, Jean-Michel. *The Ghosts of Modernity*. UP of Florida, 2010.

Rado, Lisa. "'A Perversion That Builds Chartres and Invents Lear Is a Pretty Good Thing': *Mosquitoes* and Faulkner's Androgynous Imagination." *The Faulkner Journal*, vol. 9, no. 1–2, 1993, pp. 13–30.

Randall, Alfred E. "'Promethius Re-Bound'." *The New Age*, 20 Jan. 1910, p. np.

Rees, Emma. "Birth." *Encyclopedia of Feminist Literary Theory*, edited by Elizabeth Kowalewski-Wallace, Garland, 1997, pp. 47–48.

Ricks, Christopher, and Jim McCue, eds. *The Poems of T. S. Eliot: Collected and Uncollected Poems*. Johns Hopkins UP, 2015.

Roche, Hannah. *The Outside Thing: Modernist Lesbian Romance*. Columbia UP, 2019.

Rosowski, Susan J. "Pro/Creativity and a Kinship Aesthetic." *My Ántonia*, 1918, edited by Sharon O'Brien, Norton, 2015, pp. 438–51.

Rothman, Barbara Katz. *In Labor: Women and Power in the Birthplace*. Norton, 1982.

Rubin, Gayle. "Of Catamites and Kings." *The Transgender Studies Reader*, edited by Susan Stryker and Stephen Whittle, Routledge, 2013, pp. 471–81.

Sacks, Elizabeth. *Shakespeare's Images of Pregnancy*. Macmillan, 1980.

Sanchez, Melissa E. "Antisocial Procreation in *Measure for Measure.*" *Queer Shakespeare: Desire and Sexuality*, edited by Goran Stanivukovic, Arden Shakespeare, 2017, pp. 263–78.

Satter, Beryl. *Each Mind a Kingdom: American Women, Sexual Purity, and the New Thought Movement, 1875–1920.* U of California P, 1999.

Schneider, David Murray. *A Critique of the Study of Kinship.* U of Michigan P, 1984.

Scholes, Robert. "General Introduction to The New Age 1907–1922." *The Modernist Journals Project (Searchable Database). Brown and Tulsa Universities, Ongoing.* www.modjourn.org. Accessed 6 Dec. 2021.

Schuller, Kyla. *The Biopolitics of Feeling: Race, Sex, and Science in the Nineteenth Century*, ebook, Duke UP, 2018.

Schwind, Jean. "The Benda Illustrations to *My Ántonia*: Cather's 'Silent' Supplement to Jim Burden's Narrative." *PMLA*, vol. 100, no. 1, 1985, pp. 51–67.

Seshagiri, Urmila. *Race and the Modernist Imagination.* Cornell UP, 2010.

Setz, Cathryn. " 'The Great Djuna:' Two Decades of Barnes Studies, 1993–2013." *Literature Compass*, vol. 11, no. 6, 2014, pp. 367–87.

Shin, Ery. "The Apocalypse for Barnes." *Texas Studies in Literature and Language*, vol. 57, no. 2, U of Texas P, 2015, pp. 182–209.

Showalter, Elaine. *A Literature of Their Own: British Women Novelists from Brontë to Lessing.* 1984. Princeton UP, 1999.

Silbergleid, Robin. "In Pieces: Fragmentary Meditations on Queer Mother Memoirs and Maggie Nelson's *The Argonauts.*" *Genders*, vol. 1, no. 2, 2016.

Silverman, Kaja. *Male Subjectivity at the Margins.* Routledge, 1992.

Smiler, Andrew P., et al. "Tightening and Loosening Masculinity's (k)Nots: Masculinity in the Hearst Press during the Interwar Period." *Journal of Men's Studies*, vol. 16, no. 3, Fall 2008, pp. 266–79.

Smith-Rosenberg, Carroll. *Disorderly Conduct: Visions of Gender in Victorian America.* Oxford UP, 1987.

Sniader Lanser, Susan. "Speaking in Tongues: Ladies Almanack and the Discourse of Desire." *Silence and Power: A Reevaluation of Djuna Barnes*, edited by Mary Lynn Broe, Southern Illinois UP, 1991, pp. 156–69.

Sorensen Emery-Peck, Jennifer. "Tom and Vivien Eliot Do Narrative in Different Voices: Mixing Genres in *The Waste Land*'s Pub." *Narrative*, vol. 16, no. 3, 2008, pp. 331–58.

Southall, Ashley. "She Was Forced to Give Birth in Handcuffs. Now Her Case Is Changing Police Rules." *The New York Times*, 3 July 2019. *NYTimes.com.*

Spackman, Barbara. *Fascist Virilities: Rhetoric, Ideology, and Social Fantasy in Italy.* U of Minnesota P, 1996.

Squier, Susan Merrill. *Babies in Bottles: Twentieth-Century Visions of Reproductive Technology.* Rutgers UP, 1994.

Stacey, Margaret. *The Sociology of Health and Healing.* Routledge, 1988.

Stephanson, Raymond. *The Yard of Wit: Male Creativity and Sexuality, 1650–1750*. U of Pennsylvania P, 2004.

Sterne, Laurence. *Tristram Shandy*. 1759. Wordsworth Editions, 1996.

Stevens, Robert. "The Midwives Act 1902: An Historical Landmark." *Midwives: The Magazine of the Royal College of Midwives*, Nov. 2002.

Stout, Janis P. *Willa Cather: The Writer and Her World*. U of Virginia P, 2000.

Stritzke, N., and E. Scaramuzza. "Trans*, Intersex, and the Question of Pregnancy: Beyond Repronormative Reproduction." *Transgender and Intersex: Theoretical, Practical, and Artistic Perspectives*, edited by Stefan Horlacher, Palgrave Macmillan, 2016, pp. 141–63.

Stryker, Susan. "(De)Subjugated Knowledges: An Introduction to Transgender Studies." *The Transgender Studies Reader*, edited by Susan Stryker and Stephen Whittle, Taylor & Francis, 2006, pp. 1–17.

Stryker, Susan, and Paisley Currah. "Introduction." *TSQ: Transgender Studies Quarterly*, vol. 1, no. 1–2, May 2014, pp. 1–18.

Summers, A. K. *Pregnant Butch: Nine Long Months Spent in Drag*. Soft Skull, 2014.

Swift, Daniel. *The Bughouse: The Poetry, Politics, and Madness of Ezra Pound*. Farrar, Straus and Giroux, 2017.

Terrell, Carroll F. *A Companion to* The Cantos *of Ezra Pound*. U of California P, 1993.

Thomas, Calvin. "*Modernism and Masculinity*, Ed. by Natalya Lusty and Julian Murphet (Review)." *Modernism/modernity*, vol. 23, no. 1, 2016, pp. 259–61.

Tickner, Lisa. "Men's Work? Masculinity and Modernism." *Differences*, vol. 4, no. 3, Bloomington, IN: Duke UP, 1992, pp. 42–82.

Toomer, Jean. *Cane*. 1923. Edited by Rudolph P. Byrd and Henry Louis Gates Jr., Liveright, 2011.

"To Waldo Frank." 12 Dec. 1922. *Cane*, by Jean Toomer. Edited by Rudolph P. Byrd and Henry Louis Gates Jr., Liveright, 2011. 152.

"travail, n.1." *OED Online*, Oxford UP, June 2020. www.oed.com/view/Entry/205252. Accessed 3 Sept. 2020.

van Mensvoort, Koert. "The First Pregnant Man." *Next Nature Network*, 6 May 2008.

Velasco, Sherry. *Male Delivery: Reproduction, Effeminacy, and Pregnant Men in Early Modern Spain*. Vanderbilt UP, 2006.

Vicinus, Martha. "'They Wonder to Which Sex I Belong': The Historical Roots of Modern Lesbian Identity." *The Lesbian and Gay Studies Reader*, edited by Henry Abelove et al., Routledge, 1993, pp. 432–52.

Wall, L. Lewis. "Preventing Obstetric Fistulas in Low-Resource Countries: Insights From a Haddon Matrix." *Obstetrical and Gynecological Survey*, n.d., 11.

Warren, Tracey. "Conceptualizing Breadwinning Work." *Work, Employment and Society*, vol. 21, no. 2, 2007, pp. 317–36.

Wiegman, Robyn, and Elizabeth A. Wilson. "Introduction: Antinormativity's Queer Conventions." *Differences*, vol. 26, no. 1, May 2015, pp. 1–25.

Weingarten, Karen. *Abortion in the American Imagination: Before Life and Choice, 1880–1940*. Rutgers UP, 2014.

Weston, Kath. *Families We Choose: Lesbians, Gays, Kinship*. Columbia UP, 2010.

Wette, Wolfram. *The Wehrmacht: History, Myth, Reality*. Harvard, 2007.

Wiesenthal, C. Susan. "Female Sexuality in Willa Cather's *O Pioneers!* and the Era of Scientific Sexology: A Dialogue Between Frontiers." *Ariel*, vol. 21, no. 1, 1990, pp. 41–63.

Williams, William Carlos. *I Wanted to Write a Poem*. 1958. Cape, 1967.

Wilson, Aimee Armande. "Modernism, Monsters, and Margaret Sanger." *MFS: Modern Fiction Studies*, vol. 59, no. 2, 2013, pp. 440–60.

Wilson, Aimee Armande. *Conceived in Modernism: The Aesthetics and Politics of Birth Control*. Bloomsbury Academic, 2016.

Woods, Livia Arndal. "Not-So-Great Expectations: Pregnancy and Syphilis in Sarah Grand's *The Heavenly Twins*." *Syphilis and Subjectivity: From the Victorians to the Present*, edited by Kari Nixon and Lorenzo Servitje, Springer, 2017, pp. 115–36.

Woolf, Virginia. *Orlando: A Biography*. Edited by Maria DiBattista, Harcourt, 2006.

Woolf, Virginia. *A Room of One's Own*. 1929. Harcourt, 2005.

Woolley, Paula. "'Fire and Wit': Storytelling and the American Artist in Cather's *My Ántonia*." *Cather Studies*, vol. 3, 1996, pp. 149–81.

Worden, Daniel. "'I Like to Be Like a Man': Female Masculinity in Willa Cather's *O Pioneers!* and *My Ántonia*." *Masculine Style: The American West and Literary Modernism*. Palgrave Macmillan, 2011.

Wussow, Helen. "Language, Gender, and Ethnicity in Three Fictions by Willa Cather." *Women & Language*, vol. 18, no. 1, Spring 1995, pp. 52–55.

Yaeger, Patricia. "The Poetics of Birth." *Discourses of Sexuality: From Aristotle to AIDS*. U of Michigan P, 1992.

Yuknavitch, Lidia. *The Chronology of Water: A Memoir*. 2011.

Zhang, Sarah. "The Surgeon Who Experimented on Slaves." *The Atlantic*, 18 Apr. 2018.

Zimmerman, Bonnie. *The Safe Sea of Women: Lesbian Fiction, 1969–1989*. Beacon Press, 1990.

Zunshine, Lisa. *Bastards and Foundlings: Illegitimacy in Eighteenth-Century England*. Ohio State UP, 2005.

Index

abortion: and the Comstock Act, 55;
  If I Forget Thee, Jerusalem, 27, 84,
  86–88, 90–91, 178n14; in *A Room
  of One's Own*, 173n15
Adam, Ruth, 24, 25, 49
Adler, Franklin Hugh, 152
Adorno, Theodor, 183–84
Aiken, Conrad, 174n5
Allen, Carolyn, 152
Anderson, Margaret C., 59, 63
Anderson, Sherwood, 78
Andrzejewski, Alicia, 11–12
antisemitism: 152, in *Nightwood*, 153,
  158–59, 184n10
Apollinaire, Guillaume: *The Breasts of
  Tiresias*, 163
Armstrong, Isobel, 10, 151, 182n20
Armstrong, Nancy, 22
assimilation: in *My Ántonia*, 97–98,
  104, 107–11, 112, 113, 119
Atkinson, Ted, 177n1
Auerbach, Nina, 10–11
authorship, 8–10. *See also* creativity;
  labor: creative; legitimacy: authorial;
  writing
Avise, John C., 81, 178n8

Bailey, Bruce, 174n3
Baker, Jean H., 48
Baldanzi, Jessica Hays, 177n23

Barker-Benfield, G. J., 35
Barnes, Djuna, 2, 3, 14, 15, 16,
  21, 25, 39, 41, 128–48, 150–62,
  182n2, 183n7, 184n10, 186n22,
  187n28, 187n1; *Ladies Almanack*,
  140, 185n18; *Nightwood*, 7, 14, 17,
  41, 69, 92, 98, 125, 127–60, 164,
  182n1, 183n5, 183n7, 187n29;
  Ryder, 183n3; sexuality of, 130. See
  also *Nightwood* (Barnes)
Barnes, Robert, 52
Bassett, John Earl, 177n1
bastardy, 9–10, 15, 19, 21–24,
  47–49, 69, 162, 174n23. *See also*
  illegitimacy
Baxter, Charles, 155
Beatie, Thomas, 1
Behling, Laura L., 26, 20, 32, 168n9,
  171n5, 180n7, 185n18
Benjamin, Walter: on novelistic
  narrative form, 100
Ben-Merre, David, 60
Bersani, Leo, 169
Boas, Franz, 122
Bosworth, R. J. B, 152
Bourke, Joanna, 74
Briggs, Julia, 174n3
British Medical Association, 52
Brown, George, 52
Boyde, Melissa, 174n3

Broe, Mary Lynn, 147, 186n22
Burnett, L. D., 68
Bush, Ronald, 60
butchness, 7, 95, 168n7, 172n7; in
    Pregnant Butch, 1, 4

Cane (Toomer), 45, 65–68, 170n18
Capo, Beth Widmaier, 173n15, 175n6
Carby, Hazel, 13
Carden, Mary Paniccia, 105, 118,
    181n12
Carpenter, Edward, 75
Caselli, Daniella, 128, 131, 141, 151,
    183n3, 185n16
Castle, Terry, 36–38, 67, 168n9
Cather, Willa, 2, 3, 14, 15, 16, 17,
    21, 25, 28, 30–31, 41, 69, 91,
    93–125, 127, 129, 131, 153–54,
    160, 162, 179n2, 179n3, 180n4,
    180n7, 180n10, 181n12, 181n15,
    182n21; *My Ántonia*, 3, 11, 14,
    16, 17, 31, 41, 69, 91, 93–125,
    127, 131, 153–54, 159, 160, 164,
    179n2, 179n3, 179n4, 180n5,
    180n8, 181n13, 182n21, 182n22,
    182n26; *O Pioneers!*, 93, 94,
    181n12; notions of gender, 180n10;
    sexuality of, 179n2; *Song of the
    Lark*, 93, 122. See also *My Ántonia*
    (Cather)
Caughie, Pamela, 132
Champagne, John, 184n8
Chauncey, George, 74–75
childbirth, 57, 58, 173n22, 177n25;
    in *Cane*, 65–68, 170n18;
    medicalization of, 40; metaphors
    of, 3, 8, 9, 10, 12–14, 20, 23, 25,
    36–37, 39, 45–49, 65–71, 168n10,
    170n16, 173n15, 175n5; in *My
    Ántonia*, 113–14; in *Nightwood*,
    133–36, 142, 154–56, 183n7,

187n28; and Pound, Ezra, 45–49,
    57, 58, 61–65
Christian, Barbara, 13
Christian Science, 139–40; 185n14
Coffman, Chris, 7
Cohler, Deborah, 25, 32, 172n9
Comstock Act (1873), 55, 176n13
conception, 13, 137, 169n11, 176n13;
    in *If I Forget Thee, Jerusalem*,
    178n14; in *Ladies Almanack*,
    185n18; in *Nightwood*, 141–44,
    155, 157; in *Orlando*, 89; and
    Pound, Ezra. 47; in *Pregnant Butch*,
    4, 20
Cox, Jeanette, 39–40, 173n19,
    173n21
Craig, Layne Parish, 175n6
creativity, 15, 16, 37, 91, 162, 163;
    in *Cane*, 45, 67; and Faulkner,
    William, 71, 90; and Pound, Ezra,
    46; and pregnancy, 10, 71, 88, 90,
    170n16
Currah, Paisley, 6, 95
Cusk, Rachel: *A Life's Work*, 165

Daufenbach, Claus, 177n1
Davidson, Michael, 39, 159, 168n11,
    170n20, 173n18, 174n23, 182n1,
    183n5, 188n1
De Lauretis, Teresa, 156
D'Emilio, John, 27, 29, 74, 75, 76
Dieffenbach, John, 58
Diethe, Carol, 37
disability, 39–41, 173n18, 186n21
disability discourse, 19, 39–41
Doan, Laura, 5–6, 26, 28, 32, 74, 75,
    168n9, 179n1
Dobbs, Cynthia, 177n1
Dodge, Mabel, 140
Doniger, Wendy, 136–37, 139, 140,
    184n11

Donnison, Jean, 50–51, 52, 53, 54, 175n10
Doolittle, Hilda (H. D.), 55, 176n12, 183n3
Doughty, Frances M., 130
DuPlessis, Rachel Blau, 13, 20, 35, 47, 177n22
Duvall, John, 74, 86
dystopian fiction, 2

Eddy, Mary Baker, 185
Edelman, Lee: *No Future*, 9, 18, 169n13
Eldred, Janet Carey, 178n14
Eliot, T. S., 16, 34, 43–47, 56, 72, 83, 174n3, 174n5, 176n16, 183n3; *The Waste Land*, 16, 34, 43–47, 56–59, 61, 64, 69, 72, 174n3, 174n5. See also *The Waste Land* (Eliot)
Eliot, Valerie, 174n4, 174n5
Eliot, Vivien, 46, 174n4
Ellis, Havelock, 26, 75, 82, 138–39
embodiment, 5, 15, 37, 39, 72, 73, 75, 85; epistemology of, 57; female, 1; and geography, 122; in *If I Forget Thee, Jerusalem*, 73, 85; masculine, 3; in *My Ántonia*, 17, 102, 115–16, 119, 122, 125, 133; in *Nightwood*, 158, 164, nonbinary, 2; in Pound, Ezra, 73; in *Pregnant Butch*, 1, 3, 5, 162; reproductive, 1, 3, 5, 166
essentialism: biological, 74, 91
eugenics, 8, 10, 15, 19, 21, 31–33, 35, 41, 49, 106, 139, 172n9, 182n21; in *Herland*, 121; in *My Ántonia*, 97, 106, 117–18, 120–23, 182n20, 182n21; in *Nightwood*, 145–46, 153; in Pound, Ezra, 55. See also race

Fama, Katherine, 155

Faulkner, William, 2–3, 7, 8, 10, 14, 15, 16–17, 20, 21, 24–25, 27, 37, 41, 45, 69, 71–92, 79, 93, 94, 124, 160, 162, 178n11; *Absalom! Absalom!*, 71; *As I Lay Dying*, 79, 85; on commercialism, 79; *If I Forget Thee, Jerusalem*, 3, 7, 16, 27, 69, 71–72, 73, 75, 77, 83–88, 91, 94, 124, 108n16, 177n1, 179n17; *Mosquitoes*, 8, 16, 69, 71–73, 75, 77–79, 81–82, 83, 84, 85, 87, 91, 177n1, 187n27; *Sanctuary*, 79; *The Sound and the Fury*, 79, 178n13; *The Wild Palms*, 16, 69, 71, 178n12. See also *If I Forget Thee, Jerusalem* (Faulkner)
femininity, 38, 72, 76, 77: in Black interwar texts, 12, 13; and crisis, 35; and Faulkner, William, 71, 72, 79; in *If I Forget Thee, Jerusalem*, 85–87; in *My Ántonia*, 103, 105, 115, 116, 119, 124; in *Nightwood*, 133–34, 154, 157; and pregnancy, 4, 8–9, 39, 74, 120, 161, 166; in *Pregnant Butch*, 4; and race, 4, 12, 13; in Silverman, Kaja, 11; in *Spleen*, 145, 146; standards of, 32
fertility, 27; in *If I Forget Thee, Jerusalem*, 88; male, 170n19; masculinity and, 27, 158; in *My Ántonia*, 95–97, 104, 118; in *Orlando*, 89; in Pound, Ezra, 55, 62; 177n22
fictional kinship, 14, 15, 17, 129, 147–53, 160; limits of, 153–54, 159
Finn, Margot C., 23, 49, 146, 147
Fisher-Wirth, Ann, 115
Fletcher, Angus, 180n10
Ford, Mark, 47
Forth, Christopher J., 35, 178n6

Foster, Jeanette H., 20, 168n9, 168n10, 169n11, 171n1, 172n11, 184n13
Fracastoro, Girolamo, 62
Frank, Waldo, 67
Freedman, Estelle B., 29, 74, 75
Friedman, Susan Stanford, 27, 28, 68, 168n10, 170n16, 171n5, 173n15, 175n11
Fuchs, Miriam, 153
Funke, Jana, 5
futurity, 11, 18, 39, 165, 169n13. *See also* reproductive futurism

Galchen, Rivka: *Little Labors*, 165
Garrity, Jane, 32, 173n15, 175n6, 186n21
Gelfant, Blanche H., 94
gender: in Cather, Willa, 180n10; and creativity, 16; cultural history of, 10, 15, 19–42; "deviance," 6, 28, 172n9; in Faulkner, William, 16, 72, 82; in *If I Forget Thee, Jerusalem*, 87, 91; in interwar America, 74–77; and legitimacy, 47, 111; in *My Ántonia*, 95, 96, 98–100, 102, 103, 104, 105, 107, 108, 111, 117, 119–20, 123; in nationality, 105; in *Nightwood*, 130, 133–35, 145, 157; in *Orlando*, 88, 89; in Pound, Ezra, 47, 61, 82; and race, 12; as spectrum, 161, 166. *See also* femininity; inversion; masculinity; sexology
gender studies, 5, 30
genealogy: and fiction, 10, 14, 151–54, in *Nightwood*, 128, 129, 134, 141, 148, 151–54, 159. *See also* legitimacy
Gilbert, Sandra M., 38, 157
Gilman, Charlotte Perkins, 2, 97, 121, 181n10; *Herland*, 97, 121–22, 182n24

Gioia, Dana, 177n19
Gioia, Ted, 57
Glavey, Brian, 154, 185n2
Glover, Susan, 22, 23
Goebbles, Joseph, 152
Goethe, Johann Wolfgang von: *Elective Affinities*, 139
Gold, Michael K., 47
Goody, Alex, 187n28
Gourmont, Remy de: *The Natural Philosophy of Love*, 55
Green, Tara T., 12
Greenberg, Judith G., 40
Greenwood, M., 52
Gubar, Susan, 157, 180n4
Guttman, Sondra, 79
Gwin, Minrose, 178n10

Haffenden, John, 174n5
Halberstam, Jack, 6–7, 9, 11, 30, 96, 98, 103, 106, 162, 169n13, 180n4, 181n14
Hall, Radclyffe, 20, 27, 182n2; *The Well of Loneliness*, 20
Hammer, Allison K., 95
Harbin, Persephone Emily, 186n24
Harker, Jaime, 73, 80, 91, 187n27
Harris, Andrea L., 134, 187n1
Hartman, Saidiya, 107
Hauck, Christina, 173n15, 175n6
Hawthorne, Nathaniel: *The Scarlet Letter*, 9
Heaney, Emma, 29, 170n20
Heap, Jane, 59, 63
Hemingway, Ernest, 27
Helstern, Linda Lizut, 122, 182n21
Herland (Gilman), 97, 121–22, 182n24
hermaphroditism, 80, 81, 178n8
Herring, Scott, 182n2, 183n7
Hoffman, E. T. A.: "The Doubles," 139
homophobia, 3, 5, 103

Hovey, Jaime, 29, 168n7
Huxley, Aldous: *Brave New World*, 2

ideology: of masculinity, 178n6;
  modernist, 147; reproductive, 164,
  169n13
If I Forget Thee, Jerusalem (Faulkner),
  3, 7, 16, 27, 69, 71–72, 73, 75,
  77, 83–88, 91, 94, 124, 108n16,
  177n1, 179n17 83–90; abortion
  in, 27, 84, 86–88, 90–91, 178n14;
  conception in, 178n14; embodiment
  in, 73, 85; femininity in, 85–87;
  fertility in, 88; gender in, 87,
  91; inversion in 86–87; queer
  possibilities in, 87; race in 179n16;
  sexuality in, 179n16
illegitimacy, 19, 24–25, 41, 48, 49,
  152, 174n23; in *My Ántonia*,
  104, 107, 159; in *Nightwood*,
  129, 135, 140, 152–53, 155, 158;
  reproductive, 9, 10, 14. *See also*
  bastardy; legitimacy; race
immigration, 10, 15, 33–34; in *My
  Ántonia*, 106. *See also* assimilation;
  race
incest, 85, 87, 178n13, 186n22
inheritance, 15, 17; in *My Ántonia*, 117
interwar literature, 5, 8, 15, 25, 27,
  28, 139, 165, 183n3
inversion, 5, 6, 8, 17, 28, 30, 71–77,
  131, 171n1, 172n9, 172n11,
  180n7; discourse of, 16; in *If I
  Forget Thee, Jerusalem*, 86–87; logic
  of, 74, 86–87; and *Mosquitoes*, 84;
  and *Nightwood*, 133, 135. *See also*
  sexology
Irving, Katrina, 97, 99, 104
Izenberg, Gerald N., 35

Jacobson, Matthew Frye, 33, 34,
  181n18

Jaffe, Aaron, 174n1
Jennings, Rebecca, 133
Johnson, Allen, 10
Johnson, Mark, 69
Johnson-Reed Act (1924), 33–34
Joyce, James: *Portrait of the Artist as a
  Young Man*, 139; *Ulysses*, 36, 56

Kahan, Benjamin, 169n13
Kawakami, Meiko: *Breasts and Eggs*,
  165
Kaviola, Karen, 158–59, 187n29
Keay, J. H., 52–53
Kelley, Joyce, 144, 146–47, 175n6
Kenner, Hugh, 43
Key, Ellen, 75
Kingsley, Erin, 146, 147, 186n21
kinship, 14, 147, 183n4; biological;
  critique of, 148–50, 158; queer, 17,
  18. *See also* fictional kinship
Koestenbaum, Wayne, 34, 46, 47, 57,
  59, 176n15

labor: creative, 44, 45, 114; and Eliot,
  T. S., 44, 45, 58, 72; and Faulkner,
  William, 79; manual, 79, 101, 116,
  122; movement, 178n6; in *My
  Ántonia*, 96, 101, 106–108, 116,
  122; in *Nightwood*, 136, 142–43;
  procreative, 36, 38, 44, 45, 52,
  53, 63, 72, 142, 173n22. *See also*
  childbirth
Lakoff, George, 69
Lambert, Deborah G., 95, 118
Lang, Fritz, 152
Larsen, Nella; *Quicksand*, 12, 13
Lee, William Howard, 31–32, 142
legitimacy, 8–10, 20–25, 171n2;
  authorial, 8, 16, 25, 32, 34, 37, 41,
  43, 45, 47, 49; biological, 14, 27,
  69; creative, 2, 17, 91, 93; legal,
  22–23, 164; limits of, 17, 125, 127,

legitimacy *(continued)*
135, 147–48, 150, 158, 182n2;
literary, 19, 128; and masculinity,
15, 64; and modernism, 162; in *My
Ántonia*, 98–100, 104, 107, 111–20,
125, 160; and narrative, 98, 99,
155; in *Pregnant Butch*, 1; and
rationalization, 30–31; reproductive,
32–34, 128–29, 131, 136, 141,
146–47, 154, 159–60, 162, 164,
166; women's, 73, 94. *See also*
bastardy; illegitimacy
Leitao, David D., 36
Lewis, Wyndham, 34
Lindemann, Marilee, 100, 113, 123
Lobban. Michael, 23
Love, Heather, 2–3, 96–97, 160
Lowe, Simon, 145
Loy, Mina, 140

MacKethan, Lucinda H., 66
Maclean, Marie, 22, 23
Maine, Henry Sumner, 149
male pregnancy, 5, 13–14, 39, 168n7,
168n11, 170n19; in *Cane*, 65–68,
170n18; and disability, 39, 173n18;
metaphorical, 2, 3, 43, 47, 56;
unthinkability of, 5; in *Spleen*, 145.
See also masculine pregnancy
Manne, Kate, 49
mannishness, 6, 8, 12, 19, 25–31, 65,
95, 97, 169n11, 171n5; fears of,
32; in *My Ántonia*, 97, 106, 117; in
Nightwood, 128, 131–32; and race,
32. *See also* mannish women
mannish women, 3, 14, 20, 21,
25–31, 94, 162, 168n7, 168n9,
172n9, 172n10; in *If I Forget
Thee, Jerusalem*, 73; in *Mosquitoes*,
73; in *My Ántonia*, 97, 98, 106;
in *Nightwood*, 3; as threats, 160;

unimaginability of, 4–5. *See also*
mannishness
Mansfield, Katherine: *In a German
Pension*, 144
Marcus, Sharon, 135, 140, 141, 155,
183n7
Marinetti, F. T.: *Mafarka, The Futurist*,
37, 163
Marsden, Dora, 63
Martin, Terence, 96
masculine pregnancy, 2, 14;
exclusionary depictions of, 3, 4;
and illegitimacy, 41; imaginative
depictions of, 4, 24; unthinkability
of, 4
masculinity, 4–13; anxiety over, 34,
35; in *Cane*, 65; crisis of, 19, 35,
172n14; and Faulkner, William,
71–73; female, 7, 9, 27, 31, 166,
179n2; in *If I Forget Thee, Jerusalem*,
84–91; interwar, 28, 76–77, 178n6,
184n8; and legitimacy, 15, 16, 17,
93, 162; and modernism, 34–38;
and money, 86; in *Mosquitoes*,
77–83; and motherhood, 20,
21, 27, 117–23; in *My Ántonia*,
94–108, 113, 116–20, 124; in
Nightwood, 128–35, 140–41,
143–44, 147, 154–60, 180n4; and
pregnancy, 2, 9–11, 14, 16–18,
38, 41, 43, 65, 93, 162, 163, 165,
166, 168n10; and Pound, Ezra,
48, 64; rationalization of, 31; self-
making, 77–83; of surgeons, 45, 49;
trans-, 7, 29. *See also* legitimacy;
male pregnancy; mannish women;
masculine pregnancy
Mazzoni, Christina, 127, 137–38
McCann, Carole R., 176n13
McCullers, Carson: *The Heart is a
Lonely Hunter*, 164

Mensvoort, Koert van, 167n3
Michel, Frann, 82
midwifery, 44–45, 48–50, 53–56,
  62–63, 68; in the early twentieth
  century, 50–53; intellectual, 45,
  48, 49; and Pound, Ezra, 44, 45,
  48–49, 53–56, 62–63, 68
Midwives Act (1902), 15, 50, 51, 54
Miller, Jr., James E., 47
Millington, Richard H., 100–101
Mirrlees, Hope: *Paris*, 174n3
misogyny, 35, 49–50, 63, 74, 138; in
  Faulkner, William, 74, 83, 90; in
  Marinetti, F. T., 37; in Pound, Ezra,
  49
modernism, 4–11, 19, 34–38, 162,
  173n15, 174n23, 175n6, 186n21;
  and masculinity, 19, 34–38; and
  Pound, Ezra, 44, 47, 48; and
  patriarchy, 49; and queer literature,
  9, 11. *See also* transatlantic
  modernism
Monroe, Harriet, 63
Moore, Marianne, 21, 55, 60–61,
  186n20
Moore, Olive, 2, 131, 145–47;
  Celestial, 146–47; *Spleen*, 131,
  145–47, 186n20. See also Vaughn,
  Constance
Morantz-Sanchez, Regina, 58, 59,
  176n18
Morgan, Lewis Henry, 148
Mosquitoes (Faulkner), 8, 16, 68,
  71–73, 75, 77–83, 84, 85, 87,
  91, 177n1, 187n27; inversion in,
  72, 75, 84; masculinity in, 77–83;
  misogyny in, 72, 91; reproduction
  in, 73; queer possibilities in, 73
motherhood, 36; and eugenics, 32; in
  My Ántonia, 110, 114, 116, 118,
  119; in *Nightwood*, 130, 133–34,

141, 144–45; queer, 167n5. *See also*
  childbirth; pregnancy
Muñoz, José Esteban: *Cruising Utopia*,
  169n13
Murphet, Julian, 25, 168n11
My Ántonia (Cather), 3, 11, 14,
  16, 17, 31, 41, 69, 91, 93–125,
  127, 131, 153–54, 159, 160, 164,
  179n2, 179n3, 179n4, 180n5,
  180n8, 181n13, 182n21, 182n22,
  182n26; assimilation in, 97–98, 104,
  107–11, 112, 113, 119; childbirth
  in, 113–14; embodiment in, 17,
  102, 115–16, 119, 122, 125, 133;
  immigration in, 106; eugenics in,
  97, 106, 117–18, 120–23, 182n20,
  182n21; legitimacy in, 98–100, 104,
  107, 111–20, 125, 160; motherhood
  in, 110, 114, 116, 118, 119; and
  narrative, 111–17; queerness in, 31,
  96, 97, 106; race in, 104–107, 123,
  124; sexuality in, 98, 100, 108, 110,
  180n4, 180n7

narrative: in *My Ántonia*, 111–17; and
  reproduction, 162–63. *See also* travel
  narratives
nationalism, 32, 33, 49, 128, 152. *See
  also* eugenics; immigration; race
Nelson, Maggie: *The Argonauts*, 8, 165,
  167n5
New Age, The (magazine), 54, 176n14
New Thought, 139–40, 157, 185n14
New Woman, 25, 27, 133, 171n4
Nightwood (Barnes), antisemitism
  in, 158–59; fictional kinship in,
  153–54, 159–60; illegitimacy in,
  129, 135, 140, 152–53, 155,
  158; obstetrics in, 187n1; parental
  impression in, 140–44, 147–50,
  155, 157, 159, 160; patriarchy

Nightwood (Barnes) *(continued)*
in, 135; psychoanalysis in, 134;
queerness, 135, 153, 154, 158, 159,
187n27; race in, 128, 135, 143,
152–53, 156–58, 159, 187n29;
reproduction in, 129, 134–35, 142,
151; sexuality in, 130, 133, 155;
trauma in, 154–58

O'Brien, Sharon, 100, 181n13
Obstetrical Society, 52
obstetrics, 35, 50, 57; in *Nightwood*,
187n1; and Pound, Ezra, 55, 57
Orage, A. R., 54
Orlando (Woolf), 72, 88–90;
conception in, 89; writing in, 89
Ostriker, Alicia, 57

parental impression, 15, 17, 127–32,
136–40, 184n11, 184n13, 185n15;
in *Nightwood*, 140–44, 147–50, 155,
157, 159, 160; in *Ryder*, 183n3
parthenogenesis, 121, 185n17
Pateman, T. W., 176n14
patriarchy: and Faulkner, William, 73,
91, 118; in *Nightwood*, 135
Peppis, Paul, 175n6
Pound, Ezra, 2, 3, 10, 14–17, 20,
25, 34, 37, 41, 43–69, 72, 73, 77,
83, 90, 92, 93, 160, 162, 174n1,
174n4, 176n12, 176n14, 176n16,
177n19, 187n1; "Canto V," 55,
62–63, 176n12; as "midwife," 16,
43–44, 46–49; "SAGE HOMME,"
16, 25, 44–48, 55–64, 67–69, 72,
83, 176n14; as "surgeon," 44, 47,
56–57, 59, 61, 64, 174n1, 176n14
pregnancy: and creativity, 10, 71, 88,
90, 170n16; as disability, 39–41,
173n18; male, 5, 13–14, 39,
168n7, 168n11, 170n19; masculine,

2, 14; medicalization of, 39–41;
queer, 1–3, 5, 8, 38, 164–65,
167n4, 184n11; trans, 5, 168n7.
See also childbirth; male pregnancy;
masculine pregnancy; reproduction
Pregnant Butch (Summers), 1, 4, 8,
20, 162, 165; butchness in, 1, 4;
conception in, 4, 20; embodiment
in, 1, 3, 5, 162; femininity in, 4
psychoanalysis: in *Nightwood*, 134

Quayson, Ato, 7
queer kinship, 17, 18
queer literature, 11
queerness, 11, 12, 20, 30, 31, 38,
165, 169n13; in *My Ántonia*, 31,
96, 97, 106; in *Nightwood*, 135,
153, 154, 158, 159, 187n27
queer theory, 9, 11, 31, 38, 164–65;
antisocial thesis of, 17, 164–65,
169n13
Quinn, John, 59–60, 63

Rabaté, Jean-Michel, 47, 56
race, 4, 12, 15, 19, 32, 32–34, 76,
138, 181n18; in *Herland*, 121; in *If
I Forget Thee, Jerusalem*, 179n16; in
My Ántonia, 104–107, 123, 124; in
Nightwood, 128, 135, 143, 152–53,
156–58, 159, 187n29; in *Portrait of
the Artist as a Young Man*, 139. *See
also* eugenics; immigration; whiteness
Rado, Lisa, 80
Randall, Alfred E.: "Prometheus
Re-Bound," 54
Rees, Emma E L., 37
reproduction, 8–12, 14, 74, 88; and
authorship, 9, 14, 46, 78, 82;
and biological essentialism, 74;
in *Cane*, 177n23; cultural history
of, 15, 19–42, 48; and eugenics,

106, 121; in Faulkner, William;
69, 73, 81, 82; in *If I Forget Thee,
Jerusalem*, 88; in *Herland*, 121; and
modernism, 10; in *Mosquitoes*, 69,
78, 80–82; and narrative, 162–63;
in *Nightwood*, 129, 134, 135, 142,
151, 182n1; nonbinary, 5; and
Pound, Ezra, 46, 64; queer, 5, 12,
170n21; rights, 5; self-fertilization,
80–81, 83; trans, 5. *See also*
childbirth; futurity; male pregnancy;
masculine pregnancy; parental
impression; pregnancy
reproductive futurism, 165, 169n13
Roche, Hannah, 132
Rosowski, Susan J., 113, 114, 122,
179n3
Roth, Edward Allsworth, 181n16
Rothman, Barbara Katz, 40, 41
Rubin, Gayle, 7, 95

Sacks, Elizabeth, 168n10
Sanchez, Melissa E., 11
Sanger, Margaret, 68–69
Satter, Beryl, 139, 157, 185n14
Scaramuzza, E., 5
Schneider, David W., 149
Schuller, Kyla, 4, 76, 138
Schwind, Jean, 105, 106
Seshagiri, Urmila, 33–34
Setz, Catherine, 184
sexology, 16, 20, 74, 80–82, 91, 139,
155, 175n6
sexuality: categories of, 7;
heterosexuality, 30, 169n13, 180n7;
homosexuality, 20, 74, 76, 155,
169n1, 183n3; in *If I Forget Thee,
Jerusalem*, 179n16; in interwar
America, 74–77; and mannishness,
6, 25, 28, 29; in *My Ántonia*, 98,
100, 108, 110, 180n4, 180n7; and

narrative, 96; in *Nightwood*, 130,
133, 155; and sexology, 71. *See also*
inversion; mannishness; queerness;
sexology
Silbergleid, Robin, 167n5
Silverman, Kaja, 11
Sims, J. Marion, 59, 176n18, 177n19
Smart, Elizabeth: *By Grand Central
Station I Sat Down and Wept*, 144
Smiler, Andrew P., 76, 77, 80
Smith, Sidonie, 185n20
Southall, Ashley, 173n22
Spinner, Gregory, 136, 138–340,
184n11
Spleen (Moore), 131, 145–47, 186n21
Squier, Susan Merrill, 175n6
Stephanson, Raymond, 170n19
Stephenson, Jill, 134, 135
sterility: and Faulkner, William, 87–88
sterilization, 5, 41
Sterne, Lawrence: *Tristram Shandy*, 9, 57
Stockham, Alice Bunker, 139
Stritzke, N., 5
Stryker, Susan, 6, 95, 171n7
suffragists, 25, 30
Summers, A. K.: *Pregnant Butch*, 1, 4,
8, 20, 162, 165. See also *Pregnant
Butch* (Summers)
Sutton-Ramspeck, Beth, 121

Taylor, Jenny Bourne, 23
Thomas, Calvin, 49
Toomer, Jean: *Cane*, 45, 65–68,
170n18
transfemininity, 29
transmasculinity, 29, 95, 168n7
transatlantic modernism, 2. *See also*
modernism
transphobia, 167n3
travel narratives: in *Nightwood*, 131,
144–47

Vaughn, Constance, 145
Vicinus, Martha, 24, 26, 168n9, 172n10
Waste Land, The (Eliot), 16, 34, 41, 43–49, 55, 56, 57, 64, 72, 90, 174n5; composition of, 45–48, 174n4; editing of, 41, 64, 72, 90; reproductive discourse in, 34, 175n5, 175n6. *See also* Eliot, T. S.; Pound, Ezra

Weston, Kath, 147–50, 183n4, 186n25
whiteness, 10, 14, 17, 19, 32–34, 152
Whyde, Janet M., 65
Wiesenthal, C. Susan, 93–94
Wild Palms, The (Faulkner), 16, 69, 71, 178n12. See also *If I Forget Thee, Jerusalem*
Wilde, Oscar, 20, 35

Williams, William Carlos, 36, 54–55; *Kora in Hell*, 36
Woods, Livia Arndal, 184n13
Woolf, Virginia, 2, 21, 61, 72, 88–90, 173n15, 174n3; *Orlando*, 72, 88–90; *A Room of One's Own*, 61. See also *Orlando* (Woolf)
Woolley, Judith, 124
writing: as manual labor, 79; as pregnancy, 22, 36–37, 45, 46, 68, 71, 168n10, 170n18, 173n15; as surgery, 176n14
Wussow, Helen, 104
Wyeth, John Allan, 177n19

Yaeger, Patricia, 38
Yuknavitch, Lidia: *The Chronology of Water*, 165

Zunshine, Lisa, 23

Milton Keynes UK
Ingram Content Group UK Ltd.
UKHW011406090624
443836UK00004B/154

9 781438 495606